CRITICAL VICTIMOLOGY

SOCIAL & BEHAVIORAL SCIENCES   *Sociology*

32-0614

Mawby, R.I. **Critical victimology: international perspectives,** by R.I. Mawby and
S. Walklate. Sage Publications, CA, 1994. 224p bibl index ISBN 0-8039-8511-8, $65.00;
ISBN 0-8039-8512-6 pbk, $19.95

Brit. CIP

The role and rights of victims have been increasingly important preoccupations of both criminology as an academic discipline and of the public discourse on crime. British criminologists Mawby and Walklate have published earlier books on policing and victimology. They recognize that historically, victimology and the victims' rights movement have been dominated by mainstream and generally conservative forces. Their objective is to explore some of the principal issues involved in the status of victim within a critical framework that questions conventional assumptions and considers progressive alternatives to existing policies. A fairly thorough comparison of victim-related policies and the meaning of the "victims' movement" in various countries—with special attention to the US and British experience—is arguably the most valuable contribution of this work. The authors conclude with some policy responses they believe to be authentically progressive and fair. This study complements the mainstream emphasis of such books as Albert Roberts's *Helping Crime Victims* (1990) and the focus on the American experience of Robert Elias's *Victims Still* (CH, Nov'93). Appendix; references. Upper-division undergraduates and above.—*D. O. Friedrichs, University of Scranton*

CRITICAL VICTIMOLOGY

International Perspectives

R.I. Mawby and S. Walklate

SAGE Publications
London · Thousand Oaks · New Delhi

First published 1994

SAGE Publications Ltd
6 Bonhill Street
London EC2A 4PU

SAGE Publications Inc
2455 Teller Road
Thousand Oaks, California 91320

SAGE Publications India Pvt Ltd
32, M-Block Market
Greater Kailash – I
New Delhi 110 048

British Library Cataloguing in Publication data

Mawby, R.I.
  Critical Victimology: International
  Perspectives
  I. Title II. Walklate, Sandra
  362.88

  ISBN 0–8039–8511–8
  ISBN 0–8039–8512–6 (pbk)

Library of Congress catalog card number 93–086519

Typeset by The Word Shop, Bury, Lancashire.
Printed in Great Britain by Biddles Ltd, Guildford, Surrey

Contents

1

Perspectives on Victimology

Books are very much a product of the time in which they are written. This particular text was conceived at a time in which the relatively young (sub)discipline of victimology, and the victim movements variously associated with victimological thinking, were increasingly making their presence felt on the criminal justice policies of England and Wales. That presence, however, was felt not only in England and Wales. Influenced to a certain extent by North American initiatives, it was being felt across Europe. The social circumstances affecting this particular project, then, stem from not only the political and social events of the 1980s in England and Wales, but also from the rapid changes to the political map of Europe, both East and West, that occurred during the late 1980s and early 1990s. These changes have led to a re-evaluation of theory and praxis across the East–West European divide. This may prove to be as significant in the context of understanding the operation and processes of the various criminal justice and welfare systems as in the more overtly political arenas. These developments afford an opportunity of evaluating the potential contribution of the various strands of victimological thinking, towards both understanding and influencing the direction of these changes.

Given that much has already been written about victimology, the reader may well be wondering why it is necessary to review, once again, its origins and emergence. Most texts of recent origin, for example, have paid due attention to the work of Von Hentig and Mendelsohn and to the nature of the relationship of victimology to criminology. (Karmen, 1990; Mawby and Gill, 1987; Walklate, 1989). Little attention, however, has been paid to understanding the different strands within victimological thought, the different relationship that those strands have with so-called 'victim movements', and the relationship of those movements to wider processes of social change. An attempt will be made here to map some of these connections through the development of three victimological frameworks.

Victimological frameworks

Various attempts have been made to classify the different strands of victimological thought. This began with the work of Mendelsohn and Von Hentig. Their ideas, as Schneider (1991) amongst others suggests, set the victimological agenda in two different ways: the first directing attention to a victimology of human rights and thereby establishing victimology as an independent discipline; the second being more closely concerned with victims of crime and thus seeing victimology as a sub-discipline of criminology. These different directions can be traced in the debate which follows.

Initially it is important to be aware that efforts to set a framework for victimology face a number of difficulties. One of these difficulties is that of disentangling what Fattah (1989) has called 'humanistic victimology' from 'scientific victimology'. In making this distinction Fattah is attempting to explicate what he considers to be the uncomfortable relationship between the activist and the academic in their concern for the victim of crime. The connections between academic thinking and activist concerns cannot, however, be disentangled simply because that is seen to be a preferable state of affairs. These links are deeply embedded in the theory and practice of the discipline and need to be squarely addressed. To this end Karmen (1990) identifies three tendencies within the victimological debate: the conservative, the liberal, and the radical-critical. Each of these, he argues, defines the scope of the discipline differently and connects differentially with positions within the victims' movement. It is perhaps worth summarizing Karmen's argument before developing these issues a little more fully.

For Karmen (1990) the conservative tendency within victimology defines the discipline in four ways. First, it focuses on crime as a problem with particular attention being paid to victims of street crime; secondly, it is concerned to render people accountable for their actions; thirdly it encourages self-reliance; and finally, it focuses on notions of retributive justice. He argues that the liberal tendency extends this conservative focus by including 'crimes of the suites' in their analyses; by being concerned to 'make the victim whole again'; and by considering the value of restitution and reconciliation as appropriate penal strategies. The radical-critical tendency within victimology, according to Karmen, wishes to extend the focus of the discipline even further. This tendency includes all forms of human suffering in the analysis and considers the criminal justice system to be as much a problem in constructing that suffering as the 'victimizing' event. Thus 'institutional wrong-doing that violates human rights' (Karmen, 1990: 12) is considered a legitimate area for study.

These tendencies are certainly present within victimology and they certainly draw attention to the question of the connections to be made between them and the different types of 'advocacy' position taken up within the victims' movement. A characterization of this sort, however, makes it difficult to locate a particular writer or a particular organization under one label, since the labels themselves are not mutually exclusive. In addition, what this characterization fails to unwrap more closely are the connections to be made between these labels and the presumed scientific status of the discipline they represent. Examining assumptions of this kind allows connections to be made between differing conceptions of victimology and the image of society implied by those conceptions. This provides one way of addressing the implications that these images of society have for understanding the role of the law and the role of the state in the victimization process. An attempt will be made to unwrap some of these issues and their value for understanding the development of victims' movements by identifying three 'types' of victimology: positivist, radical, and critical victimology.

Positivist victimology

Miers (1989: 3) has usefully identified what can be considered the key characteristics of positivist victimology:

> The identification of factors which contribute to a non-random pattern of victimization, a focus on interpersonal crimes of violence, and a concern to identify victims who may have contributed to their own victimization.

These characteristics dovetail with Karmen's (1990) identification of 'conservative victimology' and parallel Walklate's (1989) 'conventional victimology'. Indeed, one of the key features of this type of victimology is its focus on street crime to the exclusion of other kinds of criminal victimization like violence, rape, and various forms of abuse, which more often occur behind closed doors. In this vein the work of Hindelang, Gottfredson and Garofalo (1978) constitutes a good example of the neglect of the 'private' as an arena for victimological analysis. By the same token such conservative/conventional work largely neglects to consider victims of corporate crime. Miers (1989), however, does not fully outline what is meant by positivism in this context. This is a useful question to explore a little more fully at this point.

Keat and Urry (1975: 3) state:

> For the positivist, there are no necessary connections in nature; there

are only regularities, successions of phenomena which can be systemati-
cally represented in the universal laws of scientific theory. Any attempt
to go beyond this plunges science into the unverifiable claims of
metaphysics and religion, which are at best unscientific, and at worst
meaningless.

This view of science facilitates a concern with patterns, regularities
and precipitative characteristics of victimizing events and, consequently, the production of victim typologies. It is this view of
science which has traditionally insisted upon the separation of the
scientist from the humanist (the academic from the activist; see
Fattah, 1989). This separation is, of course, highly problematic and
constitutes a view of science which has been challenged by feminists
amongst others, a challenge that gains particular significance in the
context of victimology, as shall be seen. Here it is sufficient to
observe that whilst humanists wear their hearts on their sleeve the
scientist's commitments are frequently hidden behind notions of
objectivity and value freedom; notions which in themselves have
largely been couched in male terms, hidden by what Smith (1990)
has called the 'regime of rationality'. That feminist work has largely
been marginalized by victimology as a whole, and by positivistic
victimology in particular, is not unconnected to the desire to
separate activism from science.

The marginalization of feminism by victimology has been
commented on elsewhere. Rock (1986) implies that this has
occurred to a certain extent by choice in so far as the concept of
victim precipitation came to be regarded as 'victim blaming' and
victimology came to be seen as a 'weapon of ideological oppression'. Hostility towards such work from within victimology and the
potential for this work to be used politically as a way of further
denying the pervasiveness of patriarchal structures on women's
lives, alongside mainstream (malestream) analyses of those lives, is
hardly surprising; a hostility which is more than justified given the
deep roots such concepts seem to have. But the importance of
reflecting on the challenge of feminism draws attention to more
than just the political arena. It challenges the very conception of
science to which not only positivistic victimologists adhere.

Harding (1987, 1991) develops the feminist challenge to science
and its associated features in a number of different ways. At its
core, however, this is a debate which is concerned less with the
techniques of doing research (though it may be argued that those
techniques may be used more appropriately and/or more imagina-
tively) than to establish, at the level of methodology, the status not
only of women as knowers but of what it is that is to be known.
Thus part of the impact of feminist research lies in its concern to

make visible what has been invisible and to name that which has gone without a name. In the context of victimology in general, and positivist victimology in particular, this renders its focus on the public rather than the private highly problematic. It also renders problematic the concern to separate the 'academic' from the 'activist', an issue to which we shall return.

The problems associated with the influence of positivism within victimology does not mean that such an influence has not yielded some important information for academic and activist alike. Thus Fattah (1989) berates the activist for not having taken note of some of these findings, and the development of the criminal victimization survey in particular was certainly very influential in placing the question of criminal victimization on the policy agenda. It is quite clear, of course, that such information has been used politically in one context to downplay the risk of crime (see Hough and Mayhew, 1983) and, in another, to emphasize the risk of crime (see President's Task Force on Victims of Crime, 1982).

So positivism has been very powerful in the development of victimology. Indeed, and whether or not work from within this framework has been appreciated by particular victims' movements, organizations, or academics, the patterns and regularities yielded by positivist victimology has been used expediently in the political arena. In a general way it was certainly implicated in the move from 'crime prevention' to 'victimization prevention' (Karmen, 1990) which in the United Kingdom has been advocated by the Conservative Party as 'social responsibility' and 'active citizenship'; a move which has not been confined to the UK and North America (Van Dijk, 1991a; Bienkowska, 1991a). Overall political trends of this kind reflect more specific links with specific victims' movements.

Karmen (1990: 11), for example, connects his understanding of conservative victimology with victim movements in the following way:

> Conservatives within victimology and the victims' rights movement see the criminal justice system as the guarantor of retributive justice – satisfying victims with the knowledge that offenders are being punished for their crimes.

It is possible to argue that their relationship is somewhat stronger, in that in some circumstances victims' movements have been involved in setting the pace for the return to and giving priority to retributive justice. This was the case with the 'Victims of Violence' organization in England and Wales in the early 1980s (Jonker, 1986), which is paralleled by some elements of the feminist movement, NOVA in the United States and to a lesser extent

Die Weisser Ring in Germany (Maguire and Shapland, 1990). Traditional thinking, as reflected in the moves towards retribution, is also to be found in the way in which this kind of victimology views the nature of society. This view of society is most readily gleaned from the pre-eminence given to the construction of victim-typologies. This, of course, began with the work of Von Hentig and Mendelsohn.

As stated earlier, Von Hentig and Mendelsohn are considered the founding fathers of victimology. Each developed typological frameworks as means of generating an understanding of the victim/offender relationship. Von Hentig did this by considering the nature of victim-proneness. His typology has thirteen categories including the young, the old, the female and the mentally defective, and so on. Mendelsohn considered the extent to which the notion of culpability could inform an understanding of the victimizing event. He had six categories ranging from the 'completely innocent' to the 'most guilty victim'. The problems associated with each of these typologies has been discussed elsewhere (Walklate, 1989). The search for typologies, however, continues. One of the most recent, most sophisticated and wide-ranging typologies to be produced is contained in the work of Landau and Freeman-Longo (1990). This highly imaginative and multidimensional model nevertheless shares a key weakness of such work: an inherently static and sociologically functionalist view of society. The themes of consensus, equilibrium and incremental change, which are embedded in functionalism, are also embedded in the production of typologies since they fail to capture (or challenge) the process of the social reproduction of (criminal) victimization. They provide a way of offering a picture of regularities, hence the connection with positivism, but cannot capture the social and historical reproduction of victimization through time and space.

This view of society and its implicit conception of social change as being gradual and incremental has a number of consequences. First, it makes it difficult to recognize and analyse the definitional problems associated with the term 'victim' itself. Positivist victimo logy takes the meaning of this term as being self-evident by the mere 'fact' of individual suffering on the one hand or by recourse to the legal framework on the other. There is little sense in which either the law itself or the state in the implementation of the law constructs our understanding of the victim. Secondly, there is no sense within this view of the way in which individuals may actively resist, campaign against or survive the label 'victim'. Finally there is little sense of those processes of social change which may be dramatic and unforeseen as opposed to gradual and incremental. Radical victimology can be considered to address some if not all of these issues.

Radical victimology

The presence of a radical victimology can be traced back to the work of Mendelsohn, who argued for a victimology concerned with all victims. However, this radical strand takes on a more substantial form in the late 1960s and early 1970s and can be traced through to the 1980s. Its emergence has some parallels with the emergence of radical criminology and though Jones, MacLean and Young (1986) dispute Friedrichs's (1983) view that radical victimology had little influence on radical criminology there is some agreement that these ideas emerged at around the same time. Essentially a radical victimology concerns itself with:

> victims of police force, the victims of war, the victims of the correctional system, the victims of state violence, the victims of oppression of any sort. (Quinney, 1972: 315)

For Quinney all of these could be rendered visible by the development of an alternative perspective; and that alternative perspective would, rather as radical criminology did, call into question the role of the capitalist state, and the role of the law within capitalist societies in defining the social construction of both the offender and the victim. The elements of such a perspective were not only to be found in 'Western' criminology/victimology. Similar questions were being asked of socialist societies:

> The activities of the powerful and the privileged are either beyond the criminal law (e.g. many sorts of political, religious, national or racial oppression) or even if they are criminalized, the criminals very seldom appear in court. (Falandysz, 1982: 111)

This echoes what Reiman (1979) and Box (1983) document in drawing attention to the way in which the criminal justice system is implicated in constructing the crime (the victims) we 'see' and those we do not. Radical victimology, however, has another edge to it, and this connects more directly with the question of victims' movements.

There is a dimension to radical victimology which is concerned to establish the discipline as one in which the central concern is the question of human rights. Elias (1985: 17) states:

> A victimology that encompasses human rights would not divert attention from crime victims and their rights, but rather would explore their inextricable relationship to more universal human rights concerns.

This broader remit for victimology echoes the work of Mendelsohn and, arguably, also permits the inclusion of some of the issues addressed by the feminist movement in the area of legal rights. The human rights perspective produces for Elias, by definition, a consideration of the role of the state in the production of victims. He also argues that it is a perspective which has considerable scientific potential:

> Human rights standards can provide victimology with boundaries that include not merely official victimological definitions, but more objective measures of actual victimization. By using international covenants, we can promote more universal, and less national, definitions of victimization. (Elias, 1985: 17)

In promoting the idea of 'objective measures' Elias (1986: 245) clearly sees victimology as concerned 'to relieve human suffering' and assumes that this suffering can be objectively agreed upon. In so doing he also assumes that the universal standards to which the discipline aspires are 'the progressive goals of democracy and social change' (Elias, 1986: 244). Whilst Elias displays a critical awareness of the implementation of such ideals in the United States, the question must be asked as to whether such ideals are innately progressive. This issue is considered elsewhere by Young-Rifai (1982). It is a question which is an important one for this perspective and is returned to below. The issue for the moment is whether this strand of radicalism can provide victimology with a more appropriate theoretical and empirical agenda.

Whilst the underlying spirit of these radical ideas within victimology is to be commended, there has for the most part been a very limited research agenda developed from them (Friedrichs, 1983), with perhaps the exception of that work emanating from within the feminist movement which shares some of these concerns. But, as observed earlier, there are obvious theoretical and ideological problems in constructing a 'feminist victimology'. In addition, whilst this radical perspective does challenge the strands of positivist victimology, it too slips into positivism by assuming the applicability of universal standards without articulating how those standards may be historically specific. This strand of victimology does not see society as innately consensual but recognizes the considerable power of the law and the state to oppress. These processes are thereby implicated both in creating the victims we see and also in creating and adding to that victimization process; from the creation of 'police property' (Lee, 1981) on the one hand to the implementation of state policies which violate human rights standards on the other. The concerns of organizations like Amnesty International are not that far removed from a victimology couched in these terms.

This particular strand of victimology may have had more of a rhetorical impact than one that can be documented in research terms. There is, however, another version of 'radical' victimology whose impact has been a little more substantial. On a par with some of these ideas within victimology, ideas within criminology emerged which were concerned to address the question of the victim of crime. The emergence of 'radical left realism', which has had an impact both theoretically and empirically on work done in the UK and to a lesser extent in Canada and Australia, has been determined to take the victim of crime 'seriously'. Young (1986: 23–4) states that the radical perspective which argued for a political economy of crime in the early 1970s for the most part neglected the real victim of crime. The emergence of 'radical left realism' within criminology sought to rectify this omission with a call for an 'accurate victimology' starting from 'problems as people experience them' through a recognition of the geographically and socially focused distribution of criminal victimization. More recently, left realism has argued that this position has also embraced the concerns of feminism (Young, 1988).

Detailed criticisms and evaluations of this move towards radical left realism have been rehearsed elsewhere. The issues of relevance here concern the understanding of realism associated with these developments. At best they reflect a partial reading of what is meant by realism resulting in theoretical difficulties in defining what constitutes social reality and methodological difficulties in translating the theoretical concerns into an empirical agenda. The cumulative effect of this is a slippage into positivism (see Smart, 1990), reflected in the way in which research emanating from this perspective employs the criminal victimization survey. It has nevertheless successfully offered a much more detailed documentation of who the victims of crime are at a local level, and has done much to challenge the view that crime is a rare occurrence. For particular sections of society this is certainly not the case. More recent work from this camp has also attempted to look at the question of the extent to which those same sections of society who are victims of 'conventional' crime are also disproportionately victimized as a result of 'commercial crime' (Pearce, 1990). This version of radicalism also connects with victims' movements but in a politically much more general fashion.

Radical left realism is committed to a clear political agenda which demands an 'engaged' criminology. In England this has been reflected in the association between radical left realism and Labour-controlled local authorities. This political project has been particularly concerned to criticize the policy agenda established by

Home-Office-based 'administrative criminology' and its associated concern with patterns of criminal victimization (see above). It is perhaps similar in spirit, though not so clear in substance, to the position adopted by Elias, though left realism was more specifically designed to recapture the political terrain of law and order which right-wing radicals made their own during the 1980s in the UK. These comparisons are worth developing a little further.

The commitment to a human rights perspective for radical victimology is a very important one. Yet this political as well as conceptual question has remained analytically speaking relatively underdeveloped for both radical victimology and radical left realism within criminology. The definition of human rights which seems to be implied from within radical victimology is a very broad one. It concerns itself not just with 'life, liberty and the pursuit of happiness' but also with 'the economic, social and cultural rights indispensable for [the individual's] dignity and free development of his personality' (United Nations Declaration of Human Rights, Article 22), and a 'standard of living adequate for health and well-being of himself and his family, including food, clothing, housing, and medical care and necessary social services' (ibid., Article 25). Victims' rights are thus not the exclusive property of a right-wing law and order lobby. Radical left realism entered the debate concerning rights and citizenship, albeit briefly, by arguing for a socialist view of citizenship which concentrates on both rights and obligations. This position, like that of Elias (1986), presumes a harnessing of the democratic process to achieve such goals, and, echoing some of the ideas of Plant (1988), Corrigan, Jones and Young (1989, 17) argue that: 'it would be impossible to defend the social individualism of a person who was registered as looking for work but refused both work and training'.

This social individualism, whilst perhaps usefully tempering a claim to rights which does not consider the question of obligations, fails to lose the taint of traditional liberal principles. Thus neither radical victimology nor radical left realism in entering this debate address the question of how a collective and pluralistic notion of rights and citizenship might be achieved (Mouffe, 1988). Smart (1989) outlines some of the problems facing the feminist movement and its association with the question of women's rights and how some of the 'gains' made from this position have resulted in the simultaneous extension of power for men. Such complexities face this radical strand within victimology.

So radical victimology problematizes the state, but has historical-ly failed to consider features of the process of victimization other than class (for example gender, race and age) and has also traditionally failed to consider the way in which 'not all law is directed towards specific capitalist objectives' (Friedrichs, 1983: 111). In addition, Friedrichs also criticizes the radicals because 'the perceived insensitivity of radical criminology with regard to the immediate suffering of victims of conventional, predatory crime probably diminishes the effects of its ultimately humanistic message' (ibid.). Radical left realism attempts to overcome this last criticism and also attempts to embrace the variables of age, gender and race alongside the question of social class in measuring the extent of criminal victimization. At a theoretical level it is a perspective which also acknowledges the role of the state in 'the square of crime' (Young, 1991). But although this is acknowledged, it is an issue which is subsequently neglected. This results in a partial and distorted picture of the processes of criminal victimization (Jefferson *et al.*, 1991).

Radicalism within victimology moves us from a framework which sees victimology as being primarily concerned with victims of crime as defined by a conventional understanding of the law, to a framework which recognizes the importance of problematizing the law and the state. This recognition, however, has for the most part led to a simplistic reading of the relationship between the law and social class (Friedrichs, 1983; Sumner, 1990) and consequently a simplistic reading of the role of the state. Perhaps as a result, it has failed to develop a coherent research agenda which can usefully explore these issues. In many ways, the agenda which has been set under this radical umbrella has also failed to break away from the hold of positivism. A resolution of some of these issues may be found within the construction of what might be termed a critical perspective, a version of which, as will be seen below, argues for, amongst other things, a different interpretation of a realist scientific agenda.

Critical victimology

The term critical has been used in a number of different ways in order to develop an agenda for victimology. Miers articulates one understanding of this version of victimology as a resolution of some of the difficulties he associates with positivism: 'Many groups and individuals may claim the label, but the key questions for a critical victimology are who has the power to apply the label and what considerations are significant in that determination' (Miers, 1990: 224).

Miers is here drawing primarily on social psychology and symbolic interactionism (as popularized in the sociology of deviance in the 1960s) in attempting to redress the balance of positivism within victimology. These theoretical perspectives can certainly cast some light on the way in which conceptions of the 'ideal victim' (Christie, 1986) are present in day-to-day interpretations and understandings of the social world. But such understandings reveal little about the underlying structural formations of those definitions. This is largely a result of the liberal democratic tendencies associated with such perspectives. Symbolic interactionists may claim to have been concerned with the political processes underlying the process of labelling. Nevertheless:

> it is equally problematic that 'labelling theorists' (1) never specified in detail the ideological constitution of the moral and criminal categories, (2) never fully explored the links between these categories and the social structure, and (3) only dealt with the relationship between moral/legal condemnation and 'interest' in an instrumental way. (Sumner, 1990: 23)

These same questions pertain to a victimology which concerns itself with the labels but not with the constitution of those labels. This partly explains why the scope of victimology offered by Miers's (1990) understanding of the term 'critical' leaves victimology within the confines of the law, with the law itself remaining unchallenged. In addition his use of the term 'critical' does not facilitate the establishment of an effective and alternative scientific agenda which would connect the description of such labelling processes to the wider social structure.

The sense in which Walklate (1989, 1990) has attempted to develop an understanding of critical victimology has been concerned in the first instance to establish an understanding of the relationship between epistemology, methodology and the political agenda. This view has largely emerged from a critical understanding of the achievements of radical left realism in criminology, a Bhaskarian understanding of scientific realism, and the way in which Cain (1990) has developed some of these ideas from a feminist critique of criminology.

This view of victimology takes seriously the need for the development of an empirically based, rational and objective science, but as Keat and Urry (1975: 5) point out, for the realist: 'this will mean postulating the existence of types of unobservable entities and processes that are unfamiliar to us: but it is only by doing this that we get beyond the "mere appearance" of things, to their natures and essences'.

Key to this process for the development of an empirical science seems to be the question of what constitutes the real. This question demands that any empirical investigation must take account of a number of processes which contribute to the construction of everyday reality: people's conscious activity, their 'unconscious' activity (that is, routine activities people engage in which serve to sustain, and sometimes change, the conditions in which they act), the generative mechanisms (unobservable and unobserved) which underpin daily life, and finally, both the intended and the unintended consequences of action which feed back into people's knowledge.

A conceptual framework of this kind enables victimology to address a number of important issues. In the first instance, put in a rather simplistic fashion, it postulates the importance of understanding the processes that 'go on behind our backs' which contribute to the victims (and the crime) we 'see' as opposed to that which we do not 'see'. Thus the concerns of the radical victimologists are placed on the agenda. The concern with those processes which are seen and those which remain hidden has also been a key concern for the feminist movement. Feminist work has forced the recognition of women as occupiers of both the public and the private domain and has argued that this recognition enhances the objectivity of a discipline; rendering visible and naming processes and experiences which were once unspoken and hidden. In addition feminist work has been keen to document women's strategies of surviving and resisting the dominant social structural framework. This in turn results in an understanding of human subjectivity (conscious as well as 'unconscious' action) as a central feature of day-to-day life to be taken seriously.

Whilst these questions demand a critical rethinking of the relationship between theory and method (concepts and techniques) they do not necessarily imply the abandonment of the criminal victimization survey. What is required is a recognition that such techniques cannot capture both the generalities of victimization and the 'lived realities' (Crawford *et al.*, 1990) of human beings (see also Genn, 1988; Mawby, 1992a). Cain (1990) has suggested some general guidelines on setting realist research agendas, Pawson (1989) has examined the implications of realism for doing empirical work in general and quantitative work in particular, and Walklate (1990) has suggested how it might be possible to research the fear of crime by employing these ideas. The questions of more general relevance here are how do these ideas better inform the kinds of analysis offered within victimology, and victims' movements? And what implications do these ideas have in terms of the relationship between academic and humanist victimologists?

There are some clear indications above as to how realism might better inform the general analyses offered from within victimology.

A critical victimology informed by these ideas problematizes both the law and the role of the state, and places both conceptual and empirical questions raised by the feminist movement at the centre of the agenda. It does this, however, not in a simple or straightforward manner; for these ideas demand that account is taken of the recursive relationship between agency and structure (Giddens, 1984). It is important to document those changing relationships through an appreciation and understanding of historical and cultural processes. At an empirical level this constitutes a call for imaginative comparative and longitudinal studies. At a theoretical level it requires postulating and testing the existence of generative mechanisms which may underpin specific individual action at specific moments. In the context of documenting the emergence and development of victims' movements it demands not only an understanding of the cultural variations in style and content of policy implementation processes relating to such movements, but also connecting these to the socioeconomic framework in which such initiatives develop. Some of those broader pictures are beginning to be painted.

Jefferson and Shapland (1990) document the way in which trends within criminal justice research are clearly connected with wider political and economic concerns. One of those trends is the increasing concern with the 'consumer' of the criminal justice system, who is assumed primarily to be the victim of crime, not the perpetrator. This rising concern has developed relatively unchallenged:

> Distinctions of this order – between 'consumerism' and the free market idea itself – do not attract much attention in the language of free market theorists themselves, and they do not excite much commentary in current public, political debate as a whole. That they do not is some measure of the extraordinary success of free market theorists and politicians in western societies in mobilizing a grossly generalized and popular political language, focused around the ideas of 'freedom' and of 'choice'. (Taylor, 1990: 5)

Whilst the rise of this popular political language seems to have penetrated both 'public' and 'private' institutions from the police service through to higher education, it reflects important socioeconomic processes which form the backcloth to the phenomenal rise of Victim Support in England and Wales; similar developments – though with variations in organization and scale – are seen across Europe (see Chapter 5). Such developments have gone alongside changes in criminal justice systems and the emergence of state compensation schemes encouraged by recommendations from the Council of Europe (see Chapter 6).

Alongside the development of this consumer orientation, provisions for women, and their experiences of the criminal justice process, have also undergone some marked changes. Not only have networks emerged to support women as 'victims' of specifically sexual crime but agencies within the criminal justice system have responded to complaints about their treatment of women (and children) as victims of crime. Again, whilst these developments may vary depending upon the specific cultural and legal context in which they occur, they nevertheless represent changes that need to be connected with wider socioeconomic and political circumstances. Although women may well still be censured (Sumner, 1990) the moment of that censure may have changed. This broader picture of social change facilitates a move away from the partial analyses offered to date by victimology both politically and academically, and towards examining the underlying thesis of the relationship of such movements to wider social changes.

Critical victimology as conceived in this text constitutes an attempt to examine the wider social context in which some versions of victimology have become more dominant than others and also to understand how those versions of victimology are interwoven with questions of policy response and service delivery to victims of crime. It constitutes an attempt to appreciate how the generative mechanisms of capitalism and patriarchy set the material conditions in which different victims' movements have flourished. These notions provide the critical edge in understanding the particular impact that research agendas and policy initiatives may or may not have.

Conclusion

This work is an attempt to document some of the changes that have occurred in response to the issues of criminal victimization and to connect them, theoretically, to changes occurring in spheres outside the criminal justice system.

It is conceived within a framework which posits a particular relationship between the academic endeavour and the humanistic endeavour it is concerned to examine. This view does not rest on a claim to scientific status which is dependent upon the maintenance of the 'facts/values' distinction with which this chapter began and which is implicit in the positivist project. The view of science suggested here places the academic and the activist on the same critical plane (Cain, 1990). They are a part of social reality in which as knowledgeable actors both have the capacity to influence the processes of social change. They have much to learn from each other. It is hoped that the process of documentation engaged in here will lead others into more specifically empirical explorations of the issues addressed. The text will explore a number of issues.

First, it will examine, critically, the idea of a 'golden age' of the victim and the notion of the 'rediscovery' of the crime victim. Secondly, it will attempt to document those initiatives which appear in the literature as 'turning points' in the life and development of victims' movements. It will examine these 'turning points' not just in the context of the criminal justice system, or in relation to the characteristics of the movements themselves, but by locating them in the broader context of changing notions of welfare. Finally it will attempt to build on this by engaging in a cross-cultural analysis of the ways in which different societies currently approach the question of the crime victim.

As these issues are addressed it will become clear to the reader that whilst this chapter has presented three victimological frameworks, one of these frameworks and its associated concepts – positivist victimology – has been by far the most influential in terms of nationally funded research and in setting the agenda for centrally funded policy initiatives. This influence is self-evident in the summary of findings presented in Chapter 2 concerning the extent and impact of criminal victimization. Whilst the persistence of this influence has to be recognized the view will also be developed that the changes which have occurred and are recurring across Europe constitute a significant moment for a re-evaluation of the relevance of a victimology couched in these terms.

The challenge to understanding these changes and their impact on the processes of criminal victimization is as vital in victimology as in other academic disciplines. To disregard the potential relationship between the process of marketization, crime, fear of crime, and the development of particular kinds of victim services is to miss a vital link in the chain of understanding and explanation. The limitations inherent in positivist and radical victimology cannot unravel these changes in and of themselves. This text will also document policy initiatives taking place in Eastern Europe as a means of further evaluating the usefulness of some of the concepts discussed here. It is hoped that the case can be made in this book for a critical victimology informed by realism, which may not only facilitate a better understanding of these processes but may more clearly outline the policy possibilities for both victims and survivors of crime.

2

Crime and its Impact

The extent to which people define crime as a problem depends, in part, on what kind of crime is being referred to. Arguably, it is still fair to say that for most people their first thought about crime would relate to images of street crime ('mugging'), burglary or – in the case of women – rape. However, it is also fair to suggest that as a result of changes during the 1980s those first thoughts might, fairly rapidly, develop into broader images to include the sexually abused child or the victim of an industrial 'accident'. And although some of the research concerned with criminal victimization has attempted to incorporate such a broader understanding, much of it still reflects a concern with 'crime of the streets' and burglary rather than 'crime of the suites' and abuse. This tendency, of course, reflects the extent to which positivist victimology has influenced the research agenda, especially through the formulation of the criminal victimization survey (see Chapter 1) and is paralleled by the increasing influence of, for the most part, a structurally neutral image of the victim of crime reflected within the development of the victims' movements in the 1980s (see Chapters 4 and 5). In recognition of these tendencies this chapter will focus first of all on a selected comparative analysis of the data available concerned with the extent and impact of what is conventionally understood as the 'crime' problem.

The 'crime' problem

While there are some notable international variations, generally speaking the public in most Western societies sees crime, as conventionally defined, as a major social problem. As research in both the United States and England and Wales indicates, this is especially so when we consider public perceptions of the national picture, for example in terms of the overall crime situation or national trends (Hough and Mayhew, 1985; McPherson, 1978).

Of course, responses vary according to the precise nature of the questions that are asked. For example, perceptions of risk tend to be lower than concern about crime and fear of crime. Nevertheless, crime is seen as pervasive. Using a five-item Likert-type attitude scale designed to measure crime as a problem, a survey in Sheffield in 1975 found that some two-thirds of the population scored in the top third of scale (Bottoms *et al.*, 1987). In the London Borough of Islington, a survey in 1985 revealed that crime was identified by residents as second only to unemployment as a major problem (Jones *et al.*, 1986). By 1988 a second survey in that borough revealed that crime had supplanted unemployment as the most readily identified problem, with 81 per cent of respondents seeing it as a neighbourhood problem; 40 per cent saw crime as one of the three worst problems in the area (Crawford *et al.*, 1990: 22–3). Finally, it is noteworthy that geographical research in the UK aimed at identifying cities offering the highest 'quality of life' also suggests that both violent and other types of crime rate at the top of citizens' lists of negative features of the environment (Findlay *et al.*, 1989; Morris *et al.*, 1989; Rogerson *et al.*, 1988).

High levels of concern have also been found where surveys have asked about feelings of safety, usually specified in terms of the respondent being out alone in his or her neighbourhood (Gaquin, 1978; Garofalo, 1979; Maxfield, 1984; Skogan, 1986). Indeed, levels of fear evidenced in the 1982 British Crime Survey (BCS) led Hough and Mayhew (1983) to argue that fear of crime was perhaps a more serious problem than crime itself. Whilst dissociating themselves from this viewpoint, the Islington researchers also identified fear as prevalent (Crawford *et al.*, 1990; Jones *et al.*, 1986). Thus as well as finding that fear of being out alone at night was common, the 1988 Islington survey found that 37 per cent of respondents felt unsafe in their home, and 30 per cent of those who used public transport after dark felt unsafe when using it. Of those who did not go out alone after dark, 41 per cent said that fear of crime was a major reason, and 24 per cent said it was a significant influence (Crawford *et al.*, 1990: 44–58).

Are the public correct in their perceptions of crime? Is it the major problem that local and national surveys reveal, or is it possible that public perceptions are exaggerated? In approaching an answer to this question, the following sections focus on the extent of crime in various societies, and the impact of crime on its victims.

The extent of crime

There is a variety of sources for information on the extent of crime. None is perfect, and all have their own particular strengths and weaknesses. Official government crime statistics, for example, provide periodic time comparable data for crimes reported to and recorded by the police. They include crimes against individuals, offences against corporate victims, like shops or banks, and victimless crime. However, to the extent that victims fail to report crimes, or the police fail to discover or record crimes, they provide a seriously biased picture of crime. Thus, while homicides may be fairly accurately recorded, as will be motor vehicle thefts where insurance policies require reporting, many other crimes against individual victims are less commonly reported and recorded. Equally, corporate and victimless crimes usually escape official notification.

Self-report studies, whereby members of the public are asked to record crimes that they have *committed*, provide an alternative. Popular among criminologists in the 1960s and early 1970s, they reveal much higher levels of crime than do official statistics. However, doubts about the reliability and validity of response remain, especially where adults are surveyed, and even for juveniles there are concerns that respondents may vary in their willingness or ability to record their offending.

Victim surveys have become a more popular alternative in recent years. Since the mid-1960s they have been conducted – on both a national and local basis – in a number of different countries, although in almost all cases they are confined to individual and household victimization. That is, corporate crime and – by definition – victimless crime are excluded. In the United States, the National Crime Survey (NCS) involves panels of respondents who are periodically replaced, interviews taking place at six-monthly intervals with all adults in the households. In total, nearly 100,000 citizens are interviewed annually (Taylor, 1989). In England and Wales, separate sweeps of the BCS were conducted in 1982, 1984, 1988 and 1992, with twin surveys in Scotland in 1982 and 1988. In England and Wales in 1988 the sample consisted of 10,392 citizens sampled from the electoral register, a new feature being an additional booster sample of 1,349 ethnic minority citizens (Mayhew *et al.*, 1989). In 1989 the first large-scale *international* victim survey was undertaken. Based largely on telephone interviewing, some 28,000 respondents were interviewed in fourteen countries (Van Dijk *et al.*, 1990). While this survey mainly concentrated on Western industrial societies, the second survey, conducted in 1991–2, incorporated a number of developing societies and countries from Eastern Europe.[1]

Whether one uses recorded crime or victim survey data, the findings may still be presented in a number of different ways. One may for example look at overall rates, or rates for specific crimes. The latter is particularly feasible in the United States, where the regularity of the surveys has enabled researchers to combine data from different years and provide detailed analysis for some of the less common offences such as robbery (Harlow, 1987). One might also make a distinction between *prevalence* rates, whereby victims are counted only once and the results tell us what proportion of the population has been victimized, and *incidence* rates, where each crime is counted and the correspondingly higher crime figure reflects the number of incidents divided by the number of victims. This difference between prevalence and incidence is particularly important when comparing and contrasting studies concerned with rape, sexual assault and sexual abuse (see for example Mooney, 1993). Finally, the base rate can be varied. Most surveys provide data on victimization over a specific time period, most commonly a year. In the United States, household and personal crimes are also combined to present household risks as indicated by 'households touched by crime in any one year' (Rand, 1989). Alternatively, long-term lifetime risk may be estimated. In England and Wales, Hough and Mayhew (1983) suggested that on the basis of the 1982 BCS the average person could expect to be robbed once every five centuries, be injured in an assault every century, to have the family car stolen every sixty years and to be burgled every forty years. In the United States, similarly, Koppel (1987) used data from 1975–84 to estimate lifetime victimisation rates for a series of different crimes against the person and long-term (twenty-year) victimization rates for burglary, household larceny and motor vehicle thefts.

Whatever the time period, relating crime to some population base provides a logical and rational basis for measurement. In complete contrast, crime statistics are sometimes presented in terms of the number of incidents in a specified time period. In the United States, for example, the President's Task Force on Victims of Crime (1982), in portraying crime as a serious problem, headlined the fact that 'Every 23 minutes, someone is murdered. Every six minutes a woman is raped. While you read this statement two people will be robbed in this country and two more will be shot, stabbed or seriously beaten' (Presidents' Task Force, 1982: vi). Such figures are high in emotional appeal, but utterly meaningless unless they take account of the population at risk. By increasing the population considered – from Washington to Columbia to the United States to North America – crime takes on a more and more menacing image. When the population of the United States is four times that of England and Wales, to compare robberies per minute is misleading!

As well as relating criminal incidents to population, the extent of crime is more properly identified if there is some basis for comparison. For example, is crime more common now than in the past, and is it more prevalent here than in other countries?

Unfortunately here the problems with measuring crime are accentuated. Using official statistics, definitions of crime and reporting and recording practices will change with time, and vary between countries. Victim surveys may allow us to pinpoint short-term changes, but are too recent in origin for long-term comparisons. Additonally, as Block (1983) illustrates, surveys vary between countries, both in terms of the populations surveyed and the questions asked. As already noted, for example, the United States NCS involves interviews with all household members (aged 12 and over), using a panel of respondents. The BCS, in England and Wales in contrast, samples afresh from the electoral register, which includes all those aged 17 or more, and covers household crime but only crimes against the person where the respondents themselves were victimized. It does, however, include a wider variety of crimes, since the NCS excludes threats and criminal damage (Taylor, 1989). Clearly the international crime survey allows far more accurate international comparisons, even though restricted to a small number of countries. It is, however, limited in scale, largely dependent upon telephone interviews, and, partly as a result, subject to a low and internationally varied response rate (Van Dijk, 1991b). Although using identical questions (subject to translation) it does also assume that respondents from different countries will reply in similar fashion to similar questions.[2]

Bearing in mind these notes of caution, what can be learnt from cross-national comparison? Kalish's (1988) analysis of recorded crime reveals considerable variations in homicide rates. In the early 1980s, for example, the rate per 100,000 population in England and Wales, and indeed in most of Europe, ranged from 1 to 1.5. In contrast, in the United States the lowest figure available put the rate at 7.9. While the homicide rate in Japan was even lower than that throughout Europe, Canada and Australia registered rates of approximately double the European average, but well below that for the United States. Northern Ireland's homicide rate was also high, at about half the United States figure. Lest high rates for homicide be associated with advanced capitalism, it should also be noted that Third World countries such as Thailand, Venezuela and the Philippines had even higher rates than the United States, supporting the earlier conclusion of Archer and Gartner (1981) that while within a country homicide may be most prevalent in urban areas, more highly urbanized countries do not necessarily have higher rates. On a different level, it also seems that some Eastern bloc countries, such as the Soviet Union, had high rates for homicide prior to political change, and that these rates have recently increased (Mawby, 1990: 123).

Kalish (1988) also draws comparisons between a range of countries for other types of crime recorded by the police, illustrating the high levels in the USA for violence and street crime. Interpol figures for robbery in 1984 for example, suggest a rate for the USA of over four times that in England and Wales, with Japan again registering a very low rate. On the other hand, the USA does not stand out as having a particularly high recorded crime rate for offences such as vehicle theft or burglary. All such comparisons, nevertheless, are suspect to the extent that reporting and recording practices may vary markedly between different countries. It is consequently safer to rely on victim survey data for crimes other than homicide where there is an identified citizen victim.

The main report on the 1989 international crime survey was unfortunately restricted to Western industrialized capitalist societies (Van Dijk *et al.*, 1990), although more recent data are available for Japan (Van Dijk, 1991b). It does, however, demonstrate that even between such countries crime rates, and thus risk of being the victim of crime, vary considerably. Taking the overall prevalence rate for crimes covered in the survey, the rate for the European countries as a whole was 20.9 per cent, being lowest in Northern Ireland (15 per cent), Switzerland (15.6 per cent) and Finland (15.9 per cent) and highest in Spain (24.6 per cent) and the Netherlands (26.8 per cent). Crime was, however, apparently most common in the three non-European countries included – the USA (28.8 per cent), Canada (28.1 per cent) and Australia (27.8 per cent) – and lowest in Japan. If we focus on particular crimes which evoke public concern, such as burglary and robbery, a similar pattern emerges but with some notable variations. The incidence rate for burglary, for example, was highest in Australia (5.7 per 100 respondents) and the USA (5.5); for robbery the USA again figured prominently (3.0) but was eclipsed by Spain (3.9) (Van Dijk *et al.*, 1990).

Although the 1992 survey did not take place in all of these countries the pattern was broadly confirmed, the main exception being a disproportionate rise in victimization rates in England and Wales (Van Dijk and Mayhew, 1992; Mayhew, 1992). Interestingly, rates in the two former Eastern bloc countries included, Poland and Czechoslovakia, were broadly in line with the European norm, although higher in the former. Poland also seemed to experience higher levels of thefts from the person, whereas Czechoslovakia had the joint-highest rate in the survey for burglary (Van Dijk and Mayhew, 1992).

The 1992 survey also included personal interviews with samples drawn from selected cities in developing countries (Zvekic and Del Frate, 1992). These revealed generally *higher* rates of victimization than in industrial societies, although there were marked variations within the sample of countries, the highest risks being in Africa and South America. The most significant finding relates to corruption by state officials and consumer fraud, offences rarely mentioned in the West. Such incidents were cited far more frequently than conventional cases, leading the authors to conclude:

> Citizens are markedly running the risk of being victimized either by government officials and/or in the sector of services. Both victimizations indicate much more than the sheer sphere of conventional crime; they speak about development itself, of the citizens' position *vis-à-vis* government and commercial sector activities, the lack of consumer/client and citizen protection, and the ways in which people go about or are made to go about in satisfying their needs and rights. (Zvekic and Del Frate, 1992: 10)

These comparisons imply that when we consider how far crime is a problem, the answer will depend on the precise question asked. In terms of crime risks, there are variations between countries and between types of crime. Within capitalist societies, victim survey data and recorded crime statistics suggest at least five categories. At one extreme, the USA appears to register high crime rates across the board; at the other extreme, crime is relatively uncommon in some countries such as Japan and Switzerland. Other major European countries, including France, Germany and England and Wales, fall somewhere in between. Above them come Australia and Canada, with higher crime rates overall but with homicide rates nearer to the European mean than to US figures. Finally it is worth mentioning Northern Ireland, where the international crime survey reveals a low crime rate but where the homicide rate is well above that in the rest of Europe, a fact largely attributable to the political situation. As official reports stress, however, the homicide rate in Northern Ireland is only a third that of New York, a sixth that of Fort Worth and an eighth that of Detroit (Police Authority for Northern Ireland and the RUC, 1988: 36).

Having put the situation in some sort of international perspective, it is worth pausing to review briefly the risk of crime in England and Wales and the USA, for which most information is available. The BCS has included data on all criminal offences where there is an identified victim, including threats, but excluding from analysis thefts of milk from the doorstep. Figures for 1988 revealed that 6 per cent of crimes involved violence, 11 per cent common assault and just over 2 per cent theft from the person. Most crimes were, therefore, against household property: motor vehicle thefts (22 per cent), other vandalism (10 per cent), other thefts (28 per cent) or burglary (9 per cent). Some 37 per cent of incidents were reported to the police, with the highest rates of reporting for motor vehicle thefts (95 per cent) and completed burglaries (86 per cent). The overall incidence rates were 4,610 per 10,000 households for household offences, an increase of 22 per cent since 1981, and 1,099 per 10,000 respondents for personal offences, an increase of only 3 per cent (Mayhew *et al.,* 1989: 8–10, 69–70). Few details are available as yet from the 1992 survey. However, it seems that rates for acquisitive crime have continued to rise, and that such offences have nearly doubled during the 1981–91 period. The 1992 survey also reveals that victims have become more willing to report their crime to the police (43 per cent did so), and while this corresponds to the finding that victim survey rates have not increased to the same extent as have recorded crime rates, for acquisitive crime increases have been broadly similar (Mayhew and Maung, 1992). Moreover, combining data from the British and international crime surveys, Mayhew (1992) accepts a marked increase in crime in England and Wales, higher than in other countries included in the survey, a finding Waller (1992) relates to government policies and increased levels of poverty and inequality in England and Wales relative to other capitalist societies.

As already noted, the NCS has focused on the more serious crimes. According to estimates from the US Department of Justice in 1991 there were nearly 35 million such incidents of which 6.4 million were violent crimes, 12.5 million personal thefts and 15.8 million household crimes, a very different pattern to that in England and Wales. For those crimes included, the incidence rate was 923 per 10,000 respondents for personal crimes and 1,629 per 10,000 households for household crimes. Overall 38 per cent of incidents had been reported to the police, with motor vehicle thefts being most commonly reported (Bastian, 1992). Taking each household as a separate unit for analysis, about a quarter of households per year experienced one or more of the crimes included in the survey; 5 per cent experienced at least one burglary and 5 per cent had had a member victimized in a crime of violence (Rand, 1989). Using data from surveys between 1975 and 1984, Koppel (1987) estimates that 12-year-olds had a lifetime risk of personal theft of 99 per cent and a lifetime risk of violent crime of 83 per cent. Households had a twenty-year risk of burglary of 72 per cent and of motor vehicle theft of 19 per cent. NCS figures nevertheless reveal a fall in crime since 1981 (Bastian, 1992), a contrast with official statistics that suggest increases in crime over the same period (Laub, 1990).

One further comparison is worth drawing at this point: risk of crime compared with risk of other 'disasters'. As Maxfield (1984) demonstrated using the 1982 BCS, the public tends to see crime as more likely to occur than many other disasters. The fact that the Islington surveys show crime to rate alongside unemployment (Crawford *et al.*, 1990) may also be an indication that even in times of high unemployment crime is seen as the more likely to affect the respondent. However, it is equally evident that *in reality* serious crime in England and Wales is less common than many other problems. For example serious injury in accidents on the road, at work or in the home are more common than from violent crime, and deaths in road accidents outnumber homicide by about seven to one (Central Statistical Office, 1990). The policy implications of such balancing came to the fore in 1989 when, following the murder of a woman who left her faulty car on the motorway and walked to phone for help, some police officials advised women in a similar situation to stay in their car and lock the doors, whilst others pointed out that risk of a stationary car being hit was far greater than of any violent attack. Similarly, for the USA, Harlow (1989) quotes national statistics to illustrate that serious injuries in motor vehicles are six times as likely as violent crime victimization requiring medical treatment, and that death by homicides (while more common than in England and Wales) occur only half as often as road traffic deaths. Northern Ireland provides perhaps the best illustration of the disparity between public perception and reality: not since 1972 have more people died in public security incidents than in road traffic accidents, yet undoubtedly terrorism figures in people's minds as the key threat to safety in the province (Royal Ulster Constabulary 1989: 34). The risk of crime as conventionally defined, therefore, while varying across countries, is not perhaps as great as we think, especially when compared to other problems citizens face.

An alternative perspective is possible if we define crime some-what differently. Given the powerful tendency within both criminology and victimology to view the crime problem in a fairly narrow way, it is perhaps not surprising to be faced with a catalogue of research work which has considered the extent of crime as outlined above. But if the focus is widened to include the question of 'corporate crime' then the picture which faces us changes some-what. As already suggested, such issues do not easily lend themselves to exploration via the criminal victimization survey. Given the nature of the crime, more imaginative and varied research designs are often required, and alongside considering what official statistics are available concerning health and safety infringe-ments, for example, a much fuller picture of the extent of crime can be painted. (See Reiman, 1979; Box, 1983; for a summary of these findings, see Walklate, 1989, Chapter 4.)

Recently an attempt has been made by researchers working in Islington to deploy the criminal victimization survey to explore the extent of 'commercial' crime. They conclude that 'the victimization of individuals as consumers, tenants and workers, then can be considered to be more extensive than is true of street crimes' (Pearce, 1990: 49). They also suggest that the high reporting rate of people who believe that they have a 'right to know' about the activities and infringements of commercial and regulatory agencies was affected by the timing of the data collection (in the aftermath of the King's Cross fire). As suggested by Taylor (1991), the public debates that occurred in the aftermath of a series of 'disasters' which took place in Britain between 1985 and the end of 1988 may be considered a significant point in changing public awareness to a broader understanding of the crime problem; elsewhere the events in Bhopal in 1985 may have had a similar effect. Those events, and the associated activities of Union Carbide Corporation, changed public awareness concerning the activities of large corporations not only in India but also in the United States (Pearce and Tombs, 1989). Other specific incidents, it may be argued, also feed into changing the public perception of the broader crime equation; for example the 'Guinness affair' and the activities of pharmaceutical companies (Thalidomide, Dalken Shield). While difficult to document, it may also be fruitful to consider the ways in which these specific events tap into a broader changing political environment, in which 'green issues', and the political movements associated with bringing these issues to the fore across Europe and North America, have on occasion merged with the question of a broader conceptualization of crime.

As Box (1983) has argued, power may itself determine that the crimes of the powerful have generally been excluded from public perceptions of the crime problem and, conversely, the victimization of the powerless may be understated. Returning to the crime problem as conventionally defined, however, it must be stressed that *incidence* is only one dimension to the problem; *impact* is an important second dimension. In the following section we focus on the impact of crimes on victims.

The impact of crime

In introducing the effects of crime, we can perhaps best untangle a web of different issues by posing three questions: who is affected by crime? What is it precisely that affects them? How are the effects of crime manifested? We might expect those who are directly victimized by specific crimes to be most affected. However, a variety of studies have also noted the indirect victims of crime. Most commonly cited, and already considered in terms of the fear of crime, are those members of the public who are affected by wider concerns over crime, to the extent that they worry about it and possibly restrict their lifestyles. Other indirect victims are those who are affected by specific crimes against their kin or friends; for example the partners of rape victims.

If we consider what it is precisely that affected people, clearly those who are influenced by crime in general are affected by future possibilities, the prospect of crime. Additionally there is some evidence that those who are the direct victims of crime are particularly prone to fear of future victimization. Victims (direct or indirect) of specific crimes may also be affected by the crime itself (primary victimization) or the way in which others respond to them and their crimes (secondary victimization). In the latter case, the way that reported crimes are dealt with by the police, prosecutors and courts is of particular relevance. However, it should be stressed here that since only a minority of crimes are reported to the police, and a minority of these cleared up and subsequently prosecuted, the number of victims experiencing secondary victimization will be less. This is illustrated in Figure 2.1, taking data for England and Wales. Thus if we start with a hypothetical population of 100, the BCS suggests that some 20–30 per cent of these will be victimized within a given year. Of these, 30–40 per cent will report the crimes to the police, with a suspect identified in 30–40 per cent of these cases. Prosecution will then normally follow where the suspect is aged 17 or over, although current policy is for an increase in cautioning. The majority of juvenile offenders receive a caution in place of prosecution (Home Office, 1990a). From the original 100 citizens, or 25 victims, then, perhaps two cases will result in prosecution. Many of these will be dealt with by a guilty-plea and in other cases the victim may not be a witness. Possibly one in 25 victims will therefore experience being called as a witness in court. The number of victims who might experience secondary victimization on these different levels will be lessened by the unwillingness of most victims to report crimes, the inability of the police to clear up the crime, and the lack of necessity for many victims to appear in court. Of these, how far victims' avoidance of involvement is the result of perceptions of the process as traumatic, or even of nuisance value, is open to question.

How, then, are victims affected? A particular crime may have an effect on victims directly in a number of ways. They may be physically injured, incur expenses or lose time, as a result of the crime itself or involvement in the criminal justice process. Crime

Figure 2.1   *The career of the crime victim*

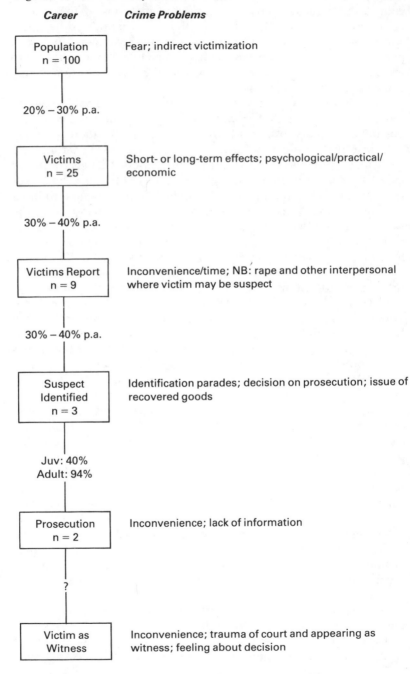

Career

Crime Problems

Population
n = 100

Fear; indirect victimization

20% – 30% p.a.

Victims
n = 25

Short- or long-term effects; psychological/practical/
economic

30% – 40% p.a.

Victims Report
n = 9

Inconvenience/time; NB: rape and other interpersonal
where victim may be suspect

30% – 40% p.a.

Suspect
Identified
n = 3

Identification parades; decision on prosecution; issue of
recovered goods

Juv: 40%
Adult: 94%

Prosecution
n = 2

Inconvenience; lack of information

?

Victim as
Witness

Inconvenience; trauma of court and appearing as
witness; feeling about decision

may also have an impact on their psychological state, undermining their state of well-being and making them unsure, apprehensive, afraid, and so on. This may itself affect future behaviour; for example, resulting in fear to go out alone after dark. These less tangible manifestations may affect those who are not directly victimized but who see crime as a particular problem and react accordingly.

However, as Wortman (1983) has spelt out in some detail, the measurement of emotional effects raises a number of methodological difficulties. How, for example, does one distinguish between the victim who is unaffected, the victim who experiences emotion but does not express it, and the victim who expresses his or her emotions in privacy?

> If a man shows little emotional reaction to the death of his infant daughter, does this mean that the death does not represent a crisis for him? Or does this mean that he was extremely upset by her death, but that he has managed to get his emotions under control? Alternatively, does the absence of emotion suggest that the man is really upset, but 'denying' the impact of the crisis? Or, is he experiencing distress but unwilling or unable to admit this because he feels that displays of distress are inappropriate or indicative of poor adjustment? (Wortman, 1983: 212–13)

This problem is compounded when we consider the nature of the emotional reactions experienced, or manifest. Crying is a more 'acceptable' response in some cultures than others, and for women rather than men. Anger may be an acceptable response that incorporates other emotions. Assessing the extent to which victims have been emotionally affected is a hazardous business, and findings from various studies must be treated with caution.

If we concentrate on those who are the direct victims of crime, what evidence is available on the effects of these crimes? In summarizing the data from the United States and Britain, it is perhaps easiest to do so separately, both because the emphasis of researchers and practitioners contrasts markedly between countries, and because the research available differs substantially. For example, in the United States more emphasis has been placed on serious crime, especially sexual offences, and the traumatic impact of such crimes, and on secondary victimization. In Britain, in contrast, much of the general data on impact comes from the BCS. Unlike the NCS, which only includes information on physical injury, financial cost and time lost due to crime, the BCS in 1984 and 1988 also incorporated questions on how victims felt they had been affected, leading to more, admittedly subjective, information on the impact of crime on victims in general.

What then of the evidence from the United States? There, the early victim movement was dominated by two issues that have influenced perspectives on the impact of crime. First, government concerns that victims and witnesses were failing to co-operate with the criminal justice system led to an emphasis on secondary victimization and policies aimed, for example, at helping victims in court. Secondly, the involvement of the women's movement resulted in a focus on sex offences and violence (Mawby and Gill, 1987: 115–34; Skogan *et al.*, 1990). These twin concerns are well illustrated in the President's Task Force on Victims of Crime (1982). Using a number of examples of sex and violent crime, the commission paints a picture of victims being drastically affected twice: once by the offender, then by the criminal justice system, with police, courtroom processes and post-sentencing procedures coming in for heavy criticism for ignoring victims' needs and allegedly prioritizing offenders' rather than victims' rights.

How are victims affected? NCS data provides some evidence on the substantial effects of crime (US Department of Justice, 1990). In 1987 some 75 per cent of personal crimes covered in the survey and 91 per cent of household crimes resulted in financial loss. For these household crimes, 31 per cent involved amounts of under $50, 20 per cent over $500. Some 6 per cent of victims had time off work as a result of the crime. In a more detailed analysis of injuries from violent crime (rape, robbery or assault) Harlow (1989) shows that between 1979 and 1986 approximately 28 per cent of violent crime victims were injured, 13 per cent suffered an injury that resulted in medical attention and 7 per cent required hospital care. Of those who were injured 85 per cent suffered bruises, cuts or scratches but at the other extreme 1 per cent received gunshot wounds, 3 per cent knife injuries and 6 per cent broken bones or teeth.

What of the emotional impact of crime? As already noted, much of the US research has focused on very serious offences, especially sex or violent crime, in many cases drawing inferences from fairly small groups of victims receiving psychiatric treatment. Krupnick and Horowitz (1980), for example, detailed the experiences of 13 victims of violent assault who received psychotherapy at a special clinic for the treatment of stress response syndromes. While focusing on more serious crime, some authors compare the impact of crime with non-crime life-threatening events or other disasters (Frederick, 1980; Janoff-Bulman and Frieze, 1983). Some of the more recent, and more extensive, studies include those by Sales, Baum and Shore (1984) on rape victims, Lurigio (1987) on victims of burglary, robbery and assault, and Resick, Kilpatrick and their colleagues on rape, robbery, violence and burglary victims (Kilpatrick *et al.*, 1987; Resick, 1987; see also Lurigio and Resick, 1990; Resick 1990).

Many of these studies start with the proposition that individuals define their world as meaningful and just. Experience of crime must therefore be understood in terms of answers to the question 'Why me?' Victims may cope with the problem of unpredictability and the consequential threat of future victimization by blaming themselves for their experiences. Researchers variously describe the effects as including fear, nervousness, anxiety, depression, confusion and paranoia, evidenced in nightmares, sleep disruption, difficulty in adjusting to work and other problems with social functioning. The combination of many of these reactions is often identified as post-traumatic stress disorder, or PTSD:

> Post-traumatic stress disorder is an anxiety disorder produced by an uncommon, extremely stressful life event and is characterised by several symptoms including: (a) re-experiencing of the traumatic event in painful recollections, flashbacks, dreams, or nightmares; (b) diminished responsiveness to the environment, with disinterest [*sic*] in significant activities, feelings of detachment and estrangement from others; and (c) symptoms such as exaggerated startle response, disturbed sleep, difficulty in concentrating or remembering, guilt about surviving when others did not, and avoidance of activities that bring the traumatic events to mind. (Kilpatrick *et al.*, 1987: 482)

Despite the impression portrayed by some writers, like Bard and Sangrey (1979), that such extreme effects are experienced by victims in general, as Lurigio (1987) recognizes, the emphasis in the American literature on more serious crime has contributed to a distorted view of the impact of crime. Thus, while Lurigio (1987) himself reports few differences between the reactions of assault, robbery and burglary victims, others see rape as among the more traumatic of crimes. Resick (1987) suggests that rape has a greater impact than robbery, but that the impact is greater still where the offences are combined, and Kilpatrick *et al.* (1987) also identify rape as having the most effect, followed by aggravated assaults, molestation and burglary, with other crimes less significant. Equally, the effects of crime may take longer to wear off for some offences, rape again being cited as having long-term effects. Indeed Sales, Baum and Shore (1984) argue that while in the short term the impact of rape may lessen, after six months victims may start to experience a further increase in trauma. This may be exacerbated by the reaction of agencies of the criminal justice system to the rape victim. In the initial stages, the role of police and medical services has been criticized (Holmstrom and Burgess, 1978); at a later stage, victims (correctly) perceive court appearances as threatening

(Resick, 1987). Similar points have been made about the ways in which victims in general have been treated by the system, and this so-called secondary victimization has been blamed for widespread unwillingness among victims and witnesses to co-operate with police and courts. These views, expressed by the 1967 President's Commission on Law Enforcement and the Administration of Justice, heralded the early 1970s Law Enforcement Assistance Administration (LEAA) programmes to improve the ways in which victims and witnesses were treated (Ash, 1972; McDonald, 1976a, 1976b; Skogan *et al.*, 1990). In this context it is interesting to note that Lurigio's (1987) research, comparing assault, robbery and burglary victims, found no differences between these and non-victims in terms of stated willingness to attend court, or views of the police, although assault victims were more critical than the rest.

What then of the British experience? Unlike the United States, except in the specific case of rape and domestic violence, little emphasis has been placed until recently on secondary victimization, although the Ralphs (1988) report, resulting from a working party set up by Victim Support, highlighted the problems faced by victims in court and has led to some changes in court practices. In other respects, the British research emphasis is distinctive, with more evidence of victims' perceptions of their experiences. Before detailing these findings, it is worth summarizing other evidence.

Given that it covers a wider range of less serious crimes than the NCS, the BCS might be expected to uncover rather lower levels of crime impact. Additionally, though, it appears that the nature of violent crime is on a different level, with fewer very serious offences. The 1988 BCS, for example, found that the offender was known to have a weapon in 5.5 per cent of crimes (17.9 per cent of personal, 0.7 per cent of household crimes).[3] Where the victim was aware of the offence at the time, a weapon was evident in 20 per cent of personal crimes and 7 per cent of household crimes. For personal crimes, the weapon involved was a knife, glass or other stabbing implement in 51 per cent of cases, a stick or other clubbing instrument in 24 per cent of cases, and a gun in only 6 per cent of cases. Violence was actually used in 57.7 per cent of personal crimes and 0.6 per cent of household crimes. For the former, 32 per cent of the total involved bruising or a black eye, 12 per cent cuts, 10 per cent scratches, and 2 per cent broken bones; 11 per cent resulted in the victim seeing a doctor, but less than 1 per cent involved overnight hospital treatment.

Turning to the financial costs of crime, the 1988 BCS reveals that crimes resulted in loss or damage in 94 per cent of household crimes and 17 per cent of personal crimes. For household crimes involving loss or damage, 36 per cent of victims said the loss was at least partly covered by insurance. Taking into account compensation received from insurance policies or elsewhere, the cost from household crime was under £25 for 54 per cent of victims who incurred loss or damage and at the other extreme at least £250 for 5 per cent. Finally, only 7 per cent of victims of personal crime and 5 per cent of victims of household crimes lost time from work as a result of the crime.

What of the wider impact of crime? As in the USA, research studies and critiques by practitioners and activists have highlighted the traumatic effects of rape and violence within the home, with similar criticisms of the aggravating effects of official response to victims (Edwards, 1989; Hanmer *et al.*, 1989; Maguire and Corbett, 1987; Mooney, 1993; Pizzey, 1974). Elsewhere Maguire (1980), in a study of burglaries that were reported to the police, found that whereas 32 per cent of victims stressed the financial consequences of the crimes, 41 per cent cited intrusion of privacy and 19 per cent emotional upset. Another study at the same time by Shapland and her colleagues, again restricted to reported crimes but concerning physical assaults, sexual assaults and robberies, involved interviewing victims over a three year period (Shapland, 1984; Shapland *et al.*, 1985). As well as demonstrating the impact of police and courts on victims' sense of well-being, the research showed 'the persistence and consistency of the prevalence of physical, social and psychological effects over time, compared to the low level and decrease over time of financial loss' (Shapland, 1984: 142).

In a later survey, Maguire and Corbett (1987: 36–82) interviewed 242 victims of burglary, robbery, assault and theft from the person, whose crimes had been both reported to the police and (in most cases) referred to victim support schemes. A large majority of those interviewed described themselves as 'very much affected' by their crime, and 40 per cent said that their first reaction was one of shock, panic and confusion. Given a checklist of reactions to the crime, victims then commonly cited anger, difficulty in sleeping, feeling unsettled or uneasy, fear, and shock. Subsequently, in a separate analysis of interviews with a small number of rape victims, Maguire and Corbett (1987: 173–208) underlined the traumatic impact of this crime on victims.

Whilst the studies described above provide considerable detail on victims of specific offences, by far the most detailed coverage is contained in the BCS, although this too has its weaknesses. As Lurigio (1987) notes, surveys that record all criminal incidents, no matter how minor, deflect the emphasis from routine crime, in the same way as, at the other extreme, research on very serious crime may overstate its effects. Moreover, as Maguire and Corbett (1987) illustrate in a comparison of their own survey with 1984 BCS data, focused studies may uncover some concerns of victims that more general studies miss. Bearing this in mind, we may turn to consider evidence from the BCS on victims' experiences, where victims have been asked a series of questions about their crimes, up to a maximum of four incidents per respondent.

In the 1984 survey, victims were asked how much they or their household had been affected, and whether the crime was still affecting them. They were subsequently asked what problems the crime had caused them, and what had been the worst problem. Overall 11 per cent of victims said that the crime had affected them 'very much' at the time, with 17 per cent replying that it had affected them 'quite a lot'. Only 7 per cent said that it was still affecting them 'very much' or 'quite a lot'. Asked further about specific effects, 42 per cent mentioned practical problems and 33 per cent emotional or personal problems. Not surprisingly, crimes that victims rate more serious, and those that were reported to the police, had more impact on victims. Additionally, the effects varied by offence-type. A broad distinction between household and personal crimes for example revealed that the latter affected victims the most. More specifically, robbery, wounding, burglary and threats affected a larger proportion of victims than did other crimes (Maguire and Corbett, 1987; Mawby and Gill, 1987).

Further evidence is available from the 1988 BCS. Victims were given a showcard that read:

> Many people have emotional reactions after incidents in which they are victims of crime. Did you or anyone else in your household, including children, have any of these reactions after the incident?

In all, 60 per cent replied in the affirmative, with 55 per cent answering that they personally had been affected. These people were then offered a further showcard and asked to say precisely which reactions they had experienced. By far the largest number, 45 per cent of all victims, cited anger, with shock mentioned by 14 per cent, fear by 9 per cent, insomnia by 7 per cent and crying by 5 per cent.

These victims were then asked how much they had been affected and how long it had taken for the worst effects to wear off. In total, 14 per cent of all victims said that they had been affected 'very much' and a further 17 per cent, 'quite a lot'; 17 per cent said that the effects had lasted for at least a week. All victims were subsequently asked what had been 'the worst thing about the incident'. In reply, 22 per cent described the crime as a nuisance and 16 per cent cited anger; at the extreme, though, 11 per cent described shock (or fear) at the time of the incident and 10 per cent fear that a further offence might be committed.

These overall figures hide a wealth of diversity. Again, crimes

Table 2.1   *The Proportion of all victims affected in various ways by their victimization*

	Personal crimes			Household crimes			
	Serious	Less serious	Total	Serious	Less serious	Total	Overall
Total crimes	345	959	1,304	1,541	1,827	3,372	4,676
	100	100	100	100	100	100	100
Victim or other household member suffered emotional reactions	248 72%	629 66%	877 67%	1,003 65%	943 52%	1,946 58%	2,823 60%
Victim experienced emotional reactions	247 72%	614 64%	861 66%	862 56%	872 48%	1,733 51%	2,594 55%
Victim affected 'very much' or 'quite a lot'	192 56%	378 39%	570 44%	478 31%	420 23%	898 27%	1,468 31%
Victim affected for at least a week	126 37%	228 24%	353 27%	251 16%	168 9%	421 12%	774 17%
Victim experienced:							
anger	188(55%)	414(43%)	602(46%)	763(49%)	760(42%)	1,523(45%)	2,124(45%)
shock	118(55%)	239(25%)	357(27%)	176(11%)	105 (6%)	281 (8%)	638(14%)
fear	81(23%)	210(22%)	290(22%)	86 (6%)	58 (3%)	144 (4%)	435 (9%)
difficulty sleeping	66(19%)	128(13%)	194(15%)	82 (5%)	65 (4%)	146 (4%)	340 (7%)
crying	57(17%)	106(11%)	163(13%)	51 (3%)	37 (2%)	88 (3%)	250 (5%)
Victim's worst reaction:							
nuisance	27 (8%)	10 (1%)	37 (3%)	494(32%)	508(28%)	1,002(30%)	1,039(22%)
anger	28 (8%)	109(11%)	136(10%)	284(18%)	331(18%)	615(18%)	751(16%)
shock	71(21%)	274(29%)	345(26%)	76 (5%)	78 (4%)	155 (5%)	500(11%)
financial loss	28 (8%)	7 (1%)	35 (3%)	220(14%)	204(11%)	424(13%)	459(10%)
fear	64(19%)	111(12%)	175(13%)	116 (8%)	166 (9%)	282 (8%)	457(10%)
invasion of privacy	9 (3%)	5 (1%)	14 (1%)	163(11%)	133 (7%)	295 (9%)	309 (7%)
sentimental loss	7 (2%)	1 (–)	9 (1%)	53 (3%)	61 (3%)	144 (3%)	123 (3%)
injury	45(13%)	41 (4%)	87 (7%)	2 (–)	2 (–)	3 (–)	90 (2%)

Source: BCS (1988)

that are reported are the ones that are more likely to affect victims, commonly because unreported crimes are considered trivial. Equally, personal crimes affect victims more than household crimes. To test out variations by offence-type, personal and household crimes were subdivided into more and less serious incidents, depending on the legal classification and the extent of physical loss or harm. For example, personal crimes involving wounding, sex offences, robbery and theft from the person were categorized as serious, those comprising common assault, attempted assaults and threats as less serious. The resulting analysis, which is portrayed in Table 2.1, clearly demonstrates that victims are most affected by more serious personal crimes, with less serious household crimes having least impact. What is also notable from Table 2.1 is that supposedly less serious personal crimes, incorporating many incidents that have traditionally been 'no-crimed' by the police, have a greater impact than do serious household crimes.

For household crime, burglary is often identified as especially traumatic. Focusing on the 380 burglaries covered by the 1988 BCS, including attempts but excluding burglaries from outside buildings, this was confirmed. Thus 64 per cent of victims said that they personally were affected, 42 per cent that they were affected 'very much' or 'quite a lot' and 35 per cent that the effects had lasted for at least a week. Moreover 26 per cent mentioned feelings of shock, 21 per cent of fear, 20 per cent sleeping difficulties and 10 per cent crying. Asked what the worst problem had been, 26 per cent mentioned fear of future victimization, 13 per cent shock at the time, and 27 per cent a concern over the invasion of privacy. With the exception of this last category, which parallels other studies of burglary victims, these responses are more akin to those of victims of personal crime than household crime.

The British evidence suggests that whilst a majority of victims suffer very little, a significant minority are affected by their experiences, and that where the crimes are particularly serious the effects are greater. Although less emphasis has been placed on PTSD than in the USA, the underlying message is not dissimilar. However, before leaving this section it is important to remember that understanding the impact of crime relates to assumed understanding of the extent of crime and the crime problem. The data available here, as in the first section, operate within a fairly narrowly defined and incident-related view of crime, perhaps with the exception of the studies dealing with the impact of rape. To understand the impact of crime, the activity or behaviour affecting the 'victim' must first of all be defined and recognized as criminal by the victim. In certain contexts this is a major stumbling block to achieving a full and complete picture of the impact of crime. Corporate crime, as Geis (1973) observed, rests on the possibility of 'victim-responsiveness'; that is a certain 'willingness' to be victimized; and whilst that willingness may be changing, it is certainly the case as Levi (1988: 17) reports being told in the context of an interview about fraud, 'Do your friends first; they're easier.' This exploitation of a relationship is one way of beginning to understand the impact of other kinds of crime which have at their base a power relationship; children who are or have been sexually abused, for example, may believe that the nature of the relationship they have with their father or father figure, is normal. Women for whom violence and rape may be an intrinsic part of their relationship, may not recognize (and up until recently were not encouraged to recognize) these activities as criminal. The impact of crime conceived in these terms cannot be measured and articulated in the same way as the impact of a burglary (even if burglary is commonplace in a particular area) since this constitutes part of what Crawford *et al.* (1990) have called the respondent's 'lived realities' (see also Genn, 1988). It is important also to remember that the impact of commercial fraud, for example, carries far more cost to the economy than burglary (Levi, 1987) and that the impact on a child of being sexually abused *may* result in a distortion of her/his own sexuality. Having said this, the same caution regarding generalization needs to be observed though some of these issues relate to the question of vulnerability (see below).

Finally, in the context of impact, it is appropriate to consider the extent of indirect victimization, where those affected are closely tied to the 'actual' victims. At least four categories have been identified in the literature: relatives of those killed in drink-driving fatalities; families of murder victims; partners of rape victims; and children caught up in crimes involving their parents. The problems faced by survivors or relatives of victims in drunken-driving cases led in the USA to the setting up of Mothers Against Drunk Driving (MADD), an organization that helps those in need and campaigns for legal change. Describing the work of MADD, Harris Lord (1986) has identified the problems faced by these indirect victims, both in responding to the fatality and in coping with the response of statutory agencies such as the courts. In such cases, as with families of homicide victims (Burgess, 1975; Riggs and Kilpatrick, 1990), reactions are likely to include grief as well as feelings of injustice and possible guilt at being a 'survivor'. Moreover, as Brown, Christie and Morris (1990) detail in a recent British study of the experiences of families of murder victims, a number of problems arise in addition to the sense of grief and loss that may accompany any bereavement. For example, the home may be sealed off during an investigation and once accessible again may contain evidence of the crime, families may be treated as suspects rather than victims, and extended investigations and court processes may prolong the stress. Yet, as the authors note, very few agencies deal sympathetically with these indirect victims, and many of the procedures exacerbate their problems.

The problems faced by partners of rape victims may be equally severe, but differ in emphasis. Summarizing the evidence, Riggs and Kilpatrick (1990) distinguish between the impact of the crime on the relationship, and on the psychological functioning of the partners themselves. In the former case, partners have reported problems of communication, sexual difficulties and the need to control emotions. In the latter, disbelief, concern, shame, anger, guilt and betrayal have been described, and indeed it appears that some partners may themselves suffer PTSD.

The problems faced by children are different again. Of course, the issue of children as direct victims of crime has been the focus of considerable research, especially where violence or sex is involved (Walklate, 1989: 52–80). In many of these cases, secondary victimization has become an issue at least in so far as courts have faced problems with regard to child testimony. A slightly different issue, which has been placed on the agenda in Britain by Victim Support, is the prospect of children being affected by crime where the actual victim is a parent or the household in general (Morgan, 1988). For example, following a burglary some children will evidence similar symptoms to adults – insomnia, nightmares, bedwetting, and so on. To test this further, respondents to the 1988 BCS were asked whether anyone else in their household had been emotionally affected following a crime. Of those with children, 10 per cent said that one or more child had been affected, with over a third of these saying the children had been affected 'very much'. Where there were children aged under 5 in the household, parents were particularly likely to describe them as affected. Interestingly, children were, according to their parents, more likely to be affected where the respondent was the victim of a crime against the person than for household crimes, although in the latter case burglaries were particularly likely to affect children. In cases of burglary, 24 per cent of children were reportedly affected, 17 per cent 'very much' 'or quite a lot', and 17 per cent for at least a week afterwards; 13 per cent were described as experiencing fear, 9 per cent insomnia and 14 per cent as having cried.

Vulnerability and crime

In the previous sections, we have argued that risk of crime as it is conventionally understood is perhaps less than many people imagine, and less than the likelihood of many other problems that might affect us, such as injury in traffic accidents. Moreover, for most crimes, indeed the majority of crimes from which official statistics are constructed, victims are not seriously affected, and it is the less common crimes such as rape, violence, robbery and burglary where the impact on victims is most marked. However, aggregate statistics can be misleading. The statistical fact that burglaries are uncommon is little comfort to those, like one of the authors, faced with a fourth burglary in as many years! It is also important to note that fear is also unevenly distributed among the population, and may contribute to a deep-seated strategy for dealing with routine daily activities among some groups, especially women (Stanko, 1990). It is therefore crucial to consider how far certain subgroups of the population are at particular risk of crime, or when victimized are highly likely to be affected. These two issues together relate to the notion of *vulnerability*.

Taking first the risk of crime, six variables have been generally identified as influential: area of residence; class or status; race; gender; age; and marital status.

Concerning area of residence, the relationship between area and crime has been a common theme of criminology, from nineteenth-century British indignation about the rookeries of large industrial cities, through the influence of the Chicago school, to present-day concern over deprived inner city areas and public housing complexes. NCS data from the United States emphasize the vulnerability of city-dwellers, who suffer more crime than suburban or rural dwellers. For example in 1988 the rate for household crimes was 299 per 1,000 households among central city-dwellers compared with 153 in the suburbs and 127 in non-metropolitan areas. Variations were most notable for robbery, where the respective rates per 1,000 persons aged 12 or more were 10, 3.9 and 2.1 (Johnson and DeBerry, 1989). Equally, within cities differences are marked (Skogan, 1990). Drawing comparisons on a rather different scale, the first international crime survey identified the highest victimization rates among those living in urban areas of 50,000 or more, least among those in communities with under 10,000 residents (Van Dijk *et al.*, 1990: 60).

In England and Wales, respondents to the BCS are subdivided according to the types of area in which they live, using the

ACORN classification of neighbourhood groups. Subsequent analysis has demonstrated marked variations by area type, with residents of the 'poorest council estates' and multiracial urban areas having the highest victimization rates, and agricultural areas, prosperous retirement areas and the affluent suburbs at the other extreme. The crime problem of the inner city is vividly illustrated in the Islington crime surveys (Crawford *et al.*, 1990; Jones *et al.*, 1986). Moreover, local surveys in London (Sparks *et al.*, 1977), Merseyside (Kinsey, 1984) and Sheffield (Bottoms *et al.*, 1987) reveal considerable disparity within the urban environment, with poor privately rented areas and unpopular public housing estates facing the worst problems.

Studies such as these suggest that where housing groups experience different rates of victimization, class differences might follow. However, whilst both the NCS and BCS reveal higher rates of victimization among those in rented accommodation and lower rates among owner-occupiers, differences by income or class are more ambiguous. In the United States, NCS data indicate that for violent crime and most non-violent personal crime, victimization rates are inversely related to income. For household crime, low-income groups are most at risk, but differences between the other income groups are negligible. Moreover, whilst burglary rates are highest for low-income groups, they are also relatively high for the highest-income groups. A similar picture emerges from the BCS; generally the inverse relationship between victimization and income or class is most evident for personal crime, less clear for household crime. Equally, as Maguire (1982) has demonstrated, high-income groups may be at particular risk of burglaries which are professionally planned. Most recently, the first international victim survey found victimization rates highest among high-income groups (Van Dijk *et al.*, 1990: 63). The unemployed do however have higher victimization rates: in the 1984 BCS 55 per 100 households for household crime and 16 per cent for personal crime, compared with the norms of 41 and 11 respectively.

Area of residence is also related to race. In the United States, detailed analysis of data for Hispanics (Bastian, 1990) and blacks (Whitaker, 1990) reveals high victimization rates for both groups, but also the influence of residence on these patterns. For Hispanics, rates of victimization between 1979 and 1986 were well above those for non-Hispanics. For example, robbery rates were 11 and 6 per 1,000 individuals respectively; for burglaries the difference was 266 compared with 205 per 1,000 households. Controlling for other variables related to victimization, like area of residence, eliminated most of these differences although Hispanics were still more likely to suffer from robberies.

For the same period, blacks also experienced more personal and household crime than whites, and violent crimes committed against blacks tended to be more serious. This is graphically illustrated in Karmen's (1990) analysis of homicide statistics. Similarly, Whitaker (1990: 10), referring to 1986 Uniform Crime Reports (UCR), concluded that 'the murder rate for blacks was nearly six times the rate for whites (31.2 versus 5.4 per 100,000)'. Concentrating on NCS figures, she also shows the violent crimes victimization rate to be higher for blacks, 44 compared with 34 per 1,000 people. However, while blacks were more likely to experience rape, robbery and aggravated assault, whites had higher rates for simple assault and theft from the person. Blacks also experienced higher rates for household crimes such as burglary (108 versus 72 per 1,000 households) and motor vehicle theft (25 versus 15 per 1,000 households). Moreover, while these differences shrank in suburban and rural areas when she controlled for other variables, 'in central cities, blacks had higher robbery and household burglary rates than whites regardless of the age or family income of the victim or household head' (Whitaker, 1990: 1).

In Britain, the evidence is more ambiguous. In the early 1980s, a Home Office (1981) report condemned the harassment experienced by ethnic minority groups, and data from the 1988 BCS reveals that minorities interpret many of the crimes against them – especially crimes against the person and vandalism – as racial harassment (Mayhew *et al.*, 1989: 40). However, the 1988 BCS, which contained a booster sample to increase the numbers of ethnic minority respondents, found that many of the differences in victimization rates between whites, blacks (Afro-Caribbean) and Asians (Indians, Pakistanis and Bangladeshis) shrank once controls were introduced for variables such as areas of residence and age:

> Both Afro-Caribbeans and Asians tend to be more at risk than whites for many types of crime. This is largely explained by social and demographic factors, particularly the areas in which they live. However, taking account of this, ethnic minority risks tend to be higher, with Asians particularly at greater risk of vandalism and robbery/theft from the person. (Mayhew *et al.*, 1989: 50)

Previously Smith (1982) had found in a local survey in Birmingham that variations by race were minimal, and similar findings were reported from Islington (Crawford *et al.*, 1990), although an earlier London survey did find that blacks suffered disproportionately from crimes against the person (Sparks *et al.*, 1977). It seems that in England and Wales, as in the USA, blacks are more at risk of crime, but that in the former case differences are largely a product of variables other than minority status as such.

What of differences by gender? Most victim surveys reveal that males experience higher levels of conventionally defined crime than females. NCS data project lifetime risk of violent crime at 89 per cent for males and 73 per cent for females (Koppel, 1987: 2). Homicide rates are also higher for males and, combining race and gender, Whitaker (1990) identifies black males as the highest-risk group. In 1986, the homicide rate per 100,000 was 2.9 for white females, 7.9 for white males, 12.3 for black females and a staggering 52.3 for black males. In Britain, crime statistics for homicide (Home Office, 1990a) and BCS data (Mawby, 1988a) similarly reveal marked gender differences. A survey on school-children in Sheffield also found crimes against boys to be most common (Mawby, 1979a). Using data from the 1982 BCS, Clarke *et al.* (1985) demonstrated the higher risk of males to street crime, though this is challenged by Worrall and Pease (1986), and the Islington surveys suggest that crimes against women may be as common as, or more common than, those against males (Jones *et al.*, 1986).[4] One of the major arguments here is that women may be reluctant to reveal their crime experiences to an interviewer, especially where the offender was a partner or other relative, a problem the Islington researchers claim to have surmounted. Mooney's (1993) recent findings are an excellent illustration. It is certainly the case for homicide and (in the BCS) other offences against the person that women are more likely to be victimized by those whom the victims know well than are males (Home Office, 1990a; Mawby, 1988a). This is well illustrated in Figure 2.2, where data on crimes against the person from the 1988 BCS have been included. It thus seems likely that while street crimes, or crimes by strangers, are more likely to be committed against males, females may be more at risk for crimes by those known to the victim, and indeed personal crimes against women are typically committed by non-strangers. Since victim surveys underestimate levels of domestic violence, sexual assault and rape, this is particularly note-worthy.

Fifthly, we can consider the influence of age. Here, contrary to popular imagery, youth is associated with high crime risk and old age with relatively low victimization rates. NCS data for 1988, for example, indicate the personal crime victimization rate to be highest for those aged 16–19 (193 per 1,000 persons) and to fall steadily to a low of 22 for those aged 65 or over. Similar trends

Figure 2.2 *Crimes against the person: extent to which offenders were known to male and to female victims*

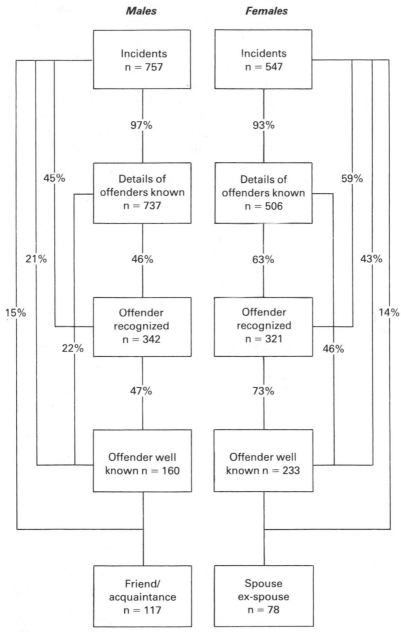

Source: BCS (1988)

have been found elsewhere, for household as well as personal crime (Brillon, 1987; Mawby, 1988b). For example, the first international crime survey compared three age groups: 16–34, 35–54 and 55 or over. Rates for contact crimes were 8.9 per cent, 4.3 per cent and 2.5 per cent respectively; for burglary 4.5 per cent, 3.9 per cent and 2.3 per cent (Van Dijk *et al.*, 1990: 60). As with gender patterns, however, we should stress that victim surveys are likely to understate non-stranger crime, and so much elder abuse is likely to remain invisible (Brillon, 1987).

For rather different reasons, official statistics also underestimate or ignore crimes which have taken place against minors (but with the exception of a range of officially recorded sexual offences, however; see below). By this, it is meant that much petty theft and violence, which is often, though not always, an intra-age activity, is either not reported, or if it is, is not taken seriously (Feyerherm and Hindelang, 1974; Kinsey, 1990; Mawby, 1979a). As a balance to this trend, however, some criminal victimization surveys do include in their sample a subset of 11–16-year-olds, and as Morgan (1988) reports, teenagers in the United States consistently report higher rates of victimization than other age groups. In addition, parents, at least in Edinburgh, seem to be aware of some of the patterns of victimization of their children. The Edinburgh Crime Survey indicates that the adults in their sample report rates of theft against their children three times higher than that for the adult population, with rates of assault and threat being about the same (Anderson *et al.*, 1990: 40). This was subsequently followed up by a survey of young people themselves, which reports that over a nine-month period half of the 11–15-year-olds surveyed 'had been victims of an assault, threatening behaviour or theft from the person' (Kinsey, 1990).

Into this broader equation of the extent of child victimization needs to be slotted the critical and more emotive edge of child physical and sexual abuse. At one end of this spectrum is the question of child murder. Pritchard (1991) reports the following comparative statistics for child murder per million children in 1986–7.

UK babies	22	infants	8	5–14-year-olds	3 (1987)
Ireland babies	0	infants	8	5–14-year-olds	5 (1986)
Japan babies	56	infants	12	5–14-year-olds	5 (1987)
West Germany babies	34	infants	8	5–14-year-olds	6 (1987)
France babies	15	infants	8	5–14-year-olds	5 (1986)
USA babies	73	infants	25	5–14-year-olds	12 (1986)

Whilst there are some obvious difficulties associated with the accuracy of these figures and the cultural variations which contribute to their make-up (the categories themselves are based on World Health Organization statistics which have been standardized), they constitute a useful comparative measure against which to locate the more general questions of child physical and child sexual abuse.

Although child murder seems to be comparatively rare, attempts to measure the extent of child physical and child sexual abuse are extremely difficult, replete with both definitional and technical problems (Walklate, 1989: Chapter 3). Added to this is the way in which the media have played a significant role, both positively and negatively, in heightening awareness of these issues. A composite estimate of the extent of child sexual abuse based primarily on survey work conducted in the US and the UK (see for example Russell, 1984) assumes a level of abuse around 1 in 4 for girls and 1 in 10 for boys. Interestingly, researchers in Islington attempted to include a measure of people's experiences of relationships which in legal terms could be defined as sexually abusive (this, therefore includes a sexual relationship between a 15-year-old male and an 18-year-old female). Defined in this way they estimate that 8 per cent of females and 12 per cent of males in Islington had experience of abuse (Crawford *et al.*, 1990)! Estimates of child physical abuse are seemingly more difficult to come by given the extent to which the physical punishment of children is increasingly frowned upon, and the extent to which the social norms and more recently legal rules governing such behaviour may or may not condone it. The physical punishment of children by parents or parental figure is illegal in Sweden, for example. The social norms and legal rules also vary with respect to defining child sexual abuse, especially the question of the 'age of consent'. The gender dimensions characteristic of child sexual abuse, have made this an area much more fully explored by feminist research.

Finally, marital status is closely associated with risk. The low rates for the widowed and high rates for single people can be largely accounted for by the age dimension. However, married people have far lower rates for both household and personal crime, with the separated or divorced having high rates. Indeed, NCS data reveal that for certain offence categories, such as assault, divorced or separated women have even higher rates than single women (US Department of Justice, 1990). Similarly, 1984 BCS figures reveal rates for divorced or separated people of 53 per hundred households for household crime and 16 for personal crime, compared with overall rates of 41 and 11.

It is clear that risk of crime rises for those living in urban areas, especially lower-status areas, and for ethnic minority groups, males, younger people and the single, divorced or separated. Combinations of these variables produce even greater levels of risk. Take for example the United States evidence on homicide that was cited earlier (Whitaker, 1990). Among blacks, the homicide rate per 100,000 people in 1986 was 31; for black males this rose to 52; adding the age dimension, the rate among black males aged 25–34 rose to 104. That is, approximately 1 per cent of black males aged 25 will die from homicide before reaching the age of 34!

The reasons for these patterns are generally associated with the concepts of lifestyle and routine activities (Gottfredson, 1984; Maxfield 1987, 1988). That is, those who spend more time out of the home both increase their risk of personal crime and, where the home is left unguarded, increase the risk of burglary. As Block (1987) argues, this may also contribute to explanations of international variations. In the Netherlands, for example, where the female rate of participation in the labour force is very low, burglaries and especially daytime burglaries, are less common than in the USA or in England and Wales. The international victim survey also highlights 'the relationship between victimization and lifestyle, measured by the frequency of outdoor visits in the evening for recreational purposes', such that 'those who went out most were more at risk' (Van Dijk *et al.* 1990: 61). For example, the rate for those who went out in the evening 'almost daily' was double that of those who went out less than once per week. In Britain, Clarke *et al.* (1985), drew on data from the 1982 BCS to illustrate the extent to which the relationship between risk and age and gender was explained by lifestyle factors of this sort. However, even when one controlled for number of evenings out, some differences remained, suggesting that more refined aspects of lifestyle will also affect risk. For example, *where* one goes in the evening, how one travels there and with whom, may each have a bearing on victimization rates, an issue which might well be addressed in future local victim surveys.

This raises the question of choice, which is relevant on at least three levels. First, it is arguable that those who fear crime restrict their activities, thereby protecting themselves and so reducing their victimization rates (Balkin, 1979; Lawton *et al.*, 1976). Secondly, however, it seems that while most routine activities are unaffected by fear, personal choice (or whether or not to go out) is only part of the issue. Some people, like shift workers, are required to commute during the hours of darkness; many who use public transport do so because they cannot afford their own cars; those who live in crime-prone areas of the city rarely choose to live there, but may be trapped by poverty and family circumstances. Awareness of the relationship between crime and lifestyle should not be used to justify blaming the victim; the poor and socially vulnerable often find themselves trapped in environments where their risk is increased and in ways they are powerless to prevent. Thirdly, where incidents occur as part of a close and continuing relationship between offender and victim, lifestyle as defined here is an inadequate explanatory tool, and it is invidious to blame the victim whose realistic choices may be minimal. With this in mind, it is appropriate to turn to the second dimension of vulnerability to crime: the impact of crime on different victims.

Much of the earlier United States writings tended to stress the universal threat of crime, with the implication that people were equally vulnerable to its effects. Whilst research on rape victims has indicated that impact varies according to the social or psychological

Table 2.2 *Proportion of victims who were affected by their crimes, according to selected characteristics*

	Emotional reactions		Affected very much/quite a lot		Affected for at least a week	
	Personal	HH	Personal	HH	Personal	HH
Income						
Low	83	55	57	34	50	21
High	70	51	37	18	10	7
Tenure						
Rented	72	54	50	32	37	18
Owner-occupier	63	50	38	24	20	10
Race						
Afro-Caribbean	89	69	59	47	41	33
Asian	70	53	56	34	29	19
White	66	51	43	26	26	12
Age						
60 or over	77	51	57	28	43	16
Under 20	50	48	28	22	12	6
Marital status						
Divorced	89	57	64	37	71	19
Married	63	50	43	26	23	11
Household type						
No other adult	86	58	66	33	53	21
Other adults	62	50	39	25	22	11
Gender						
Women	83	52	59	29	42	16
Men	54	51	32	25	17	9

Source: BCS (1988)

characteristics of victims (Burgess and Holmstrom, 1978; Sales *et al.*, 1984), in most studies differences appear minimal or ambiguous (Lurigio and Resick, 1990). Nevertheless, it appears that although victims who have suffered an earlier, quite specific stress may have gained strength from this and be better able to cope with their crime victimization, in general those whose social circumstances or previous experiences suggest that they are the more vulnerable or frail are affected most by the crime experience.

The extent to which the *social* circumstances of victims impinge upon their victimization is well illustrated in a number of British studies. In an early survey of those visited by Victim Support in Bristol, for example, Gay, Holton and Thomas (1975) suggested that women, the elderly and those living alone were most affected, and Maguire's (1980) burglary research supported this, with the addition that the separated, divorced and widowed were also adversely affected. In the first Islington crime survey, the elderly, blacks and people with low incomes were also identified as badly affected (Jones *et al.*, 1986). Detailed analysis of the 1984 BCS also revealed the close link between status and vulnerability (Mawby and Gill, 1987: 21–3).

Findings from the 1988 BCS well illustrate this point. In Table 2.2 we have compared the proportions of victims with selected characteristics who said that they experienced emotional reactions after the offence, were affected 'very much' or 'quite a lot' and who were affected for at least a week. Here we have drawn a distinction between personal and household crimes, but a similar pattern emerges if we further control for offence seriousness. In summary, those most affected are:

1   those on low incomes, compared with highest income earners;
2   those in rented accommodation, compared with owner-occupiers;
3   blacks, especially Afro-Caribbeans, compared with whites;
4   the elderly to some extent, with young victims distinctive at the other extreme;
5   the divorced compared with married victims;
6   those living in households with no other adults (either single-person households or one-parent families);
7   women compared with men.

Although these differences are most marked for personal crimes, they are also evident for household crimes. In most cases, it is those groups that are most vulnerable prior to the crime – through poverty, lack of family support or physical frailty – on whom crime has the greatest impact.

Table 2.3 *Relationship between risk of crime and impact of crime according to victim survey data*

	High risk	High impact
Class/status	Poor, living in privately rented housing	
Gender	Males	Females
Age	Young	Elderly, not young
Race	Afro-Caribbean, Asians	Afro-Caribbean
Marital/family status	Divorced: those living in households with no other adults	

The relationship between risk and impact is illustrated in Table 2.3. For two of the sets of variables considered – age and gender – it seems that those on whom crime has the most impact are the least at risk. This may go some way towards explaining the apparent inverse relationship between risk and fear that has been identified in a number of studies (Balkin, 1979; Garofalo, 1979; Hough and Mayhew, 1983; Jones *et al.*, 1986; Lawton *et al.*, 1976; Riger *et al.*, 1978). In terms of age and gender, it may be the frailty and powerlessness of the elderly and women that affects both the impact of crime and fear of crime in general. Gender and age are also, of course, variables where hidden crime presents particular problems for researchers. With respect to the other sets of variables, a clearer pattern emerges: the poor, racial minorities, and those divorced or living in one-adult households are more at risk of crime and more likely to be affected when a crime takes place. 'Poverty', defining the term broadly, affects not only the ability to adjust one's behaviour so as to limit crime risks, but also (perhaps partly because of this) one's capacity to cope with crime.

A rather different aspect of the social circumstances of the crime victim is the relationship between offender and victim. In relation to the incidence of crime, we have already noted that crimes where victims are closely tied to 'their' offenders are disproportionately under-recorded in victim surveys. However, evidence from such surveys and more qualitative research clearly demonstrates that victims of crime by non-strangers are particularly affected by their experiences. Thus in an analysis of the 1984 BCS, Mawby and Firkins (1987) showed that the impact of crime was greater when the offender was better known to the victim. Similarly, analysis of the 1988 BCS reveals a difference for both household and personal crimes. In the former case, 79 per cent of respondents who were victims of crime by offenders who were well known to them said that they or someone else in their household was affected, and 37 per cent said that they had been affected for at least a week. In the case of personal crimes, victims of spouse abuse were more seriously affected by their crimes than were other victims of crimes against the person.

The differences here may reflect both the greater impact of crimes by those who were originally seen as 'trustworthy', people on whom one depended, and the fact that where the offender is well known victims' perception of future problems are qualitatively different. A similar conclusion comes from a very different research study, specifically on rape in marriage. For example:

> The sense of betrayal combined with the many obstacles to leaving the situation when rape occurs in marriage, often causes an even stronger negative impact on the women's other (and future) intimate relationships than when the rape is perpetrated by a stranger. (Russell, 1990: 355)

Whilst crime may not be the pervasive social problem it is often portrayed as, clearly for some it is far more of a problem than for others.

Conclusion

This chapter has reviewed, for the most part, the mainstream findings concerning the extent of crime, its impact, and groups who seem to be vulnerable to crime within this broad and mainstream framework. It is evident from these findings that conventional definitions of crime have predominated within the work done in this area, and whilst some efforts have been made by the proponents of local victimization surveys to redress this balance, it is important to look beyond the findings of the criminal victimization survey if the desire is to develop a more complete picture of the extent and impact of crime. It is also clear that the influences underpinning the debates around the extent and impact of crime have varied. The feminist movement in the early 1980s in the United States, for example, has exerted much more influence on this debate in the political and policy arena than it did in England and Wales, though that influence is perhaps becoming more identifiable at a local political level. The findings of the criminal victimization surveys in Britain and their more neutral tone have, indirectly, been intertwined with the similar style of Victim Support as it has grown and developed during the 1980s. The variations in impetus for the development of victim services are one of the concerns of the following chapters, but it is also important to note the connections to be made between the academic debate and the implementation of different types of policy response. This is particularly the case in the context of the notion of 'vulnerability'. Different victim movements have made different uses of this term, and it has generally been an important consideration in the question of assessing the appropriateness of response and effective resource allocation. It will therefore constitute an important thread in assessing the effectiveness of available service provision.

Having read this chapter, the reader may be left with the impression that much of the interest in victims of crime has been of relatively recent origin. Indeed, it is almost a commonplace now for writers to assert that from the 1960s onwards there has been a 'rediscovery of the crime victim' on academic, political and policy agendas. However this assertion has been based on a partial understanding of the role of the victim in the criminal justice systems of different societies, both historically and currently.

Notes

1. The 1989 survey was conducted in England and Wales, Scotland, Northern Ireland, the Netherlands, West Germany, Switzerland, Belgium, France, Spain, Norway, Finland, USA, Canada, Australia and Japan, as well as in Warsaw and Surabaja (Indonesia). The 1992 survey also covered England, Wales, the Netherlands, Belgium, Finland, USA, Canada, Australia and Japan, and in addition Italy, Sweden and New Zealand, Czechoslovakia and Poland, and cities in a number of developing countries (Van Dijk and Mayhew, 1992; Zvekic and Del Frate, 1992).

2. For example, the willingness of victims to mention crimes committed against them by relatives, or of respondents in general to admit to fear, may vary between cultures.

3. Where unacknowledged data are included from the 1984 and 1988 BCS, these are drawn from secondary data analysis by one of the authors (RIM). We are grateful for the advice and assistance of Pat Mayhew and Mike Hough in relation to all material from the BCS. Personal crimes as here defined primarily refer to assaults and threats, but also include thefts from the person, robberies and attempted assaults. Household crimes comprise burglaries and attempts, thefts from dwellings, other thefts, attempted thefts, and criminal damage. Whilst these generally involve loss to the household rather than to a specific individual, it should be noted that some, like vehicle-related thefts, may involve property which at the time of the offence was in the possession of one household member.

4. A similar finding for contact crimes in the international crime survey is probably due to the fact that these include pickpocketing and, especially, sexual assaults, the latter only being asked of women (Van Dijk *et al.*, 1990: 61).

3

The Place of the Victim in Non-Western Societies

Alongside the cliché that the victim is ignored within modern criminal justice systems sits another: that in some far-gone primitive utopia the interests of the victim reigned supreme. Various authors, in accepting that the victim has become 'the Cinderella of the criminal law' (Schafer, 1960: 8) have looked elsewhere – in the past or in present-day Third World societies – for examples of Cinderella enthroned as of right at the centre of the criminal justice stage. Thus Christie (1977) in a seminal article in which he criticized the 'theft' of conflict by complex organizational structures, approvingly described the courtroom processes of 'modern' Tanzania, where 'victim' and 'offender' held centre stage, other members of the local community participated fully, and court officials played a backstage role.

Essentially, those who look for a victims' utopia seek it in at least one of three directions. Some, like Christie (1977) turn to primitive, or modern non-industrial societies. Others, like Harding (1982), Fry (1951) and Meiners (1978) cite Maine's (1887) *Ancient Law* as illustration of earlier, and in many ways preferable, systems in our own pasts. Finally, a few look to socialist societies such as China and Cuba for examples of how victims may be better treated.

Dispute settlement in primitive societies

Epstein (1974) described a 'contentious situation' where the alleged rights of one party are infringed, interfered with or denied by a second. This develops into a full-grown dispute only when the first party responds, thrusting it into the public arena (Gulliver, 1969). The ways in which disputes are settled, or at least an attempt at settlement is made, varies markedly between societies. Use might be made, for example, of violence, ritual or mysticism, or of talk. Violence, in the context of retribution, is perhaps at the extreme, although even this may be tightly regulated by custom. Aborigine deaths, for example, might be responded to by kin spearing the wrongdoer, but not fatally: in New Guinea, the Minj-Wahgi engaged in *Tagba boz*, whereby opposing sides performed a ritualized and tightly prescribed fight (Roberts, 1979: 57–8). Ritual or mysticism is an equally varied category. It may comprise putting pressure on individuals through the use of magic, or complex rituals that serve to replace blame or guilt with shame. Notable here is Young's (1974) account of the Kalauna people of Melanesia. Contrary to the utopian stereotype, they are characterized as 'quarrelsome and fractious, given to *endemic conflict*, preoccupied with sorcery fears and status battles, and divided rather than united by a configuration of values which stress competition rather than co-operation' (Young, 1974: 41, emphasis in original). Perhaps not surprisingly, conflict was resolved through competition, 'fighting with food' whereby the aggrieved group would attempt to shame the offending party by giving the latter more food than could be offered back. Providing the larger gift thus becomes the means of shaming the wrongdoer.

Despite such colourful examples, most of the emphasis has been placed on *talk* as the means of conflict resolution. Here again we need to make a number of distinctions. For example, the disputants may attempt to reach a settlement through 'bilateral negotiation' (Roberts, 1979: 69), perhaps incorporating group support, or they may involve a third party.

One example of the former is the *Iupunga* system of the Kaliai-speaking people of Melanesia (Counts and Counts, 1974). Here disputes are settled through negotiations which take place at the public meeting, or *Iupunga*. Whilst in a minority of cases a third party acts as mediator, in most cases a settlement is negotiated by the disputants, with all those present able to make a contribution to the discussion. Similar arrangements are described by Gulliver (1963, 1969) among the Arusha of northern Tanganyika and the Ndendeuli of southern Tanzania.

This degree of informality does nevertheless entail a number of difficulties. Counts and Counts (1974) suggest that in many cases any agreement reached is vague, and it seems easier to resolve disputes where a third party is involved. This 'regular use of non-kin third party intervention in dispute settlement' (Schwartz and Miller, 1964: 161) is defined, somewhat carelessly (see below) as mediation. In a study of 51 societies, Schwartz and Miller (1964) distinguish mediation from two other types of legal organization, counsel and police. While only 7 of the 51 societies showed evidence of specialized counsel and 22 had some form of police, no less than 36 had some form of mediation, and mediation appeared to be the first form of legal organization to develop, absent in only the most primitive societies. Even some of these involved the concept of damages, that is property payments in lieu of other sanctions.

However, the lack of money and substantial property appeared to inhibit the emergence of mediation mechanisms: 'There is much evidence to support the hypothesis that property provides something to quarrel about. In addition, it seems to provide something to mediate with as well' (Schwartz and Miller, 1964: 165).

Thus it appears that mediation systems are to be found in most primitive societies, and that these predate the emergence of more specialist law enforcement, such as police and legal counsel. But the use of the term mediation is perhaps a little misleading. Essentially, when third parties are involved in such settlements, they may adopt, and indeed be expected to adopt, one or more of a variety of styles. Gulliver (1963) distinguishes between negotiation and adjudication. The former, according to Eckhoff (1966), is the more appropriate style for the mediator, who aims for reconciliation through an appeal to a common interest and with respect to future relationships; adjudication, in contrast, is more befitting of the judge, who decides more in terms of fixed principles. Roberts (1979), whilst feeling that the contrast is perhaps overstated, largely concurs, but draws a further distinction between 'judges', as adjudicators with long-term positions, and 'umpires', chosen as arbitrators for a specific occasion. However, as Epstein (1974) points out, adjudication, negotiation and mediation are often different stages of the same process. Just as in contemporary Western societies prosecution may be cancelled if mediation is successful, and negotiation – as plea bargaining – may pre-empt a contested trial ending in adjudication, so in primitive societies alternative strategies may be adapted to suit particular circumstances. Equally, those participating may appeal to common interest, future relationships, basic principles or notions of justice, depending on the likely success of different approaches. That said, let us take two examples to illustrate dispute settlement processes in primitive societies: the Ndendeuli of southern Tanzania, described by Gulliver (1969), and the Plains Indians, described by Hoebel (1961).

The Ndendeuli are a Bantu-speaking people who live in villages of some 150 to 250 people. Because of the poor soil and rudimentary agricultural techniques, communities move at approximately three-year intervals. Communities are bonded by kinship, although precise kinship lineages often become blurred. Disputes within and between communities are settled in essentially the same way. Intra-community disputes involve issues such as claims for additional bridewealth, claims for compensation for injuries caused in a fight, requests for debt repayment and various family quarrels. Cases are discussed in moots, or *mkutano*, which take place on neutral ground, such as the house of an intermediary. Each disputant recruits his or her own 'action-set', who might be expected to speak on his or her behalf. Discussion is however open to anyone present, including neutrals. In most cases one of these takes the role of mediator. No one is specifically assigned this responsibility, although it is likely to fall to one of the informal leaders in the village, a notable or 'big man'. The power and influence of the mediator is limited:

> Their role is not at all well defined. Certainly it does not afford authority in the sense that their lead must more or less be followed, and they have no active sanctions at their disposal to support their leadership. They do not adjudicate, and they can be ignored. A notable who attempts to extend his accepted influence to authoritarianism raises resentment and opposition among his neighbours. He may well lose his influence by such an attempt, for he loses the goodwill and trust that is so necessary for the continuation of a notables' success. (Gulliver, 1969: 34).

Somewhat different arrangements existed among the Plains Indians. Among the Comanche, the most militaristic and rudimentary of the three systems described by Hoebel (1961), conflicts often occur over wife-stealing and adultery. The wronged husband would respond by demanding damages from his wife's lover, and in theory could resort to force if necessary. However, in almost all the cases recorded by Hoebel, a settlement was reached without recourse to violence. Instead, compensation would be paid, its amount depending upon the bargaining power of the protagonists.

In contrast, the less warlike Cheyenne possessed a ritualized tribal government with a complementary system of military societies. The latter acted as a police, providing summary justice as well as having responsibility for crime prevention and detection. The former, comprising a tribal council made up of tribal chiefs, provided a judiciary that could function on both a group and individual level. The council dealt with serious incidents, and could impose banishment on murders, whilst individual chiefs acted as mediators, for example in adultery cases. Whilst the Cheyenne system appears to allow less public participation, it also provides a variety of settlement strategies, ranging from the judicial to the mediatory, and starkly contrasts with many African and Asian societies.

There are clearly immense variations in the ways in which disputes are settled in primitive societies. In general though, three principles are worth mentioning that are commonly distinct from dispute settlement in industrial societies: informality; relevance of antecedents; and victims' interests.

It was the informality of the dispute settlement that so impressed

Christie (1977) in his account of Tanzania. Of course, some settings are more formal than others, and by no means all include, for example, open participation from anyone present who wishes to speak. Nevertheless, generally speaking the environment is less formal and consequently more a part of the daily lives of participants, making them less inhibited about participation.

The fact that the setting is a continuation of everyday life, rather than cut off from it, is related to the second principle: the relevance of antecedents. Unlike in modern courts of law, where the facts of the case are tightly prescribed, in most primitive settings previous interaction between disputants, and perhaps also their kin, is considered relevant (Paliwala, 1982). The present conflict is viewed as symptomatic of longer-standing relationships, so the key to resolution must be sought in the past. For example: 'Ndendeuli disputes are worked out in the full context of the continuum of community life, so that previous disputes and their settlements, and developing relationships of all kinds, impinge on any current cases' (Gulliver, 1969: 60). The informality of the setting and the relevance of antecedents may in fact be highly desirable. However, the assumption that authors such as Wright (1991) make, often implicitly, is that these principles provide the basis whereby victims' rights are more adequately met. On the contrary, if we examine the principle of victims' interests, the picture is distinct, but by no means as positive as has been implied.

One of the key features of disputes in primitive society is that they are not merely between protagonists, or offenders and their victims. Disputes threaten the very existence of the community, precisely because of the complex intermeshing of relationships within communities. Consequently, community interests may predominate over individual interests, and indeed individual 'rights' in a contemporary sense are largely unrecognized. Dispute resolution is essentially about restoring relationships within the group, and at this level the interest of individuals is relegated to backstage:

> As in all modes of disputes settlement which are an integral part of the political process in a given society, the plaintiff who is at the heart of the dispute is likely to get short shrift when political aspects of the case predominate. The main issue then becomes one of groups coming to terms, rather than one of an injured individual gaining restitution. (Young, 1974: 47–8)

In some cases, kin may actually use dispute settlements as a direct means of material gain. Hoebel (1961) for example notes that where the aggrieved Comanche calls on his kin for help, they will receive the bulk of 'his' damages. On a wider level than this, the power of group interests or the power of individuals concerned often ensures that 'might' is indeed, if not 'right', at least in with a head start! For example Hoebel (1961: 100–26), describing the settlement of land disputes among the Ifugao, a gardening society in the Philippines, reveals how high-status disputants, who have more power to cause further trouble, are likely to be treated favourably in the settlement process; Young (1974) notes that where disputes are resolved through 'fighting with food', success depends on the strength of group support, not whether or not one is in the right; and Hoebel (1961: 134) explains how among the Comanche, wrongdoers who came out of disputes by paying the least possible in compensation actually gained in status as a result. In most cases, however, it is the power of the *group* that is decisive, as analysis of social control among the Arusha of northern Tanganyika makes clear:

> When one person is alleged to have committed an injury against another – when, therefore, the two persons come into dispute – the significant jural factors are not only the kind of injury involved, but the social relationship between the two persons and the position of each in the structure of the society. By position here, I mean primarily the social status of each person, and the various groups to which he belongs. Especially are the groups important, because it is very largely through them that an Arusha has access to the ability and power to take jural action. (Gulliver, 1963: 1)

The use of the masculine pronoun here is indicative of the fact that where the individual victim happened to be female her interests almost immediately became translated into the interests of her male kin. At best then, we can say that within primitive societies in general, victims' interests are subordinate to those of the group.

Many would maintain that this is preferable to a situation where outsider interests, like those of the state, take preference. Even in primitive societies, though, the interests of third parties may be important, and may indeed predominate. For when outsiders are brought in as adjudicators or mediators, their reputations, indeed their status within the group, may hinge upon their ability to gain a settlement, where 'peace at any price' may become, ultimately, more important to them than a just solution. The literature is replete with accounts of power plays between local leaders or 'big men', where the dispute is turned into 'a political contest, a confrontation, between local leaders in a public trial of strength' (Epstein, 1974: 27).

The dispute settlement processes of primitive societies are thus not necessarily preferable to those of Western industrial societies, and may provide no panacea for the victim. This is clear from a recent investigation of customary and informal dispute settlement in the Solomon Islands, where the authors contrast the colonial justice system with its more traditional alternatives:

> In many societies where disputants may have unequal economic social status or where one party has the support of more powerful elements, access to justice in the informal system may also be unequal. Communities also frequently use informal systems to control or punish those who offend against community norms; norms which may reflect the interest of dominant groups. The institution of community based dispute settlement may also be more or less directly controlled by such dominant groups. All of these situations can be found in the Solomons despite the general popularity and effectiveness of informal and customary dispute settlement. (Clegg and Naitoro, 1992: 50–51)

But if utopia is not to be found in primitive societies, did it exist in our own past?

Past utopias?

Seeking utopia in the past, Schafer (1960) regarded the Middle Ages as 'the Golden Age of the Victim' and Harding (1982: 7) makes much of the system of composition in which an offender could 'buy back the peace he had broken by paying what was called the *wer* (payment for homicide) or *bot* (payment for injuries other than death) to the victim or his kin according to a schedule of injury tariffs'. Compensation was also paid to the state, that is, the overlord, in the form of the *wite*. Wright (1991: 2) in his discussion of the victim in the Middle Ages, reports that 'crimes of violence were held in check largely by the fear of private vengeance' and that the compensation system outlined above was largely a privilege of the nobility. As Wright states: 'As for the poor man, with no kin, who became a victim, the historians do not say how he could enforce his claim' (Wright, 1991: 2). The poor, it seems, were largely left in receipt of the worst excesses of the law whether as victims or offenders. However as early as the twelfth century it appeared that the balance was beginning to shift (though not in the victim's favour), and as the authority of the church and crown increased so fines became more important than compensation, and crime came to be seen as 'against society' rather than 'against victims', resulting, according to Fry (1951: 125) in the goal 'take it out on the offender' rather than to do 'justice to the offended'.

Despite these changes, as Wright (1991) reminds us, victims still had two options to pursue in settling their claim: the civil law and the criminal law; and until the eighteenth and nineteenth centuries victims had a prominent role to play in the prosecution process. Hay and Snyder's (1989) work indicates that the exceptions in the prosecution process in the eighteenth century were cases taken forward in the name of the crown. The norm was the private prosecution. Historians such as Rudé (1985) and Phillips (1977) provide some detail on who the victims were who pursued the prosecution process, with the gentry likely to fall back on the support of 'Associations for the Prosecution of Felons' (Schubert, 1981; Phillips, 1984). The role of the victim as principal instigator of criminal proceedings was then incorporated into early colonial law alongside restitution as being an accepted goal of the system. (Brogden *et al.*, 1988; Burnham, 1984; McDonald, 1976b; Powers, 1966).

Authors generally accredit industrialization and urbanization as heralding the decline in the importance of the victim within the criminal justice system (Roberts, 1979). In particular the emergence of the 'new' police in England and Wales early in the nineteenth century contributed to the demise of the 'associations' and they also took over the victim's role in the prosecution process. By the end of the nineteenth century, prosecutions on behalf of the Crown had become the rule rather than the exception.

Nevertheless, as Wright (1991: 3) points out, those who seek their utopias in the past are looking at systems which 'hardly deserve(s) a halo'. Such 'Golden Ages' appeared to be golden only for the rich and powerful, and although other sections of society may have turned to the criminal justice process for support and/or reparation, the circumstances in which they did were largely for crimes against property rather than crimes against the person (Phillips, 1977). These utopias, therefore share some of the characteristics of the 'primitive utopias' in that they seek a society in which the victim and offender are reintegrated into society by some system of making amends or resolving conflicts. But while in primitive societies the community interest may dominate that of the victim, the more bureaucratic and professional those systems the less the concern with the individual victim and the more with the interests of the state.

Dispute settlement in China and Cuba

Whilst Eastern bloc Communist societies, like the Soviet Union, also established local community or factory courts to deal with minor conflicts (Mawby, 1990), local community action has been more a feature of Third World Communist systems (Deacon, 1983). How far do such attempts serve victims' interests?

In Maoist China, Lubman (1967) describes how the traditional mediation processes were adapted to the new social structure. The

T'ai-hsing report of 1946 stressed the ideological superiority of mediation, seen as the best means for protecting the interests of the masses. In the first years after the Communist takeover in 1949, 'mediation small groups' were formed as part of the complex structure of institutions of social control providing a bridge between central and local communities. As the system became more formalized, mediation committees of 3–11 numbers were established in each small area of the city or administrative village, *hsiang*. Committee members, elected by local party activists, dealt with disputes which could be settled out of court. Lubman (1967) goes on to describe the ways in which mediation operated through the examples of Mediator Aunty Wu and Li Erh-ma, citing cases of domestic conflict, adultery and minor theft where mediation was applied.

How does mediation in Maoist China compare to the examples given so far? In one respect, it is clearly different. As Lubman notes, traditionally in China mediation was both open to corruption and based on the premiss that settlement was desirable at any price. Instead, the Communists 'have infused into mediation absolute criteria of right and wrong rather than allowing mediation, as it once did, to seek a compromise that would not disrupt a delicate network of personal relationships within a narrow social context' (Lubman, 1967: 1287). However, this does not mean that the interests of the victim are paramount. On the one hand, the status of the disputants, notably their affiliation to the party or their former class position, will dictate their right to justice. On the other hand, mediation mechanisms are utilized as educational tools whereby individual disputes can become the props for an illustration of appropriate relationships within the new social order. The interests of the new order thus transcend individuals' and victims' rights, and the victims may be 'used' (or abused) to serve society's interests. When a young married couple under stress due to their conflicting hours of employment are told that they must 'serve national construction'; when a landlord is told that his tenant cannot afford rent and so should not be forced to pay it; and when a wife is refused leave to divorce her adulterous husband who happens to be a party member, the interests of the 'victims' involved are clearly not being addressed.

Cuba provides a useful contrast with China because since the 1959 revolution that brought Fidel Castro to power it has been influenced by both China and the Soviet Union, and whilst financially dependent upon the latter has adopted many of the tenets of the former (Mawby, 1990). Cuba's popular tribunals, in operation since 1964, are, however, distinct. Tribunals, which deal with minor local conflicts and disputes, are presided over by local people appointed as lay judges, and function in the local neighbourhood. Settings are informal and provide the opportunity for any of those present to make a contribution. Describing the operation of the system, Berman (1969) notes cases involving thefts from neighbours, neighbour conflicts over access to water, domestic violence, black-market activities and a peeping Tom.

As with many of the examples of dispute settlement in primitive societies, it is clear that the Cuban popular tribunals allow for opportunity for maximum involvement in the process; for victim, offenders and other members of the community. It is also evident that the court takes note of antecedents and indeed one role for the public is to provide further details of the previous behaviour of the disputants. Moreover, while as in China the institution of settlement is used as much as a means of educating the people as a mechanism of conflict resolution, the examples Berman gives suggest that the victim does receive a better deal than in more conventional Western courts. It is sadly ironic to note that the popular tribunals have lost their significance as the Cuban system has become more professionalized (Salas, 1985).

Discussion

We would not concur with the common belief that victims had a better deal in the 'judicial systems' of pre-industrial societies. On the other hand, they certainly experienced *different* treatment from those responsible, within the community, for conflict resolution. The literature on primitive and non-industrialized societies indicates that in general more rudimentary and localized arrangements for dispute settlement resulted in the victim, or at least the victim's kin, playing a more significant part in the proceedings. In some respects, indeed, this was to the victim's benefit. There was less feeling of exclusion, that one had been dispossessed of one's dispute; and victims were more likely to receive compensation. However, where disputes could threaten future relationships within the community, community interests appear to have predominated over victims' rights, and in many cases adjudicators' or mediators' interests might be served rather than victims'. There is also considerable evidence that the relative status – power, influence, standing in the community, gender and age – of the victim and offender made a marked difference to the levels of compensation awarded, or in fact to decisions over blame.

What undoubtedly happened as societies became more complex, and government centralized, was that judicial processes equally became more complex. As specialists came to dominate the system, so the costs of this more formalized structure needed to be at least partially met by fines levied on offenders, and victims' compensation took a lower priority. At the same time, in a more structured setting victims lost their place at centre stage, as indeed did other local people, as community involvement ceased or became redefined as jury service. We should not see these changes as a complete break with the past, but rather as a change of emphasis. Youths and women in primitive society often had their access to the courts restricted; defining crimes as 'against the state' is no more than a formal confirmation of the mandate that community interests supersede those of the protagonists. One could argue that it is local communities, rather than victims, that have lost most in the transition.

This is well illustrated in the colonial examples cited in the literature. In many areas, of Africa for example, British colonial rule enabled local informal dispute settlement systems to coexist alongside the colonial administration, a practice often necessitated by the fragility of colonial rule (Fitzpatrick, 1982). Only where the interests of the colonial power were threatened was colonial law imposed. In contrast, the Australian administration in Papua New Guinea was openly opposed to native courts and attempted to impose its control at all levels of dispute settlement (Epstein, 1974: 3).

Rather differently, revolutionary change in China and Cuba provides a useful illustration of the way that traditional dispute settlement may be recontextualized to suit the needs of the new government (in the former case), or that local dispute settlement might be utilized as a mechanism of government influence and education.

There is a clear lesson to be learnt from the review of the literature here. The common feature of change for primitive societies and/or pre-industrial societies is the way in which the needs of state come to outweigh the needs of the community. In each example though, some groups and their interests are of marginal concern. In the examples cited here, these groups tend to be the poor, the young and the female. This too constitutes a remarkable continuity between the processes observed here and those observed elsewhere in this book. We are sceptical of the view that victim utopias either exist or have existed. Nor are we convinced that non-Western systems of dispute settlement commonly provide victims with a 'better deal' than they receive in Western industrial societies. This is not to suggest, however, that victims receive adequate treatment from our own criminal justice systems, and it is to this matter that we must now turn.

4

The 'Rebirth' of the Victim as a Significant Actor

As Chapter 3 indicated, understanding the 'demise' of the victim is problematic. At one level what is clear is that victims did not disappear from the criminal justice process. Without them much of the work of the criminal justice process would have (and still would) come to a halt (Shapland, 1986).

But despite their undoubted functional importance to the operation of that process, and a more positive presence in some of the legislation (Mawby and Gill, 1987) by 1945 there was no real sense in which victims of crime had a voice in the political or the policy arenas. This is not intended to imply that changes had not taken place which significantly affected the possibilities for redress from the legal system as a whole. This was particularly the case in the context of the achievements of the 'first wave' of the feminist movement in drawing attention not only to the question of female suffrage, but also to that of violence against women. (Frances Power Cobbe's graphically entitled, *Wife Torture in England* of 1878 is a good illustration of this point.) Some gains with respect to civil law were achieved during this period. The purpose of this chapter is to document the changes that have occurred from 1945 to date and which have resulted in the voice of 'victims' of crime being more keenly heard. In doing this we shall pay attention not only to the role that the ideas which may be associated with positivist victimology have played in establishing that voice, but also the role of the more radical (and frequently unacknowledged) concerns of the feminist movement.

The Postwar settlement: an age of conformity?

It is interesting to note that the initial ideas which gave the impetus to the development of victimology arose in the late 1940s. Mendelsohn coined the term 'victimology' in 1940 and Von Hentig's *The Criminal and his Victim* was published in 1948. Whilst it is difficult to trace the precise emergence of these ideas, put in a broader framework of a desire for a better society (Elias, 1986) and a need to make sense of the events leading up to the Second World

War, the emergence of a discipline concerned with victims is, perhaps, not so surprising. The ideas of Von Hentig and Mendelsohn, positing as they do a primarily individualistic understanding of the relationship between victim and offender (Elias, 1986; Mawby and Gill, 1987; Walklate, 1989), although not really at the forefront of policy concerns in the post-war years, nevertheless reflected the essential nature of how crime victims were conceived in the 1950s.

The major policy concerns in the immediate post-war years, particularly in Europe, centred on how to rebuild societies and their economies. A key feature of that rebuilding in the UK was the construction of the welfare state. Various analyses have considered the range of influences which led to the establishment of the 'welfare state' in Britain in the immediate post-war years. A number of strands run through these: from the notion of a post-war 'consensus' to the way in which the various policies that were implemented built upon the ideas of an earlier era (enshrining distinctions between the 'deserving' and the 'undeserving' poor), to debates around the role of women and the women's movement in influencing those policies. More recent commentaries have been concerned to reconsider the value of the ideas of Marshall (1981) in mapping an understanding of what the inception of this welfare state represented.

Marshall, whose ideas were originally presented in a series of lectures held in 1949, saw the emergence of citizenship and capitalism as intertwined. Historically, he argued, citizenship in the eighteenth century was focused on debates around civil rights, in the nineteenth century around political rights, and in the twentieth century, social rights. These social rights, set in motion at the turn of the century under the guidance of Lloyd George, it was argued, were ultimately to be achieved by the welfare state. Marshall's ideas have generated considerable debate, in particular concerning their relevance for understanding more recent changes. This debate considers the extent to which importance should be attached to understanding the relationship between Marshall's notion of social citizenship, social class, and other 'social movements' (see Chapter 8). This emphasis within Marshall's work on social rights gives an appropriate flavour to understanding the issues of the 1950s and their subsequent development.

The policies introduced in Britain at the end of the Second World War, guided and influenced by Beveridge, were intended to provide protection from 'disease, squalor, and ignorance, idleness, and want'. As is well documented, in offering this protection they extended the principle of insurance: 'Which is to say, of course, that such rights are not social rights at all but merely the individual entitlements that arise from a contractual relation' (Garland, 1985: 246). And although there was some political and social dissent concerning the policies designed to implement this protection, and the individualized, contractual relationships on which they were based, the 1950s are commonly thought of as a decade of consensus. (See, in the context of the criminal justice system, Morris, 1989.) The influence of the feminist movement on this policy formation process was largely felt in the form of 'welfare feminism' (Banks, 1981). This branch of the feminist movement had some influence on, for example, the structure of family benefits. Welfare feminism was also to exert an influence in the post-war era in the United States.

It was the inception of the welfare state which formed the general backcloth against which Margery Fry introduced her ideas on victim compensation. The publication of *Arms of the Law* in 1951 made a significant input into the debates on criminal justice policy in the 1950s and 1960s. Rock (1990) has detailed some of the influences on Margery Fry's ideas. One of her major concerns was that there must be some better way of reconciling the victim and the offender which would be both educative for the offender and meaningful for the victim. This concern had crystallized into a campaign for the establishment of a criminal injuries compensation scheme by the time she died. The scheme itself, however, did not materialize until 1964 and the reason for this may in part be understood by reference to how the crime problem was defined in the 1950s.

It is difficult to assess what exactly was happening to the crime rate in the immediate post-war period since, as always, such an analysis depends upon what is chosen as the point of comparison. Wootton (1959: 32) notes that 'most countries of Europe ended the war with significantly higher rates of criminality than they had when it began with the exception it seems of Denmark and Finland'. In addition Wootton also comments on the remarkable similarity in age and gender distribution of this criminality. She argues that by 1955, as measured by the number of people found guilty of offences and by crime reported to the police, crime had declined from this post-war peak. This lull was temporary: recorded crime rates rose again in the late 1950s, especially for crimes of violence (Morris, 1989; Rock, 1990).

What is also clear, as Rock (1990) points out, is that adolescents came to be identified as the crime problem in the 1950s. There were, of course, alternative viewpoints: 'The typical criminal of to-day is certainly not the thief, nor the thug who hits an old lady on the head in order to possess himself of her handbag or to ransack her house: the typical criminal of to-day is the motorist' (Wootton, 1959, 25). But whilst the typical criminal might well have been (and taken in this sense probably still is!) the motorist, the recorded increase in crimes of violence possibly signifies a change in public attitudes towards violence as much as it might indicate a 'real' change in the levels of such crimes. And, the fact that Wootton in 1959 was already citing the 'little old lady' as the stereotypical victim of crime indicates the extent to which the vulnerability of age had begun to feature in commonsensical thinking about crime. Interestingly enough, it was crimes of violence which ultimately became the focus of the Criminal Injuries Compensation Board.

By the end of the 1950s, prior to her death, Margery Fry had formed alliances within the Howard League for Penal Reform, and had some sympathetic support from within the Home Office in her campaign for victims and offenders, though it was Reg Prentice who presented the first criminal injuries compensation bill to Parliament in 1959 (Rock, 1990). It was legislation elsewhere, in the form of the Workmen's Compensation Act, which seemed to influence the involvement of Prentice and the thinking behind Fry's later concerns with compensation. The Prentice bill was unsuccessful, yet it did mark the extent to which the lobbying which had taken place on behalf of Margery Fry's idea was beginning to bear fruit. Fry's ideas themselves, however, underwent some transformation:

> In her last formulation of the problem, compensation would represent a collective insurance provided by society. All taxpayers would be regarded as subscribers. All taxpayers were at risk of becoming victims. Since the state forbade citizens arming themselves, it should assume responsibility for its failure to provide protection. (Rock, 1990: 66)

The connections between this thinking and the welfare thinking of the post-war era are clear. It contains within it a positive view of the 'victim as citizen', a view which was to become influential again in a slightly different guise in the 1980s. It also articulated a role for the state in its relationship to victims of crime which was not that dissimilar from the protective stance presented by Beveridge in invoking the idea of insurance and the implied notion of a contract. It certainly reflected a change of emphasis in Fry's thinking, from considering the potential beneficial effects that a compensation scheme might have on offenders, towards an almost exclusively victim-oriented stance. Gone, then, is the anthropological stereotype described in Chapter 3. In policy terms, the end product was not far removed from the policies of the welfare state on which (it has been assumed) there was some consensus. This consensus, however, can be viewed in another way. Take, for example, violence against women: 'The lowest point, oblivion, was reached just after World War II . . . the problem had shifted from being a public issue relating to the social and legal statuses of women, to being a private sorrow' (Hanmer, 1985: 142).

That this should be considered to be the case in the 1950s not only connects with the notion of individual responsibility which many of the policies implemented represented, but also reflects particular ideas of 'deserving' and 'undeserving'. The 1950s saw the emergence of a complacent assumption that poverty, and all the stresses that went along with poor living conditions, such as family violence, had been eradicated. (The question of 'family violence' occurring in families who were not poor was unlikely to be considered.) As Wilson (1983) documents, a woman beaten by her husband probably deserved what she got as a result of being an inadequate or 'slovenly' housekeeper and was likely to meet with such a response from the professionals. In this respect the notion of the culpable victim voiced in the work of Mendelsohn resonated in other arenas. When such incidents were identified they were usually considered to be deviations from the norm, and were explained and handled in terms of individual pathology rather than as a product of structural relationships. The developing professions associated with the welfare state were in part to contribute to the perpetuation of these ideas.

It is important to note that the emergence of the welfare state also marked the beginnings of a process of change, the impact of which was not to be felt for a number of years. The role of women and their involvement, not only in the inception of the welfare state, but also in the workforce and the home, represents an important moment in the movement from private to public patriarchy (Walby, 1990). In the 1950s women were subjected to considerable pressure to return to their traditional role in the home. Nowhere was this more clearly represented than in the way in which Bowlby's work on 'maternal deprivation' was translated into the political and policy arenas. Arguably, this pressure was most keenly felt by those, largely middle-class women, who had gained considerable ground from the first wave of feminism (Banks, 1981). For these women, and for those who benefited from the opening educational opportunities, the welfare state set the structural framework in which occupational opportunities, already largely defined as female (social work, education, nursing) were consolidated and expanded. Walby (1990: 191) states: 'It is only with women's access both to wage labour and state welfare payments in the post-war period, that the possibility of full economic as well as political citizenship is realized.' Thus the groundwork for the greater involvement of women in the workforce, and the consequences which were to result from this, were laid.

Yet it must be acknowledged that, as has already been suggested, the 1950s were a low point in terms of the recognition of women's experiences of this era of social rights. True, the 1950s marked some structural change, the significance of which should not be under-played, but neither should it be overplayed. Some women met both private and public patriarchy headlong in the form of partners and social workers. In the context, however, of understanding the nature and influence of victims' movements yet to unfold, the consequences of those structural changes, as suggested by Walby (1990), were considerable.

There were other challenges to the idea that the 1950s constituted an era of consensus. The 'Dixon of Dock Green' image of policing has been a powerful myth constructed around policing of that time (Reiner, 1990). But it is clear that not all communities experienced policing in quite that way. In addition the 1950s saw the first of a series of incidents of racial violence. The 'riots' of 1958 in Notting Hill and Nottingham marked the beginnings of a racial dimension to crimes of violence which was not to go away. Interestingly enough, these victims did not figure in the debates around the legislation concerned with criminal injuries compensation which ultimately came into being in the early 1960s.

What then of the post-war developments in the United States? Victims' movements, *per se*, lay rather dormant in the United States during the 1950s as they did in the United Kingdom. Banks (1981) relates that the feminist movement in the United States embraced much of the post-war welfarism as it had done in the United Kingdom, though the movement in the United States was alerted to the question of equal rights for women at a faster and earlier pace than in the UK. The 1950s were marked by McCarthyism in the United States, though there is little victimological literature documenting this. Elias (1986) comments on the impact of the Cold War and the Korean War in slowing the pace of the victims' movement, suggesting that it is not until the 1960s that victims really began to emerge on the American scene.

It must be remembered that the post-war era in the United States was marked by a very different welfare response. This response was much more squarely located in individualism as distinct from the notion of collectivism which underpinned policy developments in the United Kingdom. Responses to health care are a clear illustration of this different emphasis. This key difference informs the emphasis in and format of policy initiatives to victims of crime when they did begin to appear on the agenda in the United States, some of which subsequently included payments for health care provision, for example: something which, to date, because of the structure of the post-war welfare state, has not (yet) featured in the UK.

The 1960s: a decade of promise?

Meanwhile in the UK it was left to the pressure group Justice to pick up the banner of compensation for victims of crime left by Margery Fry after her death. Its report *Compensation for Victims of Crimes of Violence* presented in 1962 made more explicit connections with the principles of the welfare state:

> The ideas it offered were described as a simple extension of the Welfare State which was then in the making, criminal injuries compensation refracting the same principles of State protection as industrial injuries compensation, health payments, and the National Health Service. (Rock, 1990: 74)

When the final White Paper on criminal injuries compensation came before Parliament in 1964 it met with little opposition. Following on quickly from the inception of the scheme in New Zealand, where policymakers had taken on board the principle of compensation from the Justice publication, the scheme took its final form. It enshrined within it the notion of the 'innocent victim', building into its operation and practice the notion of 'deserving' and 'undeserving' victims (see Chapter 6), and was seen very much by all parties as a logical extension of the role of the welfare state. The scheme, available to victims of violent crime, emphasized the notion of innocence. In this way it further consolidated the idea of culpability in assessing the relationship between the victim and the offender. Part of the rationale for this narrow remit was that it kept the scheme relatively cheap; a feature of what Miers (1978) has referred to as the politicization of the victim. The symbolism of being seen to do something was of more concern than what it was that was actually put into place for victims of crime.

All of this, as many commentators have observed, took place without anyone asking any victims of crime in general, or violence in particular, what they wanted from the criminal justice system, and without the existence of a group whose specific aim was to lobby for victims' interests. In some respects, in the narrow context of a compensation scheme so defined, there was perhaps no need for such a voice to exist at that time. Taken in the broad context of the provisions of the welfare state, victims of crime if injured could be treated under the National Health Service, claim benefit if unable to work and so on (Mawby and Gill, 1987: 37–9). Indeed, having achieved the aim of compensation, the interest which had been aroused in victims of crime dissipated.

In some respects it is possible to view the achievement of the Criminal Injuries Compensation Board as one of the final bricks of the welfare state, cemented with post-Second World War ideals. The establishment of this scheme was the culmination of a logic built on notions of insurance, contract and individual responsibility, and as such also represented a point at which certain victimological ideas had become enmeshed in policy responses. Thus the extension of social rights as citizens had been offered to victims of crimes of violence. That this was built upon particular stereotypical images of such victims was not considered problematic. That the cementing of those ideas may also have reflected the power and regulatory potential of the state in constructing the victim of crime is a theme to which we will return.

The establishment of the Criminal Injuries Compensation Board (CICB) is one of the ways in which Waller (1988a) considers that the United Kingdom set a trail for victims of crime which other countries have subsequently followed. The CICB was not the only achievement of the 1960s in the criminal justice sphere. While many of the Labour Party policies of that decade did not bear fruit (or if they did, they did so in the 1970s), and while economic difficulties were already beginning to present problems for the feasibility of the welfare state project as initially conceived, changes were taking place in the way in which the crime problem was being debated. The Capital Punishment Act was abolished in 1965 after nearly a decade of debate and rising concern about the robustness of a number of murder convictions. Alongside this arguably more liberal stance, the general emphasis within the criminal justice system seemed to move from a retributive to a welfare orientation. This is especially notable given that according to official statistics both property crimes and crimes of violence continued on an upward trend during the 1960s. Amongst these reported rises in crime there was also a rise in the number of reported sexual offences, which reached a peak in 1970 and then declined in the 1980s up to 1985 (Morris, 1989: 96).

The broader social context of the 1960s was initially marked by a freedom of expression born out of a (short-lived) economic buoyancy, and later by an increasing radicalism, and perhaps frustration that the gradual process of change towards the fulfilment of social rights did not seem to be achieving its promise. Part of this emerging radicalism must be attributed to the rapidly expanding higher education system from which women, as much as men, were beginning to benefit. By the end of the decade the women's movement was re-asserting itself. Indeed, 'the resurgence of equal rights feminism that occurred during the 1960s was not only a return to an earlier tradition but also a reaction against some of the central concepts upon which welfare feminism was based' (Banks, 1981: 178). In the context of understanding responses to victims of crime this second wave of feminism was to be very significant. By the late 1960s it was becoming clear that the economic party was over. Poverty had been 're-discovered' (Coates and Silburn, 1970). The welfare state was not delivering (and probably could not deliver) the goods according to either governmental or social demands, and through the search for better ways of handling offenders as marked by the less punitive orientation of the legislation, the victim of crime re-entered the scene.

The United States shared some but by no means all of these developments. The first compensation scheme in the United States was introduced in California in 1965. This made provision for the payment of medical expenses for those injured as a result of crime as well as compensation, and also made payments to families of murder victims. (This marked one of the key differences to the post-war welfarism of the United States as compared with the UK.) Several other states introduced compensation schemes in the 1960s although by the 1980s this by no means constituted complete coverage with respect to compensation across all the states of the United States (McCormack, 1989).

The victims' movement itself found a political voice in the form of Barry Goldwater, who in 1964 made 'crime in the streets' part of his campaign (Geis, 1990). President Johnson set up a commission on Law Enforcement and the Administration of Justice out of which came the first National Crime Survey in the United States in 1966. A tough law and order policy also featured in the Nixon campaign in 1968, and in 1969 massive funding was initiated for the Law Enforcement Assistance Administration. Under this programme funding was provided for, amongst other things, the development of rape crisis centres. In 1969 the first victim assistance program was established (Roberts, 1990: 44).

Geis (1990) suggests a number of reasons for this interest in victims of crime. In a time of increasing crime and increasing awareness that government administrations could do little to reduce the rising crime rate, he states: 'The plight of the crime victim is dramatic and determinable. Their relief is feasible. It has strong social, political, and personal appeal. Any of us, at any time, could become a crime victim. And so a movement was born and grew' (Geis, 1990: 260). There were, however, other social movements emerging in the United States, as in the UK which helped this movement to grow. One of these movements was feminism.

Equal pay legislation was passed in the United States in 1963, and alongside the declining birth rate and increased participation in the labour force the 'women's liberation movement' was beginning to make its mark, as was the civil rights movement. Neither of these movements had victims of crime at the forefront of its concern, but both were to have an impact on the law, its enforcement and the responses to those processes. The full impact of these movements, however, was not to be felt until the next decade.

The 1970s: a radical challenge?

In the United Kingdom, the late 1960s saw the emergence of two important trends which were to have a marked subsequent impact on the criminal justice system in England and Wales. The first of these started with the Bristol Victims–Offenders Group. This group comprised 'the first criminal justice reformers to consider victims without inventing them. They were *listening* to victims' (Rock, 1990: 102). This group felt that criminal justice reform could only be achieved effectively if victims were listened to. In January 1970 a NACRO (National Association for the Care and Resettlement of Offenders) regional paper was produced by Philip Priestley entitled, 'What about the victim?' and in September 1973 the National Victims Association was formed. This short-lived organization was superseded in style and form by the establishment of the Bristol Victim Support Scheme which was formed in December 1973 and made its first visits to victims of crime in January 1974 (Rock, 1990).

From rather tentative and unstable financial origins the path was set for the emergence of the fastest-growing voluntary organization of the next fifteen years. The concern of these reformers with victims and offenders echoes the earlier concerns of Margery Fry. The question remains as to why this particular model of responding to victims of crime captured the public and policy imagination. The work of these reformers proceeded very much in a quiet and reserved manner. Not so the questions which were being raised by those of a more radical persuasion.

This was the second strand to influence criminal justice policy from the 1970s onwards. The early 1970s saw the consolidation of the feminist movement and its return to questions relating to equal rights. This movement, at the time, was considered to be successful in contributing to the securing of the Equal Pay Act, the Employment Protection Act and the Sex Discrimination Act. (That this legislation did not achieve the promise if offered was a view developed with the benefit of hindsight.) There was, however, another emergent strand of feminism which interpreted the question of rights and their realization in a more radical form. This strand grew out of an increasing awareness that the problem facing women was not discrimination but oppression. Radical feminists concerned themselves with the oppression of women by men which was typified by women's experiences of male violence, particularly rape, sexual assault and what was then referred to as 'wife-battering'. Women-only organizations grew up around these issues during the 1970s. The first women's refuge opened in Chiswick in 1972 and the first rape crisis centre opened in London in 1976. There was even a Select Committee on Violence in Marriage in 1975 which recommended that one family place should be available in a refuge for every 10,000 population. These developments not only constituted a challenge to male domination, they also challenged the 'blaming the victim' syndrome which was (and some would say, still is) a feature of the welfare response to these issues. The year 1973 also brought to the fore of public attention the question of the battered child in the form of Maria Colwell.

Thus the 1970s began to lay bare the inadequacies of the welfare state in a set of socioeconomic conditions which were unlikely to suggest a massive state response to those inadequacies. In the context of responses to victims of crime the Bristol initiative and the initiatives of the women's movement were both funded initially, like many other organizations in the voluntary sector, largely on a charitable basis. As the economic circumstances changed and the pattern of the 1980s was established it was the Bristol response which was to fare the better.

As far as the United States is concerned Mawby and Gill (1987) identified at least four influences on the development of victim policies during the 1970s, in addition to the feminist movement. They labelled these the offender-focus, the system efficiency priority, the law and order emphasis and the victims' rights lobby. In many respects it was the law and order lobby along with the feminist movement which was to have a marked impact on the development of service for victims of crime in general and women as 'victims' of crime in particular. The first rape crisis centre in the US was set up in California in 1972, and a federally funded Centre for the Prevention and Control of Rape was established in 1976. Alongside these developments, initiatives to establish refuges and safe houses emerged for women who had been battered. A National Coalition against Domestic Violence was established in 1978 to lobby for policy and legislative changes to help women and children who had been battered (Karmen, 1990: 33). By 1976 NOVA (National Organization for Victim Assistance) had been established. This body was designed to oversee and act as an information exchange and resource centre for the range of victim assistance programmes that was emerging. The subsequent influence of NOVA was to be considerable. And whilst many of these initiatives suffered under the fiscal policies of the early 1980s, with some having to close (Roberts, 1990: 27), by the end of the 1980s they were much more firmly established.

The 1980s: constructing the consumer?

The underlying ideology and spirit of Victim Support as compared with initiatives emanating from the feminist movement were distinctive in their influence in the United Kingdom (Mawby and Gill, 1987). Victim Support positively eschewed political involvement of any sort. It was this neutrality which, in part, constituted the secret of it successfully gaining the co-operation of other agencies, especially the police (Maguire and Corbett, 1987) and ultimately the Home Office (Rock, 1990). So the fact that Victim Support did not constitute a critical challenge to the workings of the criminal justice system is one key to understanding its success. This, however, did have a particular consequence for the focus of Victim Support:

> A very particular kind of victim emerged out of the NAVSS's response to those feminist politics and campaigns. It was an androgynous victim, the sexually neutral subject of burglary, theft, and robbery. The victims described in the campaigns of the NAVSS had no discernible gender. (Rock, 1990: 185)

What is interesting, is that Victim Support secured Home Office funding in the 1980s when government ideology and financial uncertainty were leading other areas of public service to a curtailment of service delivery and a reduced level of state involvement. This cannot be explained solely by reference to the organization's acceptable political hue, though this certainly was influential. The underlying philosophy of Victim Support was also important.

Victim Support represented a community-based, voluntary movement, at a time when the government was sounding the 'trumpet voluntary'. This was certainly an additional reason why this organization found governmental favour. This response to the victim of crime was built on an intent to reintegrate the victim into the community, not to create dependency. The then Prime Minister, Margaret Thatcher, had as one of her personal goals the elimination of the dependency culture. In this sense then, Victim

Support was certainly more appealing than the more right-wing Victims of Violence organization (Jonker, 1986).[1] Additionally Victim Support represented a voluntary response which emphasized individuals helping other individuals from within their own community. This gelled quite well with one of the unfolding themes of the decade: the move from the social citizenship of the 1950s to the 'active' citizenship of the 1980s. Victim Support benefited from the meshing together of ideas on which its own organization was based and the ideas which were emanating from central government. But it is necessary to go beyond these themes for a full appreciation of the successful funding of Victim Support.

The 1980s began with conflicts on a scale which took many by surprise. The riots of 1981 which took place in Liverpool and London and were repeated in Birmingham, Liverpool and London in 1985 clearly marked, for even the most conservative observer of events, the end of attempts to view society in terms of consensus. The 1980s also saw a continuing rise in crime, escalating unemployment, and a growing gap between rich and poor. One of the key underlying questions for these years was how to maintain law and order. The Tory Party that was elected in 1979 had as one of its central tenets the whole question of law and order. The continuing success of the Tory Party electorally has in part been explained by the way in which, politically, this party espoused an 'authoritarian populism' (Hall, 1988). Thatcherism successfully exploited the conservative politics of the working class to this end. But it was not just populism which brought the Tory Party three successive general election successes. It was a range of political, economic and ideological mechanisms which were put in place to secure social order. These mechanisms were, arguably, held together by a number of themes but one theme in particular, consumerism, became very influential in the criminal justice system:

> The idea of consumers of the criminal justice system is one of the more important initiatives of the 1980s. Agencies, for the first time, are being conjoined to care about lay people using their 'services' . . . Consumerism has also had a certain pay-off economically. If the cost of controlling a rising crime rate were apparently spiralling out of reach, demonstrating consumer satisfaction might just prove a more feasible (cheaper) alternative. (Jefferson and Shapland, 1990: 12)

Support for this notion of the lay person as the consumer made unusual bedfellows of Sir Peter Imbert (Metropolitan Police Commissioner) and radical left realists such as Crawford *et al.* (1990). In the context of the criminal justice system, this move towards consumerism began with the post-Scarman initiatives and the first British Crime Survey (BCS).

Lay visitors to police stations, community consultative committees and the findings of the first BCS were at least partly concerned with allaying fears: fear of the police on the one hand and fear of crime on the other. As stated earlier, the findings of the first BCS were presented in such a way as to downplay the risk from crime, and the post-Scarman initiatives opened up a previously closed world to the public. (That this public was the largely secure middle classes was established by some of the research done in their wake: see Walklate, 1986; Kemp and Morgan, 1990.) These initiatives marked a movement in the debate on accountability which neutralized the public to whom the police and the criminal justice process were to be accountable. Whilst the riots of 1981 by no means represented a neutral public, opening up the police station to accredited members of the public and asking the public about their experiences of crime effectively glossed over the structural inequalities which those riots symbolized.

The ideological basis of these strategies connects neatly with the funding of Victim Support in 1986. The neutral world of Victim Support gave the right kind of message in responding to victims of crime. This funding, it must be noted, explicitly included the development of services for victims of rape from within victim support services which up until that time had been provided for, with little government funding, from initiatives within the feminist movement. Victim Support had indeed significantly developed the service it offered to women, and has subsequently established a Victim Support Working Party on Domestic Violence, though the extension of services in this area at this time looks limited.

Other developments also took place during the 1980s which specifically concerned women and children as 'victims' of crime. The development of 'rape suites' in police stations in part connects with the public response to the televised Thames Valley Police interview of a rape victim in 1982, but that public response itself must be connected with changing levels of acceptance of police practice and changing attitudes of and towards women. Other events of the 1980s mark points at which the influence of feminism can be seen if not heard. The 'rediscovery' of child sexual abuse in the events surrounding Cleveland in 1987 has resulted in an ongoing re-examination of children's experiences of the criminal justice process, with some courts now offering the facility of giving evidence by video link in appropriate cases. The Home Office (1990c) Circular 60, *Domestic Violence,* not only reminded chief constables of their powers of arrest but directed them to use those powers in the same way as they would for violent incidents in the street.

These developments do, of course, have their limitations from a feminist perspective. But it is important to recognize that they have taken place. One way of beginning to analyse some of them would be to argue that via Victim Support the state has co-opted some of the issues raised by the women's movement of the 1970s. Women's needs are being met but in such a way that they no longer constitute a challenge to the state. This view, however, would not accommodate all the changes experienced in the 1980s. It makes some sense to see them *in toto* as a further extension of the consumerist ideology.

Alongside these developments other legislative changes gave more formal prominence to the victim of crime. The 1982 Criminal Justice Act stated that where the court had ordered compensation to be paid to the victim and also imposed a fine, then the compensation was to take priority. The 1988 Criminal Justice Act requires courts to give reasons why they have not ordered compensation to be paid in circumstances where they could have done this. In addition this piece of legislation brought in tougher provisions to ensure the anonymity of rape victims from the moment they report the offence, for the rest of their lives if they so wish. Legislative changes of this sort were supplemented in 1990 with the publication of the Home Office (1990b) *Victim's Charter* which drew together varying initiatives in one document.

To summarize some of these developments: it was during the 1980s that the National Association of Victim Support Schemes (NAVSS), now known as Victim Support, rapidly expanded in size. By 1990 there were over 300 such schemes in England and Wales with similar developments having taken place in Northern Ireland and Scotland. The national office itself and its director, Helen Reeves, had gained stature and influence in the formulation of government policy and in representing that voice of the victim of crime which was absent during the 1950s. The work of the national organization, in establishing and sponsoring 'demonstration projects', also heralded an enhancement of status as the expert agency to promote research. Projects concerning the families of murder victims, the victim/witness in court, children as victims of crime, and racial harassment give a considerable flavour to the current range of issues on the national association's agenda. They also represent, to some extent, the way in which Victim Support had, by the end of the 1980s, become *the* victim organization in England and Wales. This is not intended to suggest that rape crisis centres and women's refuges are no longer important. They certainly are. But in terms of central policymaking they are clearly not represented on the same level as Victim Support.

All of the changes outlined here have so far been portrayed in terms of the ideological construction of the consumer. That such a construction became necessary relates to the economic circumstances of the 1980s. The 1980s began with an emphasis on 'cuts', particularly cutbacks in public expenditure. As the decade unfolded theorists began to argue that what these cuts represented were not so much 'real' cuts as changes in direction, a reorientation of the welfare state of the 1950s. This reorientation, marked by 'privatization' and demands for economy and efficiency in all aspects of public expenditure, set the framework in which public services strove to find alternative strategies for assessing service delivery. In the context of policing in particular, the public became consumers of a police service and the issue of public satisfaction with that service delivery became more important than the increasingly questioned and questionable 'clear-up rates'. Thus the police are currently as concerned with satisfaction rates with service delivery in the context of domestic violence as they are in other aspects of their work. The satisfaction of the consumer is not only an ideological strategy; it is a product of real economic constraints on services forcing them to look for alternative ways of justifying their budgets. However, the construction of this consumerism also marks a change of direction for the debate surrounding citizenship, with which this chapter began.

The construction of the consumer has a pervasive character to it, and it has proceeded in a surprisingly unchallenged way (Taylor, 1990). This is partly because to talk of consumers of a police service, for example, removes any stigma which might be attached to such contact, in a rather similar way that discussion of citizens in the late 1940s removed the stigma of being a recipient of state benefits. It has also been successful because of the way in which capitalism itself has nourished the belief that market forces create and permit variety. As consumers we are permitted to choose within the variety of goods and services which are on offer. As Conservative MP Sir Ian Gilmour and critic of Thatcherism has stated: 'under this philosophy everybody is a consumer and the world a giant supermarket. Life is nothing but a prolonged pursuit of groceries whereby one chooses education from Tesco's and local government from Sainsbury's.[2]

Edgar (1991) points out that this cult of the customer limits the power of the consumer to that of individual preference, discriminates between individuals according to how much they have paid, and homogenizes the relationships we have with the outside world. It would be useful to add to that list that this move towards the customer/consumer also usefully serves to mask the structural dimensions to the 'paying power' individuals might have. It provides a gloss of equality where none exists (see for example, Lister, 1990). In this vein it is non-problematic for Victim Support schemes to concern themselves with women who have been raped, since these women are in receipt of a service which has been tried and tested on other victims and shown to work successfully. In some ways this constitutes the normalization of rape.

This view of the consumer is, of course, enmeshed with the notion of the 'active citizen'. In 1989 Sir Geoffrey Hurd stated: 'the idea of active citizenship is a necessary complement to that of the enterprise culture. Public service may once have been the duty of an elite, but today it is the responsibility of all who have time or money to spare.'[3] So the notion of the consumer is given a human face: it carries with it a view of the citizen who not only has rights but also responsibilities.

The United Kingdom has, during the 1980s, experienced a decade which has seen a significant reorientation of the processes which began in the 1950s. This reorientation has been both economically and politically driven, though not necessarily in a smooth and consistent fashion. As far as victims' movements are concerned it has been a decade of remarkable growth, but a growth in which the main organization to benefit has as a consequence become enmeshed in the processes of regulation and control through the promotion of a neutral image of the victim. This does not mean that these mechanisms have been all-embracing or totally effective. The continued presence of what some have called 'the underclass' (despite the problems with this term) presents a constant threat to the effectiveness of such strategies.

It is also worth remembering at this juncture that the end of the decade saw a number of 'disasters' in the UK: the sinking of the *Herald of Free Enterprise* (1987), the Clapham rail crash (1988), the King's Cross fire (1989), Hillsborough football ground (1989), and the sinking of the *Marchioness* ferry (1989). These led to a greater public awareness and perhaps questioning of what constituted the 'criminal' and a broad-based response to the victims of these events involving both voluntary and professional agencies as well as 'ordinary' members of communities. In some respects the impact of these events has been rather more limited than the impact of the events in Bhopal, not only in India but also in the United States in a rash of 'right to know' legislation (Pearce and Tombs, 1989). But in other respects the developments of the 1980s in the United States look similar to these which occurred in the UK.

The 1980s in the United States also saw the introduction of significant legislation which ensured that the victim of crime would no longer be neglected. The 1982 President's Task Force on Victims of Crime recommended action to be taken at federal, state, and local level to ensure that the needs and rights of victims and witnesses were being met. As a part of the Federal Comprehensive Crime Control Act 1984 federal funding was made available for state and local victim/witness support programmes through the Victims of Crime Act (VOCA) and the Justice Assistance Act (Roberts, 1990: 46). This, alongside the work of NOVA and increased public and professional awareness of victim issues, put these initiatives on a sounder financial basis. By 1987 there were over 600 such organizations in the United States. Roberts (1990) also reports that by 1989, 48 states had funding for domestic violence intervention programmes and 25 had funding for local sexual assault crisis services.

In addition Karmen (1990: 332–4) lists the range of rights now possessed by victims of crime. These include: to be notified when a prisoner will be appearing before a parole board (44 states); to be notified of a negotiated plea (28 states); to compensation (45 states); to be protected during pre-trial from the accused (46 states); to have any royalties and fees paid to notorious criminals confiscated and used to repay the victim or to fund victim services (42 states).

This period also heralded the 'rediscovery' of a number of 'special' categories of crime victims: murdered and missing children, elder abuse, child sexual abuse, marital rape, date rape, victims of drunk driving, victims of bias crime (racial, religious or sexual orientation bias). It is useful to connect these 'discoveries' to wider social changes. The discovery of AIDS, for example, is not unconnected to 'gay bashing'. The increasing disparity between rich and poor which has marked the 1980s in the United States, as it has in the UK, must also play a part in understanding these discoveries and that country's response to them.

Summary: the UK and the USA

Whilst Chapters 5 and 6 will be concerned with a more detailed comparative analysis of some of these developments, it is useful at this juncture to make some comparative comment on the developments in the United States and in the United Kingdom. It is worth noting first of all that responses to crimes affecting women have been given equal prominence in the development of victim initiatives in the United States alongside other concerns. Indeed it would appear that both there and in Canada the structural position of women in the decision-making process, alongside the nature of the women's movements themselves, have resulted in policy changes being more effectively felt than in the UK. Secondly, although the USA and the UK 'suffered' from Reaganomics on the one hand and Thatcherism on the other, the victims of crime still continue to be seen as those who suffer at the hands of the lawless, not those who suffer at the hands of the state. In other words, whilst feminism in some respect achieved a respectability, if not least because women form 52 per cent of the voting public, the increasing marginalization of the poorest sections of the population, which also disproportionately included those from ethnic minorities, was a marked feature of both societies during the 1980s. Finally, it is important to note that whilst there are some similarities in the issues influencing the development of responses to victims of crime in both of these countries, the response has been marked by one key difference. The response in the United Kingdom has been a reaction to the collectivist welfare tradition marked by voluntarism whereas the response in the United States has been moulded by an individualist welfare tradition marked by legalism (and to a lesser extent voluntarism).

The following chapters will unfold in greater detail a comparative analysis of such policy responses. But before leaving this historical appreciation of the emergence of the crime victim as a significant actor, it is worth spending a little time commenting on developments worldwide.

European and United Nations initiatives

International debates on the role of the victim in the criminal justice system are, of course, no new phenomena. At international penal congresses in the late nineteenth century a variety of activists, including William Tallack from Britain, Sir George Arney from New Zealand and the Italian criminologist Raffaelo Garofalo, proposed a series of reforms largely centring on the principle of compensation by the offender (Meiners, 1978; Schafer, 1960). However, it is not until the 1970s and 1980s, particularly through the World Society of Victimology (WSV), the Council of Europe and the United Nations, that victims re-emerged in force on to the centre of the world stage. Heidensohn (1991) notes that the women's movement across Europe has been responsible for initiating responses to rape, domestic violence and child abuse, and although these responses may not be so frequently discussed they nevertheless constitute an important response to victims of crime.

The women's movement was also involved in the formation of the World Society of Victimology. This emerged in the early 1970s in the USA where local academics like John Dussich liaised with victimologists in other countries. The first International Symposium on Victimology was held in Israel in 1972. This subsequently led to the formation of the WSV with members from a range of nations in the developing and the developed world, and congresses held every three years. At its fourth symposium in Tokyo and Kyoto in 1982 the WSV set up a committee on Codes of Conduct for Victims, which led to the endorsement of victim issues by the World Federation of Mental Health in 1983. However it was on a wider stage, through the United Nations, that the WSV sought further recognition of victims' rights (Lamborn, 1985; Schneider, 1984; Waller, 1982, 1984).

The role of the United Nations is fully documented by Joutsen (1987: 58–69, 293–324). Unlike its predecessor, the League of Nations, the UN was more directly concerned to promote human rights and welfare standards. The Economic and Social Council of the UN covers crime and related issues and reports back to the General Assembly. The council itself is responsible for a number of organizations including the Centre for Social Development and Humanitarian Affairs and its Crime Prevention and Criminal Justice branch. The Helsinki Institute for Crime Prevention and Control (HEUNI), based in Finland and established in 1981, is the European regional institute for the crime and criminal justice programme.

Until the 1980s the focus within the UN had been on crime itself and the standards that existed for the treatment of suspects or prisoners. However the fifth UN congress in 1975 touched on victim-related issues in focusing on the economic and social consequences of crime, and the sixth congress in 1980 considered, among other items, the abuse of power. Victims became the focus of attention through meetings organized by the Committee on Crime Prevention and Control in 1982 and 1984, and through a European seminar hosted by HEUNI in 1983. In particular the 1984 Ottawa Interregional Meeting of Experts, with WSV influence, drew up an agenda for the 1985 congress that fused the issues of victims' rights and the abuse of power. The seventh UN congress held in Milan in 1985 subsequently included victim issues as one of its main topic areas.

The *Declaration of Basic Principles of Justice for Victims of Crime and the Abuse of Power* (A/RES/40/34) evolving from the 1980 congress, the 1982 Tokyo conference and the 1984 Ottawa planning meeting, was then adopted by the General Assembly. The Declaration incorporates a general introduction and two main sections on victims of crime and victims of abuse of power. On victims of crime the Declaration advocates compassionate and respectful treatment of victims by the police, prosecutors and courts, with emphasis placed on providing victims with information, assistance and compensation. In 1987 the Economic and Social Council granted the WSV consultative status with the UN. In 1988 it invited member states to specify how they had implemented the Declaration. In 1990 the Secretariat presented a guide for practitioners on the implementation of the Declaration (Joutsen, 1991). The eighth UN congress held in Havana in 1990 included in its discussions the recommendations and their implementation and passed further resolutions to be appended to the 1985 Declaration aimed at encouraging its adoption worldwide.

Whilst the WSV and the UN have been instrumental in broadcasting the needs of crime victims on a worldwide platform, within Europe the Council of Europe has played a part of equal or greater significance. The council, which currently has 25 member countries, is an international organization dealing with areas of common interest, formulating treaties and adopting programmes of common action (Joutsen, 1987). It also organizes conventions on crime problems, and victim policies were first considered in detail at its second criminological colloquium in 1975. It was also a major item at the thirteenth International Criminological Research Conference in 1978 and the sixteenth in 1984. Prior to this the Council of Europe passed a resolution on state compensation in 1977 (Tsitsoura, 1989). In 1982, however, the Division of Crime Problems established a select committee to develop this initiative further, the result being the *European Convention on the Victim of Violent Crime* which was adopted by the Committee of Ministers in 1983 and came into force in 1988. Interestingly, in debating the need for state compensation the council rejected the idea of compensation as a right and instead justified it in the interests of 'equity and social solidarity' (Willis, 1984: 213), a phrase that resonates with the themes surrounding the emergence of the Criminal Injuries Compensation Board (CICB) in the UK though not completely stated in those terms.

Subsequently the Council of Europe established a select committee to consider the victim and criminal and social policy. The result was *Recommendation R (85) 11 of the Committee of Ministers to Member States on the Position of the Victim in the Framework of Criminal Law Procedure*. Preceding the UN declaration by some six months, this covers broadly similar ground, focusing on the police, prosecution and court proceedings (Joutsen, 1987: 69–71, 325–9). It was followed by a series of recommendations of relevance to specific groups of victims, for example on violence in the family

-R(85)4- and consumer protection -R(88)15- and more generally recommendation R(87)21 on assistance to victims through the provision of services offering immediate assistance, promotion of efforts to improve the co-ordination of services and the encouragement of mediation experiments (Tsitsoura, 1989).

One further international victim agency in Europe is the European Forum for Victim Services. This emerged from the first European Conference of Victim Support Workers held in the Netherlands in 1987, and provides a forum whereby policymakers and practitioners in victim support can meet and exchange ideas. Noting that welfare-focused international organizations had failed to address issues surrounding crime victims, and the WSV was an organization of individual members rather than nations, Holtom (1989) proposed the formation of a separate body. It aims to provide public education on victims' needs (there is now, following the US model, a European Victims' Day), facilitate reciprocal relationships between member organizations, and act as a pressure group *vis-à-vis* the Council of Europe and the European Community. To date some 12 nations are affiliated, with Hungary accepted in 1992 as the first member from the former Eastern bloc.

According to Van Dijk (1988: 121) these international developments 'reflect those new consumer demands upon the criminal justice system'. Conversely they may act as a stimulus to public opinion by formally acknowledging the importance of the victim movement. In this respect the 1983 Council of Europe Convention 'may be regarded as a milestone for the victim movement in Western Europe' (Van Dijk, 1985a: 7). Like the Council of Europe, the UN provides a prestigious champion in the development of local policies:

> The UN covenants have become models for developing and revising constitutions of individual states. A declaration could provide the prestige of the United Nations to support the activities of the private sector, government agencies and legislators, who are trying to make reforms to assist crime victims. It would provide a model for specifying victims' rights whether in revising charters, human rights codes or specialised bills. (Waller, 1984: 6)

However, while the recommendations of these international bodies may have 'symbolic significance in the guiding of legal policy' (Joutsen, 1987: 27) neither UN nor Council of Europe instruments are legally binding. Take the former, for example:

> The adoption of the Declaration is a symbolic measure, and will not in itself change the status of the victim in any country. It is not legally binding. In the absence of other pressures working in the same direction,

it would be visionary to assume that it would lead to a direct change of the law or practice of any jurisdiction. (Joutsen, 1987: 68)

More recently, in a critical review of such international agreements Joutsen (1991) notes that agreements reached tend to be compatible with two key principles: the consensus norm that dictates that it is important to express international compatibility, and the 'my country first' norm that seeks to preserve the national status quo. One example of this is international differences in interest over the draft UN Declaration, where British representatives, particularly the NAVSS, were concerned to minimize the place in the recommendations of victims' rights (specifically through the availability of victim impact statements) and mediation and reparation initiatives (as illustrated by Reeves, 1985). As a result the UN Declaration voiced an underground concern that something ought to be done for victims but allowed different interpretations of appropriate action.

So whilst some countries and provinces such as the USA and Manitoba in Canada (Waller, 1988a, 1988b) have used the Declaration as a basis for legislation, a review of the Declaration by Dr Irene Melup (1991), UN Secretary-General, suggests that its major influence to date has been to encourage debate on victim issues and keep such matters high on the agenda rather than to effect policies or unify practice. This in itself is an important and necessary achievement, but it does not mean that national variations in the existence and form of victim policies will not continue. We would therefore agree with Joutsen (1991: 1) when he argues: 'My own view is that just as national criminal justice systems will withstand the pressure towards national standardisation, the position of the victim within and outside of the criminal justice system will retain its unique national features.'

The extent of national variation will become clearer in the more detailed analyses of Chapters 5 and 6. Here however it is appropriate to conclude this review by reiterating some of the parallel themes which we have identified.

Conclusion

The 1980s saw the introduction of a number of trends, some of which continue to be in play in the 1990s. These incorporate at least six issues of particular interest to a broad understanding of the development of victims' movements. First there is the influence of the feminist movement. In some respects Walby's (1990) analysis of the trends within patriarchy as representing a move from private patriarchy to public patriarchy can be keenly observed in the changes and debates around the criminal justice system. Indeed, along this dimension it may be argued that the subsuming of women as consumers of the criminal justice system represents not only an extension of public patriarchy but potentially a more subtle and invidious co-option of those issues and concerns.

Secondly, the theme of citizenship runs through the emergence of the various developments documented here. This starts with the social citizenship of the welfare state and ends with the active citizenship of a reoriented welfare state. In both contexts movements pertaining to victims of crime have benefited: in the first context in the form of the emergence of the Criminal Injuries Compensation Board, in the second in the form of the rapid expansion and development of Victim Support.

The third important feature of these developments and one which remains effectively hidden, is the relationship between the policy responses to victims of crime and the meshing of those interests with the questions of regulation and control. This is best epitomized by the distinctions between deserving and undeserving victim within ideas around compensation but is also present in the neutral image of the victim represented by Victim Support. Indeed the focus on social solidarity in relation to the purpose of compensation is more openly admitted by the Council of Europe. The neutral images and traditional distinctions commented upon here, of course, also gel quite nicely with the positivist victimology outlined in Chapter 1. As feminism has struggled on the sidelines of that discipline so feminist responses in the policy arena have faced a continued struggle for recognition rather than co-option. The importance of this theme gains in its strength and impact as it becomes married with the fourth thread which runs through this presentation.

The fourth feature of these developments emerges late in this historical period; that is the social construction of the consumer. This has become an important strategy whereby the economic circumstances of the 1980s have been rendered manageable by public services and from which, arguably, the victim of crime has gained some benefit. Attention to this theme stresses the importance of viewing policy initiatives as a part of a wider spectrum of changes which have emerged from within a particular social context. Not all societies have responded to the recession of the 1980s in exactly the same way; there are some valuable lessons to be learnt from comparing and contrasting the ways in which other societies have responded to such changes.

The fifth issue to be addressed here concerns itself with what has been significantly omitted from these developments:

Victim initiatives seem to perpetuate biased crime definitions conveyed in legislation, enforcement patterns, or the media, which limit our concept of victimization to street crime, usually ignoring the much more harmful 'suite' crime, be it corporate or governmental. They further narrow those victims to whom we will devote our attention: not to lower class minorities, who are among the most victimized, but rather to the elderly and the victims of child, female, and sexual abuse who are not. (Elias, 1990: 243)

Whilst it would be possible to enter into a considerable debate with Elias as to the validity of the last part of this statement the overall tenor of his observation is sound in that many of the initiatives which have been documented here have been 'safe'. In this sense victims' movements like Victim Support are not neutral at all but are bound up in supporting the status quo. The lack of recognition of victims of corporate crime as victims of crime could only be challenged effectively by many of the victim initiatives discussed here by moving their frame of reference to one which is concerned with entitlements and not needs. But to paraphrase Donzelot (1979: 64) there is no guarantee that rights will not be made 'to operate as a means of social integration and no longer a cause of insurrection'. (The question of rights emerges again in Chapter 8.)

Finally this chapter has drawn upon ideas and processes outside of the criminal justice system in order to facilitate an understanding of the kinds of policy response which have been structured both within that system and to effect change in that system. In so doing it has been interesting to note some of the comparable and contrasting historical features of different societies resulting in different emphases in responses to victims of crime. So whilst this chapter has been concerned to centre both the role of feminism and the role of the state in the changes that have been documented here, it is clear that both of these influences may result in a range of different policy formations.

In the following two chapters we shall focus in more detail on specific policies as they have emerged in a number of Western societies. Chapter 5 is concerned with the problems victims face and the services they are provided with when a crime occurs. Chapter 6 covers the courtroom and tribunal processes concerned with the prosecution of defendants and compensation for victims. In each of these chapters the emphasis is on the situation in England and Wales and the United States where most of the available research has taken place. However, where appropriate we shall also refer to a range of other countries including Canada and, in Europe, particularly the Netherlands, France and Germany. The findings from these two chapters will then be used to inform our critique of victim policies and suggestions for reform which are further developed in later chapters.

Notes

1. Victims of Violence has continued as a Merseyside-based service, providing support and ultimately residential accommodation for elderly victims.

2. Cited in *Hansard*, December 1987.

3. As cited in the *Independent*, 13 September 1989.

5

Immediate Help for the Victims of Crime

The effects of crime may be long-lasting, but the evidence shows that for most victims the initial impact is the greatest. What happens then – how different agencies and their representatives react to the immediate crime situation – is of crucial importance in underpinning victims' experiences. The first focal point here is the role of the police. This is partly because the police are usually the first official agency to be notified and to become involved, and partly because where the police are not involved it is relatively unlikely that any other agency will be drawn in. There are of course exceptions to this. Victims of violence may, for example, go to a doctor or a hospital for help with injuries but neither desire nor receive police attention. Similarly, victims of certain crimes, such as domestic violence or rape, may choose not to involve the police and go for help instead to an agency dealing specifically with that type of crime. Nevertheless, for most victims who choose to involve an official organization in 'their' crime, the police are the first agency to be called. It is with the police, therefore, that this chapter begins. Once the police are involved, and in some cases independently of police involvement, other agencies may be contacted. Generally these may be divided into those that provide services that are appropriate, among others, for crime victims (for example, medical facilities), those that are organized specifically to help victims of crime (for example, victim support services) and those that deal exclusively with certain offence-types or categories of victims, like rape crisis centres. The second half of the chapter focuses on these organizations.

The police response to crime victims

The police are highly dependent upon crime victims. Excluding motoring and public order offences, most crime is reported to the police by members of the public, in a large majority of these cases the victim; and victims frequently provide the key evidence in identifying the offender (Mawby, 1979b). In a sense then, the police *need* crime victims, and need to ensure the co-operation of these victims.

But crime victims also require a positive response from the police:

> They are generally the first representatives of the State to come into contact with the complainant. Furthermore, their intervention will come at a time when the complainant is most likely to be suffering from the immediate shock of the offence. Their attitude will considerably influence not only what the complainant decides to do but also what impression he receives of the administration of justice and of how the community as a whole regards the offence. (Joutsen, 1987: 212)

We may distinguish three levels to the police response. First, the police react to the information they receive by *intervention* (or non-intervention); secondly they adopt particular *styles* in their interaction with victims; thirdly they provide *services*, particularly *information*, to victims. How can we evaluate the police response on these three levels?

First is the question of police intervention. The assumption behind much of the literature in victimology is that police intervention is the norm, and that the key issues surround *how* the police intervene. However, this is to confuse victims' definitions of themselves as victims with police definitions of whether there is a 'real' victim and a 'real' crime. Essentially, when an incident is reported or discovered, the police define the situation according to their occupation-based definitions of crime and its seriousness and the moral worth of the complainant. Whether or not the police then do anything will depend on the balance between these interpretations and other demands on police time. Self-defined victims may then be deflected on the grounds that the matter is 'not police business', allegedly because it is 'a civil matter', because no crime has been committed, because there is no proof that a crime has been committed, or because there is little that the police can do. Research on violence or threats suggest that deflection of this sort is common, especially where the offender and victim are known to one another, particularly when they are members of the same household or neighbours. But a similar process occurs in many examples of property crime; for instance where thefts from the person are defined as lost property. Even where the fact that a crime has been committed is accepted, the police may do nothing more than record the incident. Thus while in Britain it is seen as routine for the police to visit a home where a burglary has been reported, in France the Police Nationale would not consider this usual or always necessary.[1]

In some cases, police reaction may backfire and the police be held liable when further harm befalls the victim. In the Thurman case in Connecticut, USA, for example, a battered wife successfully sued her local police department when their failure to respond to her call for help led to her being seriously injured. In this example, a $2.3 million lawsuit resulted in a swift change in police policy!

But even when the police do intervene, there is considerable evidence that their intervention is not framed by the interests of the victim. Rather, given the predominance of a police culture, in which emphasis is placed on action, a crime-fighting role for the police, and detection, it is scarcely surprising that until recently the idea of the police providing a service for victims was rare. This trend is exacerbated by the fact that the police, to whom crime is routine, often fail to recognize the impact of crime on its victims. For example, responses from police in one survey in the south-west of England revealed that generally the police underestimated the problems faced by victims, and identified only the most vulnerable and frail victims as requiring special services (Mawby and Gill, 1987: 170–5). Moreover, findings that the police are insensitive to victims are common to studies across a wide range of countries, with very different policing structures, leading one international commentator to compare actual with ideal police styles:

> There is ample evidence from in-depth interviews that victims are particularly sensitive to the way they are personally approached by police officers. According to several researchers, many victims experience an acute need to be 'reassured' by the police. Others state that victims expect the police to recognize their status as someone who has been wronged by a fellow citizen. Many victims express dissatisfaction with police officers who are distrustful, callous or cynical. Such observations are often viewed as evidence of secondary victimization . . . Police officers must be taught that their deskside manners are as important to victims as bedside manners of doctors are to patients. (Van Dijk, 1985b: 154, 162)

If police *style* is important, so is the concrete help that police provide for victims. But while providing services for victims within the police organization is usually seen as a police responsibility in only a limited and restricted sense (see below), being a source of *information* for victims has increasingly come to be seen as a crucial police task. This is certainly the case on at least two levels. First, many victims want feedback from the police on the progress made (or not made) on their case. Secondly, the police are a key provider of information on other services available for victims.

What then of police services on these levels? In terms of services provided directly by the police for crime victims, it appears that, generally speaking, the police perceive crime prevention services to be their responsibility, and there is fairly common acceptance of the need to respond to victims' requests for advice on how to reduce the chance of a further crime. This is clearly most appropriate in the case of property crimes, such as burglary, and individual victims may be linked in with specialist services, such as crime prevention, or continuous programmes like Neighbourhood Watch. Significantly here, Mawby and Gill (1987: 173) found that their sample of police officers most commonly recognized victims' needs associated with practical crime prevention issues, such as getting new locks fitted, and saw this as the main area of victim support where the police had responsibility. On the other hand, in some countries wider services for victims may be provided by the police, or at the very least housed within the police department. This is certainly the case in North America (Dussich, 1976; McClenahan, 1987; Roberts, 1990). In Clearwater, Florida, for example, the Victim Advocacy Program is the responsibility of a police officer, designated a deputy victim assistant, who deals with all serious violent crime and other crimes that are referred to her at the discretion of the investigating officer (Mawby and Gill, 1987: 124–5). In Japan, a country with a somewhat different policing philosophy (Mawby, 1990), some victim services are also located within the police organization. So where the police emphasize their service and welfare responsibilities, and indeed have a tradition for providing mediation and counselling, specialist staff are assigned at station and prefecture level to counselling duties (Bayley, 1976; Clifford, 1976; National Police Agency, 1984).

With regard to rape, studies in Britain and North America have criticized police practices and advocated legal changes (Chambers and Millar, 1983; Clark and Lewis, 1977; Holmstrom and Burgess, 1978; Minch, 1987). In North America this has had the effect of pressuring the police to improve their procedures and develop co-operative relationships with rape crisis centres, but in Britain, where the latter tend to be more radical there has been more emphasis on police procedures. For example, a number of forces, including the London Metropolitan Police, have recently set up special rape and child abuse suites. Located away from police stations, these provide facilities for interviewing, medical examinations and support in a less threatening environment.

Similar criticisms have been levelled at the police in respect of their handling of domestic violence (Brown, 1984; Hanmer *et al.*, 1989; Hanmer and Maynard, 1987; Walker, 1984). Indeed concern at police inaction in North America led to a number of changes, including in many forces attempts to make arrest of the offender mandatory (Berk and Newton, 1985; Breci, 1987; Burris and Jaffe, 1983; Jaffe *et al.*, 1986; Ursel and Farough, 1986), an interesting contrast with earlier attempts to train the police to deploy mediation in such cases (Bard, 1971, 1975).

Research in England and Wales has tended to echo Pizzey's (1974) earlier critique in revealing a reluctance among the police to prosecute males who have abused their partners, regarding this as 'not real crime' (Edwards, 1989). However, the police response has been somewhat different to that of the US. For example, a domestic violence unit set up in Northumbria in 1989, and staffed by two plainclothes female officers, emphasizes the service role of the police and a multi-agency approach. The unit is separate from routine policing, arrests being carried out by uniformed regular officers (Nicholls, 1991). This, and earlier specialist units in the London Metropolitan Police, form the basis for some of the recommendations in Home Office (1990c) Circular 60.

In England and Wales, circular instructions are instruments used by central government to set standards and impose consistency on locally based agencies. They are not legally binding, precisely because – in contrast to much of continental Europe – agencies such as the police are not, in theory at least, nationally controlled (Mawby, 1992b; Reiner, 1991). Nevertheless, there is considerable evidence that circulars can be effective in ensuring the implementation of government policies, not least because central government, while responsible for over half the police budget, is required to satisfy itself as to the efficiency of each police force.

Circular 60 can thus be seen as an important directive, reflecting government and Home Office policy. Among other things, it recommends that forces consider the establishment of domestic violence units, and stresses the fact that domestic violence should be treated before the law in exactly the same way as other violent incidents. At the time of writing it has been accepted by most forces. It is, of course, too early to assess its effects, but clearly it is more permissive than US mandatory arrest directives; while a step in the right direction, it seems unlikely to have a dramatic effect on police practices.

Circular 60 also covers inter-agency relationships and the need for police to provide victims with details of other agencies where they might receive help. The extent to which the police do provide such information, and indeed details of their own actions, is of relevance across a wide range of offences.

In fact, in most countries the role of the police is limited to providing information. Yet even here there have been criticisms that the police fail to keep victims fully informed. A variety of studies have found that victims are not kept up to date on developments in their case, and that this is a source of resentment. Shapland, Willmore and Duff (1985) for example, in their study of crimes against the person, identified this as the major source of victims' criticism of the police, and more recently in a small study of those receiving compensation orders, Newburn and De Peyrecave (1988) found that less than half of their sample were informed of the court date and even fewer knew of any sentence other than compensation. More generally, the 1988 BCS found that among those who reported crimes to the police, 46 per cent said that the police had not kept them very well informed of the progress of their investigation, compared with 30 per cent who felt that the police had kept them very or fairly well informed. Indeed, overall 35 per cent were dissatisfied with the way the police had handled their crime; of those 44 per cent thought that the police did not do enough; 41 per cent that they were not interested, and 32 per cent that they failed to keep the victim informed. In contrast, 20 per cent of dissatisfied victims complained that the police had not apprehended the offender and 13 per cent that property was not recovered, both concerns that would, perhaps, receive a higher rating among the police themselves.

If the police have been criticized for not providing victims with enough information on their own actions, we might expect a similar lack of information *vis-à-vis* the goods and services available to victims from other sources. Thus whilst Dussich (1976) notes that one advantage of police-based victim support is the ease of referral, services based outside the control of the police but which are, for all practical purposes, dependent upon the police for referral, are more vulnerable. In England and Wales, for example, whilst the police view victim support very positively and have adopted various measures to inform victims of their rights, this commitment is less evident among lower ranks, where most contacts with victims occur (Mawby and Gill, 1987; Newburn, 1989; Shapland and Cohen, 1987). In recent years then, emphasis has been placed, here and in other countries, on ensuring that information is passed on from police to victims; through more focused police training, the availability of leaflets in police stations, or making it a duty for police to pass on specified information.

Concerns to improve the ways in which the police respond to crime victims have been expressed in a number of international and national policy documents. Among the first of these were the Council of Europe recommendations adopted by the Committee of Ministers in 1985, which included, at the police level:

1. Police officers should be trained to deal with victims in a sympathetic, constructive and reassuring manner;
2. The police should inform the victim about the possibilities of obtaining assistance, practical and legal advice, compensation from the offender and state compensation;

3. The victim should be able to obtain information on the outcome of the police investigation. (Joutsen, 1987: 325-6)

While less explicit, the United Nations resolution also recommends that police and other relevant agencies 'should receive training to sensitize them to the needs of victims, and guidelines to ensure proper and prompt aid' (Joutsen, 1987: 297). Similarly, the International Association of Chiefs of Police (IACP) advises forces to provide information on social and financial services for victims and on the progress of their case (Waller, 1990: 139-40).

The IACP is particularly strong in North America, and its recommendations are reflected in policies implemented in the USA and Canada in the 1980s. In the USA, for example, both federal and state legislation sets standards for the treatment of victims by the police (Waller, 1990: 148). However, perhaps the most notable examples of government initiatives in this area are to be found in Europe, especially in the Netherlands and in England and Wales.

In the Netherlands, police response to crime victims was addressed by two committees, the Beaufort Committee of 1981, which focused on sex offences, and the Vaillant Committee of 1983 (Wemmers and Zeilstra, 1991). As a result, a series of guidelines for police and prosecutors – what Penders (1989) terms 'pseudo-laws' – was issued in 1986, covering, among other things, the rights of victims of sex offences to receive information on their cases. In 1987 these guidelines were expanded to include the victims of all crimes. The circular contains separate instructions for the police and Prosecutors' office. The duties of the police are specified as including the following:

a) To treat victims in the proper manner and to record their crime reports carefully; this duty includes referral, if necessary, of the victim to assistance agencies, in particular in the case of serious crime.
b) To give the victim general information on the procedure following the crime report: to ask the victim explicitly whether he wants to claim damages and whether or not he wants to be kept informed about the progress in the investigating procedures; to inform the victim about ways and means for the settlement of damages; to promote and – if appropriate – to mediate in the settlement . . . (Van Dijk, 1989b: 75)

According to Penders (1989) the circular acts as a public expansion of government policy whereby government agencies are required to act in accordance with that policy. Indeed, victims have a legal right to cite the circular in any subsequent legal action against the police. However, whilst this sounds impressive, a careful government review of the current situation suggests that the effect of the circular on police action has been minimal:

In these guidelines, specific duties for police and public prosecutors regarding the correct treatment of victims are outlined. Further specifications regarding optional procedure or organisation to be followed in the application of the guidelines are, however, not provided in the guidelines. Each organisation is free to interpret the guidelines into its existing structure as it sees fit . . .

As regards the police:

> Once again the guidelines do not provide concrete instructions as to how to fill the duties. As a result, each police unit tends to interpret the guidelines in its own way. Consequently the procedure followed and the extent to which compensation of the victim is achieved, can differ greatly between individual police units. (Wemmers and Zeilstra, 1991: 7, 5)

For example, reviewing smaller studies that evaluated the effects of the Vaillant guidelines, Wemmers and Zeilstra (1991) show that in a jurisdiction where the police agreed to keep victims informed by letter, only a minority of victims received a letter, and suggest that the shortfall is largely due to victims' lack of awareness of the new procedures compounded by police vagueness in their recording of whether or not victims wish to be kept informed.

The Dutch experience is particularly interesting given that the British government subsequently adopted a similar strategy in publishing the *Victim's Charter* (Home Office, 1990b). Preceding that, however, was Home Office (1988) Circular 20 on *Victims of Crime*, which can be seen as an important directive to each force *vis-à-vis* the treatment of crime victims. In it recommendations are made regarding relationships between police and victim support and concerning police co-operation with the courts in providing sufficient information on which decisions on compensation might be based. Of particular relevance here, police forces are also urged to ensure that victims are informed of the possibility of compensation, and to this end a leaflet was produced to be made available in police stations. Additionally it was recommended that forces provide victims, where appropriate, with feedback on the case outcome:

> Where someone has been the victim of a serious offence, knowing what is happening in the case can be an important reassurance and an aid to recovery, while conversely a lack of information can exacerbate the victim's feelings of anxiety and distress. There are therefore benefits to be gained, both for the welfare of the victim and for the police – public relationship, from making a purposeful effort to provide victims with information about progress, especially if the offence is a serious one or if for any reason the effects of the offence seem likely to remain with the victim . . . A number of forces have adopted systematic procedures for keeping victims informed of progress, some as a result of experimenting with pilot schemes within their force area. Chief officers are encouraged to review their present arrangements, with a view to making them as

effective as possible within the constraints of existing resources. (Home Office, 1988: 5)

Circular 20 is reiterated in the *Victim's Charter* (Home Office, 1990b) which draws together a range of policies *vis-à-vis* crime victims as they impinge on the operation of various agencies and stages of the criminal justice system. We consider the Charter in more detail in Chapter 8. Here it is important to mention its relevance for police services.

Following the outlining of government policy, Part III of the Charter on 'Standards for the Criminal Justice Services' includes a checklist by which one might evaluate the treatment victims receive. Regarding the police, this includes: whether or not victims feel sympathetically treated; whether and how follow-up visits are arranged; whether victims are given an informative leaflet; how victim details are recorded; what information is fed back to victims on the case proceedings; whether or not the victim is given a contact name at the police station; and whether police decisions on the case are fed back and explained to the victim.

These recommendations have received additional impetus from central government. Following government concern to improve the effectiveness and efficiency of the police and to more rigorously monitor and evaluate police performance (Home Office, 1983; Horton, 1989; Jones and Silverman, 1984; Sinclair and Miller, 1984), a number of central government bodies have recommended the expansion of police performance indicators, possibly to include victims' perceptions of police response (Audit Commission, 1990; Bunt and Mawby, 1993). It would thus become a responsibility of the police to monitor victims' reactions, perhaps through interviewing samples of complainants about the service they received from the police.

Whilst some forces have moved towards monitoring on this level, for most this is at best a future possibility, and current practices are to be evaluated in the context of Circular 20 (Home Office, 1988) and the *Victim's Charter* (Home Office, 1990b). There has, in fact, been no relevant research in this area since the 1988 BCS, although on an impressionistic level there seems little evidence of any major shift in police behaviour, and in a selective survey one year after the publication of the Charter, Victim Support (1991: 10) 'found its implementation decidedly patchy' with the *Victims of Crime* leaflet given out to victims in some areas but not others and with advance notice on court hearings only sometimes given. In the light of the Dutch experience, such a depressing finding is scarcely surprising.

But if government circulars fail to dramatically alter police response to victims, how else might change be introduced? One alternative is to place the emphasis on police *training*, a strategy deployed in numerous countries including Sweden (Falkner, 1989) and France (Piffaut, 1989) and recommended in both the Council of Europe and United Nations documents (Joutsen, 1987: 319, 325). In this respect, research in the USA and the Netherlands provides some insight into the effects of focused training.

Rosenbaum's (1987) research on the Detroit police is based on a model derived from the President's Task Force on Victims of Crime (1982) and the recommendations of NOVA. Two groups of police recruits were tested in the research – one group that had received a special three-day training programme on aid for victims, and a control group that instead attended a training programme on record-keeping practices. Immediately after the training had been completed officers from the two groups completed questionnaires measuring victim-mindedness. Reassuringly, the experimental group appeared more sympathetic to the needs of victims and saw their role more in terms of providing a service to victims than did the control group. However, when matched samples of victims were interviewed concerning the impact of victimization, levels of readjustment and attitudes towards the criminal justice system, the results were disappointing. Victims' psychological and behavioural reactions to victimization did not appear to vary according to whether or not 'their' police had received the special training programme. Moreover:

> The police intervention had absolutely no effect on victims' attitudes towards the police or the courts. Neither victims' confidence in police effectiveness nor their satisfaction with police services was changed as a result of their interaction with a trained police officer. (Rosenbaum, 1987: 513)

Perhaps the final twist is provided in the results of the follow-up survey, where the police were interviewed four months later. By this time, *both* groups of officers had become less sensitive to victims' emotional needs, with deterioration most marked amongst the experimental group.

Slightly more positive findings are reported from Zaarstrad municipal police in the Netherlands (Winkel, 1989, 1991). Here again, police were subjected to an intensive training programme but in this case all police participated in the programme and a comparison was drawn between a control group of crime victims and an experimental group where victims were recontacted by the police some weeks later and offered emotional, informational and tangible support. An overwhelming majority of the latter felt that this service had been useful, and Winkel (1989) reports that it had a beneficial effect on victims' perceptions of their current situation and their attitudes towards the police. Moreover he suggests that more vulnerable victims derived the most benefit from the initiative and recommends the expansion of the service to target victims with 'prior negative life events'.

It does seem as though victims may benefit from a shift in police priorities and a greater emphasis upon the service aspects rather than the crime-fighting role of the police. However, it is also clear that the police as an *organization* is resistant to change and that police subculture, with its impact on individual police styles, may negate the effects of victim-focused training initiatives. What is also evident is a feeling within the police that the emergence of victim support 'lets them off the hook' and that the police needs only to become more victim-oriented in terms of its referral practices. This is well illustrated in an address by Sir Kenneth Newman, then Commissioner of the London Metropolitan Police, to NAVSS:

> As the demands on the Police Service have grown, it has become increasingly difficult for the Service to meet the needs of all victims of crime. It is vitally important, therefore, to harness the support of the community in responding to the needs of victims . . .
>
> There are enormous pressures on the young men and women who police large cities and their reluctance to spend much time with the victims of crime often results from their heavy workloads, not from any lack of sympathy or understanding. (Newman, 1983, 23–4)

What then of the role of these other agencies?

Alternative services for crime victims

Crime victims may ask for, and receive, help from a variety of sources. Many state-based, private sector, or voluntary agencies providing help for a range of clients, for example, include within this clientele those who suffer physical injury, financial loss or psychological problems. Yet much of the research in victimology has, explicitly or by default, excluded any consideration of such agencies. Doerner *et al.* (1976) for example, in an early evaluation of needs and services in Milwaukee, consciously excluded agencies that did not provide *specific* programmes for crime victims.

More recently, the 1988 BCS included open-ended questions covering the help victims had received from different sources. Only a minority of victims who reported their crimes to the police, and even less whose crimes went unreported, said they had received any such assistance. For crimes reported to the police, in only 27 per cent of crimes against the person and 13 per cent of household crimes was any help given. Excluding the police themselves and

Victim Support, housing departments and medical services were cited most frequently, with small minorities mentioning neighbourhood watch schemes, employers and private solicitors.

The British context, within which public housing exists for a considerable minority of the population and health services are largely free, is somewhat different to that elsewhere. In the US for example, public housing accounts for a much lower percentage of citizens, and hence victims, and private medicine is expensive. Additionally the help that such agencies can give may be limited. For example, in Britain housing departments may be unwilling or unable to respond quickly to requests to be rehoused. Whilst responses to the BCS suggest that victims rated positively the help they received from medical services, more detailed studies, for example in the context of rape, point to the failings of such agencies to address more than the physical needs of victims. Holmstrom and Burgess (1978) suggested that the response of health professionals was even worse than that of the police, and similar points have been made in the context of domestic violence (Klein, 1982; Martin, 1978).

Since then, particularly in North America, the women's movement has had a significant impact on the nature of services provided for female victims by health agencies as well as the police. Agencies like Rape Crisis and refuges for the victims of domestic violence represent the efforts of (initially) feminist organizations to influence the ways in which the public and public sector agencies respond to women victims and provide their own services for abused women.

Refuges and centres for raped or battered women are becoming increasingly common throughout Western societies (Hanmer *et al.*, 1989; Hyland, 1989; Joutsen, 1987; Lägerback, 1989; Peters and Meyvis, 1989; Soetenhorst, 1985). They are perhaps best featured in North America, and in England and Wales. In the USA, the early 1970s saw the spread of shelters, largely influenced by two women's groups, the National Organization for Women (NOW) and the Women's Political Causes (WPC). But the need to secure government funding, and the availability of such funding at the time through the President's Commission's LEAA initiative, led to a dilution of feminist principles. Refuges thus became closely linked with other agencies, such as the police and medical facilities, with management committees representing this broader set of influences (Adleman, 1976; Arbarbanel, 1976; Buzawa and Buzawa, 1990; Gornick *et al.*, 1985; Hafer, 1976; Hirschel, 1978; Martin, 1978; Morley and Mullender, 1991; O'Sullivan, 1978; Roberts and Roberts, 1990). A similar shift can be seen in Canada (Amir and Amir, 1979).

In England and Wales, the first refuge for battered women was opened in Chiswick in the early 1970s. Although influenced by the women's movement, its founder, Erin Pizzey, later distanced herself from the feminist lobby. By the late 1970s there were about 150 refuges in the country (Binney *et al.*, 1985), and while most were attached to the National Federation of Women's Aids Group some, like Chiswick, were fiercely independent. Nevertheless the majority adhered to a narrow feminist ideology, were relatively independent of state funding, and run by women for women, in the mould of the Kent Women's Centre described by Pahl (1978). Similarly, rape crisis centres, imported to Britain from the US, developed according to feminist principles, and whilst there are again some variations (Blair, 1985) most are characterized by a feminist underpinning, minimal outside funding, and poor relations with state agencies such as the police. The result is that there is a marked contrast between provisions for abused women in the UK and North America, with the former more specialist and the latter more closely integrated with both state agencies and the wider victims' movement (Mawby and Gill, 1987). In terms of goals there are perhaps fewer contrasts. Most shelters and refuges see their role as including political lobbying and to provide an educational service (Pahl, 1978). Despite the emphasis on *residential* provision, refuges accommodate only a small minority of the women who contact them, providing legal advice, counselling and more general advice for the majority (Loseke and Berk, 1982). They are, however, even in North America, usually distinct from more general services for crime victims, and indeed, along with services for child victims and the elderly, provide the clearest example of services targeted exclusively at specific victim groups (Roberts, 1990). The rest of this chapter focuses on these other, more generic services.

Victim support services: an overview

There are considerable variations in emphasis between the victim support services, both within and between nations, and a number of authors have attempted to categorize alternative models (Dussich, 1981; Mawby and Gill, 1987; Viney, 1991). Essentially, we might identify four broad areas within which to describe the key features of such services. First is the organizational structure of the agency; second is its location *vis-à-vis* other organizations, that is its relationships with other agencies; third is the nature of the service provided; fourth is the nature of the victim population targeted, or prioritized, by the organization.

Taking the organizational structure of the agency, we might first distinguish between public services and voluntary or private services. In the United States and Canada some services *are* provided by public service agencies such as the police or prosecutor's office (Dussich, 1981; Roberts, 1990). Elsewhere the recently formed Oficina Ayunda Victimas in Valencia, Spain, is a local government-run service (Vidosa, 1989), whilst in Belgium it appears that where services exist they are part of state-run social work agencies (Peters and Meyvis, 1989). In Germany, whilst the Weisser Ring, the largest such agency, is a voluntary organization (Doering-Striening, 1989; Maguire and Shapland, 1990), local government services are provided by the state in Hanau (Schädler, 1989a). Services in France were also initiated by the government, in this case central government, but although they still receive state support they are now a separate entity (Joutsen, 1987; Piffaut, 1989).

Indeed, it seems that most victim support services are provided by non-state agencies, and although the profit-making private sector is sometimes involved, at least at the specialist end of the market,[2] most services are based in the voluntary, or non-profit-making private sector.[3] This itself raises a number of questions about the running and financing of such services (Gill and Mawby, 1990; Mawby and Gill, 1987). Generally speaking, services are heavily dependent upon government funding. In the Netherlands, for example, services receive financial support from three central government departments: the Ministries of Justice, Home Affairs and Welfare (Van Dijk, 1989b; Penders, 1989). In other countries, specific taxes or fines may go directly to fund victim services. This has been common practice in the US, while in German the Weisser Ring receives funding from court fines (Doering-Striening, 1989). Nevertheless, government financial support is rarely on a scale that allows for a service based on professional paid staff, and in almost all countries where support services are provided there is a heavy dependence on volunteers. In Germany, for example, the voluntary organization the Weisser Ring numbers over 1,000 volunteers although most of these provide financial support rather than counselling services, while the local-government-based Hanau Victim Assistance Centre is also dependent upon volunteer commitment (Schädler, 1989a). In Canada, McClenahan (1987) reports that in Vancouver, services funded by the Solicitor-General were based on the assumption that 140 volunteers could be recruited. Thus, while the voluntary basis of victim support in the UK is often identified as one of the central features of the service (Mawby and Gill, 1987; Viney, 1991), it is clear that *internationally* victim support services have emerged as voluntary agencies with a heavy reliance on volunteers.

The implications of this are wide. For example, in most cases funding is on a short-term basis and may be withdrawn with a change of political climate, or it may be provided for a limited period on the expectation that the agency will become self-financing in the long term. Voluntary bodies may therefore spend considerable amounts of time fund-raising rather than providing services! Equally important, the dependence on volunteers means that services may be competing with rival agencies to recruit from a far from bottomless pit, and lack of availability of volunteers may restrict the provision of services in some areas (Gill and Mawby, 1990). Partly because of the dangers of fragmentation, many countries have created national co-ordinating bodies that provide national standards, advice, examples of best practice, direct routes to central government, and links with similar agencies abroad such as through the European Forum. In France, for example, the National Institute for Assistance for Victims (INAVEM) was created in 1986 as a co-ordinating body for the (at that time) 60 local associations (Piffaut, 1989); in the Netherlands the equivalent body is the National Organization for Victim Support (NOVS) (Van Dijk, 1989b).

The United States does not have an equivalent national organization. The National Organization for Victim Assistance (NOVA), as a national umbrella organization, provides a similar role for a much wider range of victim services, including specialist ones concerned with rape and domestic violence, services provided specifically for victims at later stages in the criminal justice process, and services provided by state agencies. Ironically perhaps, whereas domestic violence and rape services have their own national bodies, there is no equivalent in the US of Victim Support in England.

One advantage of NOVA is that it makes for a better relationship between different types of victim service agency, and this is further facilitated by the less militant style adopted by refuges and rape crisis centres in North America. In Ireland too, where Rape Crisis is not strongly feminist, good relations appear to exist with Victim Support (Hyland, 1989).

Perhaps the most notable aspect of the relationship between victim support services and external agencies, is their link with the police. In North America, where some services are actually run as parts of the police departments, in many others victim support is a distinct agency physically located within the police station (Dussich, 1976; Waller, 1982). The key advantage of this is that co-ordination of services, and particularly co-operation between police and victim service, is enhanced, although at the other extreme some victims may be reluctant to contact an agency which appears to be part of the police organization. Elsewhere, some victim services, like the

Hanau Victim Assistance Centre, operate as a 'shop-front', depending on publicity for their clientele (Schädler, 1989a). Some other countries report difficulties with ensuring that the police refer appropriately to victim support; in Scotland, for example, the police have traditionally been reluctant to contact victim support without the victims' explicit permission (Moody, 1989). In Germany similarly, laws on privacy restrict the extent to which the police can pass on victim details to helping agencies, and even the Weisser Ring, with strong police links, experiences difficulties gaining significant numbers of referrals.[4] Ireland has a relatively low police referral rate, but compensates for this with a high level of self-referrals (Hyland, 1989). In England and Wales, Victim Support has built up good relations with individual police forces such that most of the initial police suspicion has been eliminated and referral levels are high, allegedly producing the best of both worlds (Mawby and Gill, 1987).

What then of the types of service provided by Victim Support? Whilst in Britain the emphasis has traditionally been placed on a combination of sympathetic support and advice, in North America each of these aspects has been given its distinctive focus. Thus 'support' has tended to include a greater emphasis on crisis counselling, with professional therapists seen as a common resource (Dobash and Dobash, 1992; Young and Stein, 1983) and 'advice' has often incorporated an integrated approach to the needs victims face at all stages of the criminal justice process, from incident to court appearance through to parole considerations.

The types of service offered are broadly similar in the Netherlands, but in much of Western Europe emphasis has been on the provision of legal advice and financial assistance rather than *emotional* support (Maguire and Shapland, 1990). This is certainly the case in France (Piffaut, 1989) and in Spain the main service offered concerns advice on legal rights (Vidosa, 1989). In Germany, the Weisser Ring provides emergency financial support for victims in need, including legal costs (Doering-Striening, 1989), and the Hanau Centre, which does provide counselling services, apparently refers on about half its clientele to other, more specialist agencies (Schädler, 1989a).

Finally, we can compare the nature of the victim population targeted or prioritized. Although there are some variations according to the social characteristics of the victims – in the US many programmes are geared exclusively to the elderly for example – the main contrast here is by offence type. For, with victim services emerging independently in many countries, particular national 'problems', plus perceptions of the precise impact of different offences, mean that agency interpretations of need vary markedly. For example, in Britain the emphasis was originally very much on the victims of burglaries, whereas in North America sexual and violent offences were prioritized. In Germany the Hanau scheme deals disproportionately with victims of violent crime (Schädler 1987, 1989a), as does the Weisser Ring, and in Ireland Hyland (1989) reports that interpersonal crimes are commonly dealt with, the difference between Ireland and England being largely due to the high rate of self-referrals in the former. In the Netherlands early schemes prioritized violent crime but later shifts followed the British model of emphasizing burglaries. Dutch schemes also concentrated considerable resources on the victims of road traffic accidents, a group not covered at present in Britain but the subject of current debate (Groenhuijsen, 1990). Some French schemes also concentrated on traffic accident victims.

Traffic accidents are not, of course, necessarily crimes, and it is also pertinent to note the extent to which victim support has been willing to provide help to non-crime victims, a debate with its roots in the formative years of victimology itself. In England, many of the rural, less pressurized schemes have tended to cover non-crime victims and while this has been a contentious issue nationally, in times of national disaster such as Hillsborough in 1988 when many football fans were killed or injured when barriers gave way, Victim Support has been to the forefront in providing support services. Similarly in France INAVEM has made contingency plans to deal with any disasters (Piffaut, 1989) and in the US Crisis Response teams have been organized by NOVA 'to assist communities beset by such disasters as plane crashes, bus or car accidents, shootings, electrocutions, and forest fires' (Davis and Henley, 1990: 164).

Even when we focus on victim support schemes then, there are marked variations between different countries. To provide further illustration of such differences, and a more detailed picture, the following sections concentrate on countries within which victim schemes are perhaps most fully developed: the UK, the USA and the Netherlands.

Victim Support in the UK

As we noted in Chapter 4, whilst criminal injuries compensation developed from the work of Margery Fry in the 1950s and 1960s, victim support services were of later origin. They arose out of the Bristol Victims–Offenders Group, formed in 1970 in co-operation with the local branch and national body NACRO, the National Victims' Association, again based in Bristol and established in 1973

(Rock, 1990). A service based on self-referral was established in the area, and although only poorly publicized and irregularly used this provided the basis for later developments.

The first victim support scheme was launched in Bristol in 1973–4 as an independent agency relying on the co-operation of statutory agencies such as the police, probation service and magistracy. Despite the fact that more victims were referred to the scheme than had been anticipated, the scheme faltered, and was temporarily suspended while the organizers sought wider support and funding. It reopened in 1975 and, following national television coverage and national administrative support from NACRO, new schemes were initiated in other areas.

By 1977 national guidelines for the establishment of schemes had been prepared and a regional structure created, and in 1979 the National Association of Victim Support Schemes (NAVSS) was formed. By 1980 there were 256 schemes and an annual rate of referral of 125,000 (Mawby and Gill, 1987: 87–8). Not surprisingly, this phenomenal rate of increase could not be maintained, and the growth in the number of schemes decelerated. Nevertheless, by 1991 there were over 350 schemes, including one on Jersey, seven in Northern Ireland, and twenty-four in Wales (Victim Support, 1991). Scotland has its own, separate organization with about 57 schemes, the majority in the Strathclyde area around Glasgow (Victim Support Scotland, 1991). During the year 1990–91 some 600,000 cases were referred to Victim Support and in addition approximately 21,000 to Victim Support Scotland.

The National Association of Victim Support Schemes operates as a co-ordinating and validating body. Over the 1970s and 1980s it developed a close relationship with the Home Office, whilst maintaining its independence, and it is separately funded by the Home Office. It employs some 20–30 staff, based in its London office. At the other extreme lie individual schemes, which are linked to the centre via a county structure and a number of national committees, including the National Council, the Executive Committee and the Funding Panel. There is a Code of Practice, which includes requirements covering service provision, training and management structure, and individual schemes that do not conform to the code will be excluded from the organization, and, effectively, from receiving police support. The national organization is also responsible for allocating central government funding to individual schemes, which gives it an additional level of control. At local level, each scheme has a management committee, at least one co-ordinator, and a number of visitors who make direct contact with crime victims.

Throughout the UK, victim support schemes are voluntary organizations and registered charities, the latter allowing them to claim tax relief. Financial support was originally gained from a number of private sponsors and from the government; nationally from the Home Office and the (then) Department of Health and Social Security (DHSS), locally from local authorities, partly using various national–local partnership grants (Russell, 1990). The most significant development came in 1986 when the government announced a £9 million grant to Victim Support over the period 1987–90.[5] In the year ending March 1991, local schemes received over £4.4 million in Home Office grants with an additional £570,000 going to the national organization (Victim Support, 1991). A year later, Home Office grants totalled nearly £5.4 million (Victim Support, 1992). By autumn 1991 the Home Secretary had projected a £6.5 million grant for 1992–3, although some of this money is for court-based services (see Chapter 6).[6]

These developments herald both a significant shift in government commitment to Victim Support and a major change in the nature of the organization (Rock, 1990; Russell, 1990). Nevertheless, the bulk of the work of individual schemes depends on volunteers. In 1991–2 the Home Office grant to local schemes was used to fund 427 posts in 309 separate schemes. However, while this meant that a *majority* of schemes had paid co-ordinators, a large minority did not, and there were considerable regional variations. For example, in 1991, Devon, with 10 schemes, had *one* paid co-ordinator, whilst the busier Merseyside area, with 23 schemes had 23 paid co-ordinators and 17 deputy co-ordinators, some of whom job-share. Moreover, whilst there were, overall, 556 paid staff by 1992, local schemes together registered 12,566 volunteers, of whom 8,266 visited victims, 342 were volunteer office staff and 3,958 members of management committees (Victim Support, 1992: 7–8).

What of the *location* of Victim Support *vis-à-vis* other agencies? Two of the key features of Victim Support, evident from the first Bristol scheme, were the fusion of independence and co-operation. While some schemes, especially in the early years, were located in probation offices, schemes were independent of both police and probation. At the same time, they built up good relationships with these and other agencies within the criminal justice system, and the close co-operation between the police and Victim Support has been a notable feature, contributing much to the successful establishment of the organization (Mawby and Gill, 1987; Rock, 1990). The Code of Practice specifies that the police and either probation or social services should be represented on schemes' management committees. The House of Commons Home Affairs Committee (1984: vii, x) noted that 'the organization with which a victim support scheme maintains the closest relationship is the police', but was also 'aware that a close working relationship often exists between victim support scheme co-ordinators and the probation service'. In contrast, the links between Victim Support and the courts have been more distant (Shapland and Cohen, 1987).

The importance of the police to Victim Support is centred on the role of the police as referrers of clients. Unlike many other European countries, almost all victims assisted by Victim Support are referred to schemes by the police. Originally the police were reluctant to relinquish control of referrals, and passed on to schemes victims whom officers felt to be in need of help, a practice that resulted in a disproportionate number of elderly, and clearly fragile, victims being seen by Victim Support (Maguire and Corbett, 1987; Mawby and Gill, 1987). In Scotland there is still a reluctance to refer victims without their explicit consent (Moody, 1989). However, in the rest of the UK it is now common practice for scheme co-ordinators to liaise directly with the police and record all known victims of predetermined crime-types as referrals, a system known as the 'direct referral system'. Schemes will then decide for themselves which victims will be contacted or, more commonly, what sort of contact will be made. For example, in 1991–2, 28 per cent of victims were visited at home; 10 per cent were visited but no face-to-face contact was made so a letter was left; 8 per cent were contacted by telephone; 50 per cent were initially contacted by letter; and 4 per cent were not contacted at all (Victim Support, 1992: 6). Whilst clearly preferable to the original practice, this does raise some difficulties. First, given that referrals have increased at a faster rate than volunteers (Russell, 1990), schemes are increasingly having to make decisions about who gets visited, or what means of contact is preferable. Secondly, whilst the police no longer act as gatekeepers, co-ordinators in the schemes are themselves increasingly deciding, on the basis of very little information, which victims are 'in need' of personal contact within a day or two of the offence being reported (Maguire and Wilkinson, 1992). Despite these problems, however, it is arguable that the British system has achieved a successful balance and remains a distinctly separate organization while receiving full co-operation, by way of referrals, from the police.

In contrast, relationships with other agencies working with victims, largely from the voluntary sector, are patchy, partly because agencies may be competing for the same clients (Russell, 1990), and correspondingly for what limited funding is available, partly because of marked variations in the philosophies of the different organizations. Thus whilst victim support has engaged in discussions with a range of other agencies, and drawn representatives of such agencies into its formal structure through annual conferences, specialist working parties, and so on, relationships with Rape Crisis and the Refuge Movement especially are tenuous and most fragile where Victim Support has moved in to accept victims of those crimes referred from the police (see below). On an organizational level, though, there is no equivalent agency to NOVA in the US that provides an umbrella for the various agencies and services in the victims' movements.

In relation to the nature of the services provided, Victim Support in Britain is also distinct from its North American equivalent in emphasizing the service nature of its work, rather than educational or political goals (Mawby and Gill, 1987). This does not mean that Victim Support is apolitical. On the contrary, as Rock (1990) points out, it has quietly and uncontroversially built itself an impressive power base within the political establishment. It is consulted by the Home Office over impending changes to the law, and has on various occasions campaigned publicly or instigated working parties to push for changes that would improve the lot of the crime victim. But any such political role is tightly circumscribed. The national Code of Practice bars members from expressing party political viewpoints when representing Victim Support and from commenting on sentencing policy, other than where it is of direct relevance to victims.

For Victim Support then, the most important focus is on the service provided by volunteers for victims. Co-ordinators receive details of victims from the police, or directly from police files, within a day or so of the crime being reported, and decide how contact is to be made. If a victim is considered in need of a visit, the co-ordinator arranges for a volunteer to pay the victim a visit, which will normally take place within the following 24 hours. Only in exceptional circumstances will a victim be visited when the crime is 'live'. Where contact is made, most victims will be seen only once (Maguire and Corbett, 1987), although in areas with less crime return visits are more normal (Mawby and Gill, 1987), and more serious crimes, where victims are more severely affected, are allocated markedly more time (Victim Support, 1991: 16). Russell (1990: 20–21) also suggests that those in inner city areas, where victimization is only one of a number of problems faced, may be visited more frequently. In most cases, however, the emphasis is on four levels of support: personal support, reassurance and the demonstration that 'someone cares'; immediate practical help where the victim needs to repair windows, fit secure locks or take other crime prevention measures; the provision of information and advice on what resources or services might be available, for example on compensation; and as a link between victim and police to feed back details of case progress to victims. Two examples taken from the 1990–91 annual report of Victim Support provide a good illustration of the range of services offered, and their appropriateness in different contexts:

> John, a 42 year old bachelor, had been burgled. When I arrived, I found him busy fixing new locks to the doors and windows. He was clearly very disturbed by what on the face of it seemed like a relatively minor burglary. However, it turned out that, amongst other possessions, a few pieces of jewellery belonging to his late mother had been stolen. This had triggered sad memories of his parents' deaths within a week of each other some six years previous. He told me that, since the burglary, he had suddenly been aware of his parents' presence in the house.
>
> Although it was in some way comforting, it had also made him surprisingly tearful. He thought he was cracking up. I spend time with John, reassuring him that his reactions to burglary were far from unusual. As I left, he said he felt much better and thanked me for coming.
>
> I had methylated spirit deliberately thrown over me at work and was then set on fire. My right arm was badly burnt.
>
> In hospital I had to have skin grafts and my arm is still in a pressure bandage. One of the Victim Support volunteers came to see me in hospital, and when I came home the volunteer called round with information about Criminal Injuries Compensation. He also sat and listened to me while I talked about how angry and upset I felt. I couldn't go back to work when the doctor eventually signed me off, as the person who did this to me still worked there – (as far as I knew) and the court case still hadn't happened. The Department of Social Security sent me a letter telling me that, if I was voluntarily giving up work, I wouldn't normally be entitled to any benefit, and asked me to fill in forms giving reasons. I didn't know what to do, so I took the letter to Victim Support and they replied on my behalf, giving all the details because I didn't feel able to do that. The DSS accepted the reasons – so that got sorted out. (Victim Support 1991: 2,3)

These two examples, of a burglary and a violent assault, represent the traditional and changing faces of Victim Support. The original scheme, in Bristol, prioritized burglary victims, partly because of the need to restrict services to a manageable proportion, partly to match needs to what help could realistically be offered. It was 'accepted' that victims of certain types of crime, such as vehicle-based offences, were little affected and would not require assistance, whereas at the other extreme sex and violence offences were considered too difficult for volunteers to deal with (Gay *et al.*, 1975; Maguire and Corbett, 1987). As a result, as Victim Support became a national service, burglaries came to dominate its case files. In 1984–5, for example, some 80 per cent of referrals were of victims of burglary (NAVSS, 1986: 20). At the same time, only 8 per cent of victims were victims of violent crime, 11 per cent of other property crime and 1 per cent non-crime victims, the latter being more common in rural, low-crime areas (Mawby and Gill, 1987).

Since then, the most dramatic change has been in the increase in help for victims of more serious crimes, including violence. Partly in recognition of the unmet needs of such victims, partly in an attempt to expand services and extend credibility, and partly in response to Home Office and police willingness to turn to Victim Support for help rather than rely on more militant feminist alternatives, Victim Support has shifted its emphasis to include domestic violence, rape, homicide and so on. Special courses have been provided to train delegated volunteers for this more intensive and demanding work; working parties have been used to set agendas, improve credibility and effect liaison with other agencies; and special projects have focused on needs and service provision. For example, there have been recent reports on the families of murder victims (Brown *et al.*, 1990), victims of racial harassment (Kimber and Cooper, 1991) and problems in high-crime, inner city areas (Sampson and Farrell, 1990). Partly reflecting these shifts, in 1990–91 only 61 per cent of Victim Support's referrals were burglary victims with 16 per cent sex or violence crimes. Moreover, it appears that while 66 per cent of recorded burglaries were referred to Victim Support, schemes also dealt with 62 per cent of homicides, 51 per cent of rapes and 39 per cent of recorded violent crime (Victim Support, 1991: 16).

At the other end of the spectrum, Victim Support has explored the possibility of providing a service for the relatives of those involved in traffic fatalities. Based on the Dutch model, this initiative was prioritized at the 1990 annual conference and despite considerable objections from many local schemes that felt pressurized by current crime referrals, a multi-agency working party has been set up by national council to review future possibilities.

Just as Victim Support in Britain has moved away from a focus on specific types of crime, so it has further emphasized its provision of services for all types of *victim*. Unlike Victims of Violence (Jonker, 1986) with its emphasis on elderly victims, Victim Support has always advertised a universal service. Despite this, in the early years the policies of some police forces and indeed the decisions of some schemes to prioritize services, meant that certain groups, such as the elderly, received a disproportionate amount of attention. Equally, schemes and police sometimes conspired to exclude certain other groups of 'undeserving' victims, such as known offenders, from receiving support. However, with national policies emphasizing the fact that it is *not* just women and the elderly who are badly affected by crime, and with a move to include interpersonal crimes where the victim is not always blameless, Victim Support is increasingly drawing nearer to providing a comprehensive service for all crime victims.

Victim Support in the Netherlands

Although in many fundamental respects the criminal justice system of the Netherlands resembles its continental neighbours, it has – especially in recent years – also been influenced by ideas from Britain and the United States (Mawby, 1990). It is therefore no surprise to see victim support services emerging earlier than elsewhere on mainland Europe and with some features in common with England and Wales (Van Dijk, 1989a; Groenhuijsen, 1990). For example, the Netherlands had a strong women's movement from the 1970s, and with political influence refuges for battered women were set up relatively early on (Soetenhorst, 1985).

Victim Support services also emerged in the 1970s with the first experimental projects created in 1975 in the city of Hoorn and the province of South Limburg. In each case the probation service was heavily involved and schemes included a commitment to mediation (Van Dijk, 1989c). In 1979 Humanitas, a voluntary agency, set out a model for future initiatives, which in many respects paralleled developments in England. Schemes were to focus on the material and emotional problems of crime victims, and be independent organizations run by one paid co-ordinator and dependent upon volunteers. Police stations were seen as the ideal location for schemes.

The Ministry of Justice agreed to finance three pilot projects in Rotterdam, Groningen and Alkmaar, using this model, but these, and other schemes in Amsterdam, the Hague and Breda evidenced a degree of variation not experienced in Britain (Van Dijk, 1989c). Overall, as we consider victim support in the Netherlands, the picture is one of considerable diversity.

This is confirmed by the stance taken by the national co-ordinating body. The National Platform for Victim Assistance (LOS), now renamed the National Organization of Victim Support, was formed in 1983–4 by the individual schemes with the active encouragement of the Ministry of Justice. In 1985 a national office was established to promote local developments. Even then, however, it was made explicit that LOS would not attempt to impose a uniform structure upon local schemes. The Ministry of

Justice funded four staff posts in the national office, and in 1985 provided a grant for the establishment of local schemes; in 1987–9 some £1.2 million was provided and in 1990 this was increased to £1.2 million per annum, to pay for the staff at the national office and one co-ordinator each for local schemes, with the assumption that local councils would pay the administrative costs of each scheme.

What of the individual schemes? Of the first six schemes, five were based around the use of volunteers, but the Breda scheme relied on professional social workers visiting victims. Two schemes, in Amsterdam and Groningen, were independent of the police and were more critical of police response to victims' needs. In contrast the Rotterdam scheme enjoyed close co-operation with the police, while the Breda scheme was the first in the Netherlands to collect referrals directly from the station, according to the English prototype. The schemes in Alkmaar and the Hague were more akin to many in North America, with co-ordinators employed by the local police (Van Dijk, 1989c).

In 1985 there were 23 schemes in the Netherlands, a figure that had risen to 75 by 1989. In the same period, referrals had increased from 1,800 to 17,000 (Groenhuijsen, 1990). By the end of the 1980s, about a third of schemes were independent, with most of the remainder based in either welfare or police departments. Almost all schemes utilized volunteers, and indeed use of volunteers had been encouraged by the government. Funding is available only for scheme co-ordinators, and only where the scheme is based on volunteer workers. The number of volunteers, correspondingly, increased from 295 in 1987 to 579 in 1989. In comparison, there were then some 60 paid workers in victim support schemes (Groenhuijsen, 1990).

In the context of the relationship between schemes and other agencies, it is interesting to note that volunteer involvement has not been a feature of Dutch welfare schemes (Mawby, 1990). Yet, most welfare schemes are based around local, relatively small voluntary organizations which are heavily subsidized by central government (Brenton, 1982), and victim support appears to fit in with this model for provision. Partly for this reason, partly because many schemes are based in welfare departments, and partly because schemes initially covered a wide range of property *and* interpersonal crimes, relationships with other welfare and voluntary agencies appear to be relatively close.

Relationships with the police seem to be mixed. Some schemes are run completely independent of the police and rely on self-referrals for their clientele, and where the police are involved official policy seems to be that victims will not be referred unless they *explicitly* give their permission (Steinmetz, 1989).

The main advantage of police-based services is, allegedly, the fact that police–victim support co-operation is enhanced. However, in an assessment of the scheme in the Hague, Hauber and Wemmers (1988) cast some doubt on this generalization. From 1982 to 1985 the scheme in the Hague was based within the municipal force, but located centrally. An evaluation of this situation suggested that the distance between police and volunteers was too great and that victims were not being referred, and so in 1986 volunteers were directly assigned to local stations in four areas of the city. On the positive side, this resulted in better contact between police and volunteers, and a more positive outlook by the police regarding the value of the scheme. On the other hand, the researchers found the police still reluctant to refer victims to the scheme, and the police also appeared no more supportive in their attitudes towards victims: 'The data showed no difference between police units with V.A.P. volunteers and those without with respect to the victim-mindedness of police. The police were in mind and action not supportive of the idea of giving information about victim assistance to every victim' (Hauber and Wemmers, 1988: 69).

This to some extent helps explain the striking difference in referral patterns between the Netherlands and Britain. With regard to the nature of the service provided, there is a greater level of accord. Descriptions of services include an emphasis on information and advice and emotional support, a 'listening and caring ear'. Assistance with practical problems, such as the installation of locks or the preparation of insurance claims, is stressed (Van Dijk, 1989c; Groenhuijsen, 1990). There are, however, perhaps two slight shifts of emphasis. On the one hand, rather more emphasis is placed on the limitations in the skills of volunteers and the consequent need to refer victims with serious problems to professional agencies; indeed some 20 per cent of clients *are* referred to welfare agencies. On the other hand, mediation is often seen as a key feature of victim support (Van Dijk, 1989c). In each of these examples, one might speculate that the closer link between schemes and welfare agencies may have contributed to the difference.

Finally, what about the cases dealt with by victim support schemes? Unlike in the UK, early schemes were involved with victims of violent crime and different schemes appeared to cater for markedly different client profiles. In Rotterdam, for example, 70 per cent of referrals in the early years were victims of violence, mostly domestic; the Breda scheme also prioritized more serious crime. In contrast, victim support in Amsterdam and Groningen catered for victims of burglary, robbery and theft. As a result, in the Netherlands the proportion of clients who are the victims of property crime is much lower than in Britain, with only 40 per cent being victims of robbery or burglary (Van Dijk, 1989c).

Another feature of the Dutch situation, as already mentioned, is the inclusion of victims of road traffic accidents. This began in the police-based Hague scheme, but these victims now account for about 11 per cent of all referrals. Groenhuijsen (1990) argues that this extension of victim support was due to a number of factors: it was demanded by victims; the police and road traffic organizations supported it; no other agency was willing to accept any responsibility; and the problem was an extensive one. Most of the problems raised by this group of victims appear to centre around difficulties with settling claims.

The variety of victims served by schemes in the Netherlands is, in fact, encouraged by government policy (Van Dijk, 1989c). Schemes are only eligible for funding from the Ministry of Justice if they offer help to all categories of crime victim. Although rape crisis centres and Women's Refuges may be separately financed by the Ministry of Health, or the Directorate for Women's Affairs, the incentive is for other victim services to provide 'general victim-support'.

Clearly in many respects victim support in the Netherlands has developed in similar ways to the UK. In other ways, however, there are differences, and in some instances there are similarities with provisions in North America.

Victim services in North America

Policies aimed at helping the victims of crime emerged in North America in the 1960s and early 1970s, with a number of progammes geared towards helping specific groups of victims – such as rape victims, battered spouses or abused children – or rectifying faults in the criminal justice system (Davis and Henley, 1990; Dussich, 1981; Roberts, 1990; Young, 1990). Combined with victim-initiated services for parents of murdered children and relatives of those killed in drunken-driving incidents, the range of victim initiatives has been considerable:

> There is no established operational model for these programs. The approaches differ from one another in relation to the target audience, the types of services provided, program organization, the purposes of the program, and the underlying rationale for the services being provided. (Schneider and Schneider, 1981: 365)

Moreover:

> Crisis intervention programs probably vary more in terms of victim clientele and the variety of services afforded to cope with difficulties sustained by victims than any other single program type. (Ziegenhagen and Benyi, 1981: 377)

This variety is to some extent exaggerated by the fact that membership of NOVA incorporates a range of service areas outside the scope of the NAVSS in England and Wales. Nonetheless, it seems that, as in the Netherlands, there is considerably less uniformity than is found in the UK, a point to be borne in mind as we consider the North American situation in more detail.

In Canada, central government initiatives were behind the early impetus in victim services (Rock, 1986). Similarly, in the US it was a government funding programme, the LEAA, that stimulated service development in the period 1970–77, when almost $50 million was provided for schemes that aimed to promote greater public co-operation with the criminal justice system (Schneider and Schneider, 1981). Then, when the LEAA initiative shifted its priorities, and victim support funding began to be phased out, the 1984 Victims of Crime Act (VOCA) and the 1984 Justice Assistance Act provided new central government sources of funding, with a variety of local taxes and court fines being used by individual states or counties (McCormack, 1988; Young, 1990). In his review of victim support and victim witness programmes, Roberts (1990: 87–8) found that 70 per cent of funds came from government sources, with most of this being generated at local level. In Pima County, for example, services were originally developed with the aid of an LEAA grant of some $150,000 in 1975, and when LEAA sponsorship ended in 1978 local government took over financial responsibility (Lowenberg, 1981). For 1985, Roberts (1990: 86) found that almost two-thirds of programmes had an annual budget over $50,000, with 15 per cent receiving at least $250,000. While the extent of funding, and the correspondingly high numbers of paid professional project staff, make such examples stand out from the situation in the UK, there is an equal degree of uncertainty attached to the funding, and NOVA has regularly had to 'fight its corner' when government restrictions have threatened to savage victim services monies.

Yet while the volunteer element is more often stressed in Britain than in the US, many services do depend on volunteer support. Whilst Roberts (1990: 122–7) describes the victim assistance unit within the police department of Rochester, New York, which is staffed by paid workers with only one volunteer in support, and Davis and Henley (1990) also note the key role of professional workers within agencies, elsewhere volunteers appear to play a key role. For example, in Vancouver in Canada, services are based around some 140 volunteers (McClenahan, 1987). On a lesser scale, the crime victim centres of Minneapolis and St Paul, Minnesota, incorporated 11 full- or part-time workers, 30 volunteers and 3 student interns (Roberts, 1990: 129) and in Pima County the original service was based around 8 paid workers and 30 volunteers (Bolin, 1980; Lowenberg, 1981). Indeed, by making eligibility for federal funds dependent upon the use of volunteers within applying agencies, VOCA demonstrates a government commitment to the volunteer principle.

Nevertheless, a variety of organizational forms can be distinguished. Roberts's (1990: 90–91) survey of a range of agencies reveals that whilst almost three-quarters employed no more than five paid staff, only 52 per cent relied on volunteers, and in a third of these there were fewer than five volunteers. It seems likely that while volunteers are relatively common in agencies specializing in domestic violence or rape, when identification with victims' needs provided a spur to action, or in organizations like Parents of Murdered Children and Mothers Against Drink Driving (MADD) that were based on the self-help model, agencies that serve a wider range of crime victims may be more dependent on paid staff and, correspondingly, on wide-scale funding.

Roberts's (1990) survey also reveals that most services were based in government agencies (see also Dussich, 1981). A majority, many of which were court-based services for victims or witnesses, which we cover in more detail in the following chapter, were based in prosecutors' offices or with the state attorney, 7 per cent were in police departments and 4 per cent in probation departments, with only 13 per cent in independent agencies, these tending to be grass-roots organizations more reliant on volunteers and private donations. Whilst many of the programmes that are physically located in public service agencies *are* independent, and have a separate management committee, this nonetheless illustrates a marked difference between North America and most of Europe. In Vancouver, for example, early initiatives by the John Howard Society, a voluntary organization, and the probation service, faltered, and the victim support service that eventually emerged was based within the police department, albeit as a separate organization (McClenahan, 1987). In the US, the Pima County programme was the result of a joint initiative from the police and the Attorney's Office (Bolin, 1980; Lowenberg, 1981), and in Minnesota the programme was also heavily dependent upon police initiatives (Chesney and Schneider, 1981).

As already noted, this may have the advantage of ensuring close co-operation with the police and enhancing a high level of referrals. But as in the Netherlands, this is not necessarily the case, and in Minnesota Chesney and Schneider (1981: 401) report that a *lack* of referrals led the scheme to shift towards personal checking of police files. There is also evidence of schemes having their priorities defined for them by the police. In Minnesota the police insisted that the scheme should be 'on call' at all hours (Chesney and Schneider, 1981: 403) and in Pima County the police appeared to define the victim support service as an agency whose role was to take any clients with whom the police did not want to deal (Bolin, 1980).

Basing a service in a criminal justice or health service agency, with its own predefined priorities, may also of course affect the relationship that the service can develop with victims or other agencies. In general, studies from the US suggest a fair degree of co-operation between different agencies, and the fact that NOVA incorporates such a disparate range of services means that it provides a forum for the interchange of ideas. In some areas agencies may be structured so as to prioritize inter-agency co-operation. In Pima County inter-agency relations are defined as a key part of the service, and individual staff are assigned responsibilities *vis-à-vis* certain named agencies with which the victim support service is expected to interact (Lowenberg, 1981). Chesney and Schneider (1981) also note that relations with welfare agencies are good in the Minnesota scheme, although they point out that where the police see the scheme as most appropriate to refer sexual assault victims to, this inevitably raises conflict with specialist grass-roots organizations in the area.

What of the range of services provided? Unlike in the UK, where victim support was based on the principle of a personal visit one or two days after the crime, and where excess demand has only recently called for a review of these principles, in North America a variety of response options appear to have been followed from the beginning (Mawby and Gill, 1987). Services range from routine letters or phone calls with only a few personal contacts (and those generally requiring the victims to attend the victim support office), to provisions for counsellors to visit the victim immediately the crime is reported (Roberts, 1990: 64). To some extent this latter option was included because of the focus on victims of more serious offences, such as rape or other physical violence, and is used with discretion. Nevertheless, the use of counsellors (volunteers or professionals) 'on call', in rapid-response cars, is a feature of a number of programmes, for example in Vancouver (McClenahan, 1987), Minnesota (Roberts, 1990: 127–30) and Pima County (Bolin, 1980).

Another feature of the North American situation, promulgated by the early emphasis on court-based services, is the fact that many agencies either provide a co-ordinated service from time of offence to sentence and beyond, or operate within a network which provides such comprehensive coverage (Young, 1990). If we focus on the most immediate victim support end of the spectrum, however, the services offered follow a broadly similar pattern to those in the UK and the Netherlands:

> The services provided include such things as transportation from the scene of the crime, counselling to relieve fears and emotional trauma, emergency facilities, referrals to other community agencies that can provide short-term or longer term social welfare services . . . (Schneider and Schneider, 1981: 368)

In Minnesota:

> The types of services delivered were expected to be characterized by crisis intervention-service delivery immediately after the victimization designed to stabilize the victim's emotional state, reduce the trauma of victimization, and initiate contact for later staff follow up . . .
>
> Those involved in the planning process also determined a need for temporary home repairs immediately after a burglary or break-in. Because many victims are unskilled or elderly and unable to make temporary repairs, such as boarding a window or replacing a door lock, program budgets included monies for plywood, locks, and tools. (Chesney and Schneider, 1981: 400–1)

Indeed, the emphasis upon immediate support and crisis counselling, very much a feature of North American initiatives, follows from the early focus on violent crime but, as the above authors note, often produces a mismatch between needs and services. In fact, in reviewing much of the material, Davis and Henley (1990) suggest that the predominance of a mental health lobby within the victims' movement may have meant that more commonly requested basic services, are not always available. Roberts (1990: 47) reported that 54 per cent of his sample provided crisis intervention, but that only 25 per cent provided emergency money and 12 per cent lock repairs.

These issues and concerns are also reflected in the types of incident dealt with by different schemes. Initially, many services focused on interpersonal crimes – violence or sex-related – and even now services for more general crime victims may prioritize more vulnerable groups. Roberts (1990: 76–84) describes a number of services specializing in helping elderly victims, while in Pima County a specialist service for the elderly was provided by separate additional funding (Bolin, 1980). The emphasis upon special groups or offences is indeed a core issue in discussions in the US, where VOCA enshrined the 'first among equals' principle whereby in allocating funding services for victims of sexual offences, domestic violence or child abuse get priority (Young, 1990). But although many services specialize in such cases, even among more general victim services the range of offences covered is fairly broad. For example, Chesney and Schneider (1981: 401) report that in 1977 in the two Minnesota victim crisis centres the most common offences dealt with were burglary (45 per cent) and assaults (21 per cent), while in Pima County Bolin (1980) notes that 30 per cent of incidents were domestic violence. Here also, largely due to 'requests' from the police, victim support covers a whole range of non-crime victims, termed PINAS, or 'persons in need of assistance' – such as the poor, elderly, the suicidal, or families of accident victims. As in the UK, whilst organized response to major disasters is seen as a legitimate role for victim support, routine services for non-crime victims are a matter of some controversy (Young, 1990).

Summary

In this chapter we have focused on the problems faced by victims at the time of the offence, and the types of aid available from police, welfare services and specialist agencies dealing with specific offences or crime victims in general. In some respects, the picture described suggests a degree of uniformity. The experiences of victims appear similar across a range of industrial societies, and the response of agencies such as the police has been universally criticized.

However, there are also notable differences. For example, police reactions to criticism of their handling of domestic violence varies between countries: in some there has been little change, in North America a move towards mandatory arrest, in England and Wales a more service-oriented shift. Equally, the development of victim services through specialist agencies reveals marked differences. To illustrate this we have distinguished services according to the organizational structure of the agency, relationships with other agencies, the nature of the service provided, and the victims targeted. Moreover, while a more detailed review of the situation in Great Britain, the Netherlands and North America reveals both similarities and differences, it is equally clear that developments through much of continental Europe have been more patchy and also more diverse. The fact that the so-called 'victims' movement' is so varied is further illustrated as we move on to consider victims in court- and state-based compensation schemes.

Notes

1. Personal communication from Jean-Claude Salomon, Institut des Hautes Études de la Sécurité Intérieure.

2. An example of specialist services in the private sector is provided in the Netherlands where a specialist within the Ministry of Justice, Carl Steinmetz, left to set up his own private agency.

3. In the US the term 'private sector' is generally used to cover all non-government agencies. In Britain non-profitmaking agencies of this sort are *usually* defined as voluntary agencies, although the definition is by no means unambiguous – see Gill and Mawby (1990).

4. Based on discussions with Gerd Kirchhoff and a visit to the chair of the Monchengladback chapter of the Weisser Ring, November 1992.

5. The original grant was for £9 million over a three-year period: £2 million for 1987–8, £3 million for 1988–9 and £4 million for 1989–90. The money was to be used for co-ordinators' salaries, with priority given to full-time posts and one co-ordinator per scheme.

6. According to the Chancellor of the Exchequer's Autumn Statement, 6 November 1991, Victim Support funding for 1992–3 was to be £7.3 million, this sum to include continuation of the victim/witness in court project described in detail in Chapter 6.

6

Victims, Courts and Compensation

As we noted in Chapter 2, the fact that only a minority of crime is reported to the police combined with low detection rates for reported crime means that only a small proportion of victims face the possibility of a court appearance. Where a suspect has been identified, victims *may* be informed or (less likely) involved in police or prosecutor decisions on whether to proceed with the case. Where they are not required as witnesses they *may* be informed of the date of the trial and/or the outcome and invited to make claims for compensation. Where the offender is not caught the victim is sometimes – usually only for some crimes involving physical injury – able to claim compensation from the state through boards set up independently of the criminal justice system. In all these cases, victim experiences are prolonged; an incident that occurred in perhaps a few minutes becomes the subject of a series of inquiries that may last months, possibly years after the event. While the last chapter was concerned with more immediate help for victims, where the main question was whether victims' immediate *needs* were addressed, here the issue is more one of *justice*. Do victims' experiences of the criminal justice system make them feel that their crimes have been dealt with appropriately and their concerns adequately addressed, or does the system act as a form of secondary victimization that further distresses or disillusions them?

Here we shall concentrate separately on these later processes. First we shall address the way victims are received by the prosecution process in a broad sense. Then we shall focus in more detail on continental Europe, where the Roman law system has traditionally offered victims a more substantial place in the process; the US, where victim witness programmes formed a major part of victim initiatives in the 1970s; and the UK, where such initiatives have been relatively recent. On continental Europe, one major difference concerns the question of compensation by the offender, and we shall proceed by considering reparation initiatives and compensation orders as alternatives to this approach, largely based in Britain and the US. Finally, we shall discuss criminal injuries compensation schemes that are largely dealt with outside the court process and entail compensation paid by the state.

The victim in the prosecution process

Joutsen (1987: 182–96) distinguishes between three different roles that victims might be expected – or allowed – to play in the prosecution process: prosecutor, civil claimant and witness. In almost all criminal justice systems victims are expected, sometimes pressured, to adopt the role of witness. The key question here is how victim witnesses are treated by the system. In some criminal justice systems, especially in continental Europe, the victim may additionally be allowed, or required, to act as prosecutor or civil claimant in the criminal court. The key questions here relate to the extent to which this occurs and the difference it makes to the victim's treatment.

We shall return to this second set of questions when considering in more detail examples from continental Europe. What is, however, evident across a variety of criminal justice systems is the inadequacy of provision for victim witnesses, and indeed witnesses and other court users in general (Raine and Walker, 1990). This is partly because the Anglo-Saxon adversarial judicial system defines victims as *alleged* victims, whose innocence is not established until the guilt of the defendant is decreed:

> Trials involve adversaries and adversity, defeats and victories, winners and losers . . . It is the business of the defence to cast doubt on those allegations and discredit witnesses and their evidence . . . It is to make witnesses appear so inconsistent, forgetful, muddled, spiteful or greedy that their words cannot safely be believed. Victims and defendants, prosecution and defence witnesses alike face accusations of mendacity, impropriety, and malice. Victims who come to court supposing that a trial will be an assertion of their wrongs will discover that it is *their* probity that is at issue as well. In a contested trial, they will almost certainly be exposed to a bruising interrogation in which there is no presumption that they are the injured party. At best, they will be the *alleged* victim. (Rock, 1991a: 267)

Even in the inquisitorial system of justice common to most countries of continental Europe, similar issues have been identified. Moreover victims face the same problems of entering the courts as non-professional outsiders (Christie, 1977) where they lack knowledge of the court as a building and the courtroom as a process.

In general, once a crime has been reported to the police, most victims are unaware of the processes involved in detection and in deciding whether or not to prosecute; they are dependent upon police and prosecutors for information, and, as research indicates, may receive very little. Even where a suspect is identified, victims may not be made aware of the situation unless they are required as witnesses, and indeed defendants may be successfully prosecuted without the victim's knowledge. Then where the victim is required as a witness little effort has traditionally been made to inform him or her of the procedure. Victims may find that cases are dealt with at inconvenient times, or adjourned at the last minute. They may have difficulty arranging to attend court, finding someone to look after children, getting transport to court and so on. Once at the court building they may have difficulty clarifying what is going on; where and when their case is being handled. They may also feel alone and threatened in an environment where no one appears to be interested in their welfare but where they may find themselves in close proximity to the defendant and his or her friends and relatives. All this before the trauma of giving evidence under oath!

In order to improve the ways in which victims are treated in the prosecution process, the United Nations, Council of Europe, and European Victim Support Workers Forum have all made recommendations. Section A6 of the UN Resolution addresses five areas where improvements are needed:

(i)   providing information on the proceedings;
(ii)   allowing the views of victims to be heard;
(iii)   providing victims with assistance throughout the legal process;
(iv)   minimizing inconvenience and maximizing the personal safety of victims;
(v)   avoiding unnecessary delay. (quoted in Joutsen, 1987: 295–6)

Similarly the Council of Europe Declaration recommends that victims should be involved in the decision on whether or not to prosecute the offender, informed of their rights to compensation and of the date and place of the trial, and treated with consideration and respect within the court (Joutsen, 1987: 325–7). The first European Conference of Victim Support Workers (1989: 21) called for prosecutors and judges to improve their treatment of victims by providing adequate information, considering compensation, remaining aware of the stress that many victims are under, and treating victims with courtesy.

This search for international standards implies that different nations share common problems, yet the role that the victim is assigned within the process does vary markedly. One distinction that is commonly made, for example, is between the Roman law tradition that underpins much of European law and the Anglo-Saxon common law tradition, with socialist law a possible third alternative (Cole *et al.*, 1987; Joutsen, 1987). We shall focus first on the situation in continental Europe, including some references to Eastern Europe, before discussing the more familiar systems of the US and Britain.

The prosecution process: continental Europe

Of course, the prerequisite for just treatment of victims within the court is that victims are informed of where and when court proceedings will take place. Contrary to popular assumptions, only a minority of victims are required to give evidence in court, and historically it appears that the remainder have been given very little, if any, information. In England and Wales, despite the recommendations of the *Victim's Charter* (Home Office, 1990b), the situation has been exacerbated with the introduction of the Crown Prosecution Service (CPS) in 1987, with the CPS resisting moves to take responsibilities for providing victims with information, and the police now often lacking the information even where they are willing to keep victims informed (Joutsen and Shapland, 1989). In contrast, on continental Europe where the role of prosecutor is more firmly established and entails wider responsibilities, some countries require prosecutors to provide certain details to victims. In Sweden, Austria and Germany the prosecutor is expected to inform victims of their rights *vis-à-vis* compensation claims and in Germany, Finland, France, Hungary, Romania, Sweden and Turkey the prosecutor is required to tell victims when he or she is *not* intending to prosecute. However Joutsen (1987: 177–8) queries the extent to which these requirements are actually met in practice.

Perhaps the most significant change in this respect is in the Netherlands with the 'pseudo law' introduced in the Vaillant guidelines of 1987, discussed in relation to police duties in the previous chapter (Van Dijk, 1989b; Penders, 1989). Accordingly each local office of the public prosecutor has been allowed to employ a victim policy co-ordinator, whose major responsibility is to keep victims informed. Specifically, the prosecutor's office is required to keep victims informed of progress, provide details of compensation possibilities and any other relevant information, invite victims of more serious crimes to discuss the case with the prosecution, express sympathy where relevant, and generally bear in mind the interests of the victim. Where the prosecutor has failed to make victims aware of their rights to claim compensation, victims may complain to the Ombudsman, and in some cases the state has subsequently been required to pay compensation (Joutsen and Shapland, 1989). Van Dijk (1989b) notes that during 1987 some 15,000 victims responded to letters from the public prosecutor by asking for more information or help, and while compensation was the most common topic raised some 10–15 per cent of victims so invited requested a personal meeting with the prosecutor. On the other hand, Wemmers and Zeilstra (1991) cite research to suggest that very few such meetings actually take place, and generally imply that prosecutors feel the guidelines sometimes place them in an uncomfortable position.

As already noted, victim support services in a number of European countries concentrate their attention on providing victims with information on the court system. The Hanau Victim Assistance Center of Hessen in Germany, is one example of this. Schädler (1988, 1989b) describes a two-year programme introduced by his own Ministry of Justice in the Limburg Regional Court aimed at improving facilities by providing witnesses with social work support, a separate waiting room, child play facilities and a central paying system. Also referring to the Hessen initiative, however, Joutsen and Shapland (1989) see it as exceptional in a country in which victims and witnesses receive little support from the courts, a point equally applicable to most European nations.

Another area to which attention has been drawn is the way victims are treated when they give evidence. This is a difficult issue, since defendants are not guilty until so proven and consequently in interpersonal crimes victims are considered 'alleged victims' when appearing as witnesses, resulting in a form of secondary victimization. In a wider context, the victims' right to privacy has been noted, and here it appears that safeguards in Europe may be more extensive than elsewhere (Joutsen and Shapland, 1989).

As in adversarial legal systems, controversy over the treatment of victims and witnesses has centred on victims of sexual offences. In Denmark, Norway and Sweden, the 1980s saw the introduction of new laws to help victims of sexual assaults by providing them with an advocate or 'support person' (Joutsen, 1987: 175). In Sweden sexual assault victims have been the subject of special attention, and as from 1988 victim assistants can be appointed by the court once the pre-trial investigation has begun, charged with looking after the victim's interests at this stage and throughout the trial (Falkner, 1989; Lägerback, 1989). In the Netherlands, the 1986 Vaillant guidelines, while concerned with the general treatment of victims of sexual offences, also introduced safeguards into the courtroom processes (Van Dijk, 1989b; Penders, 1989).

So far, the emphasis has been on the role of the victim as witness. However, as already noted, in a number of countries the victim may be allowed, or even required, to play a more substantial role, as either prosecutor or civil claimant. How does this affect the situation?

Taking the role of prosecutor first, a number of countries identify circumstances in which the onus of prosecution falls on the victim. There are at least two ways in which this might be specified. First, in many (but by no means all) countries the victim may have the opportunity to bring a private prosecution should the state not wish to prosecute (Tak, 1986). This exists across different legal systems: in England and Wales, Germany – where it is known as *Privatklage* (Sessar, 1987) – and Poland (Bienkowska, 1989) for example. Secondly, in a number of East and West European countries a distinction is made between different offence categories, such that for some allegedly less serious offences prosecution can only take place with the agreement of the victim. These so-called 'complainant offences' are to be found in former Eastern bloc countries such as Hungary and Poland, and throughout the rest of continental Europe with the exception of France, although the precise offence-types which they encapsulate vary (Joutsen, 1987: 151–6).

An alternative prosecution role open to the victim in many European countries is as a joint or subsidiary prosecutor. This possibility exists in former socialist countries such as Poland (Bienkowska, 1989) and Czechoslovakia (Fico, 1989) as well as the Netherlands, Germany, Austria and Sweden (Joutsen, 1987: 190–1). The main advantage here is that the victim does not carry the onus of responsibility for prosecution but is allowed to take a more active part in the process, being enabled to examine the evidence, suggest questions to be put to witnesses, and so on. In Germany, where the system is known as *Nebenklage*, it was extended from minor to more serious crimes in the 1987 Victim Protection Act (Schädler, 1989b; Sessar, 1987). Victims may also be represented by a lawyer. The effects of the new Act remain to be seen, but it appears that the system has in the past been relatively frequently instigated.

Of even more significance within countries where the legal system is based on Roman law is the possibility of the victim acting as a civil claimant in the criminal courts. This system is known as the *partie civile* in France, Belgium, Italy and Spain (d'Hautville and Bertrand, 1989; Piffaut, 1989; Schafer, 1960; Vidosa, 1989) and as the adhesion procedure in Germany, the Netherlands and Czechoslovakia (Groenhuijsen, 1988; Sessar, 1987):

> In both, the main proceedings are the criminal one [*sic*], where the prosecutor deals with the defendant's criminal liability. At the discretion of the court, the complainant is allowed to present his civil claim during the criminal procedure. The court will thereupon decide on both at the same time. However if the consideration of the civil claim will considerably prolong the process, the court can generally divert it to separate civil proceedings. (Joutsen, 1987: 192–3)

The prominence of a *partie-civile*-type option within the criminal justice system varies markedly across Europe. In Poland the evidence that the victim can offer as a civil claimant is tightly prescribed (Bienkowska, 1989); in the Netherlands it was down-graded as French influence lapsed after 1838. It is clearly subsidiary to the main interests of the court, and is constrained by a maximum award level (Groenhuijsen, 1988). At the other extreme it is a long-established tradition in the German courts (Sessar, 1987; Schafer, 1960) and in France, where the victim may request damages for material and financial loss, phsyical injury and mental distress. Compensation is kept separate from the criminal sentence of the court, although the latter may be adjusted in the light of the civil decision (Piffaut, 1989).

Clearly the *partie civile* or adhesion process provides a very different emphasis to that of Anglo-Saxon based legal systems, and since Schafer's (1960) early account a number of American victimologists have looked to Europe as providing a 'better deal' for victims. However, as many European commentators have more recently acknowledged, the system, while promising much in abstract, in practice appears of little benefit to victims. This is partly due to the cost, both monetary and in terms of time and effort, partly because, as with other forms of compensation from the offender, its success depends on the offender being able to pay compensation. In this context, d'Hautville and Bertrand (1989) note that in France since the victim, not the government, is responsible for collecting the award from the offender, in most cases it remains unpaid! The same authors also point out that since less than a third of victims are actually present in court – and many of these are required to attend as witnesses – active and voluntary participation by victims is not great. In Germany, too, Sessar (1987) admits that adhesion is rarely opted for, and Van Dijk (1989b) suggests that in the Netherlands compensation, which could be as a condition of a suspended sentence or via the adhesion process, is less common than in the UK, a finding perhaps influential in leading to the more recent change in Dutch law. The fact that the Netherlands has shifted towards a system of compensation orders, integrated with its traditional adhesion process, indeed suggests that compensation as a criminal sentence may be a more successful option.

It thus seems that while the possibility of the victim appearing as a co-prosecutor or claimant may improve the status of the victim within the court system for some victims, in general the European evidence suggests that victims experience the same difficulties with the system as elsewhere. Moreover, whilst in some cases victims may have more of a say in decision-making – in France victims may state their views on bail applications, for example (Joutsen, 1987: 207) –

there is very little evidence of victim power in the courts. What is also notable is that there is no European equivalent of the North American pressure groups that have led to extensive court services and victim advocacy in the form of victim impact statements.

Victim/witness assistance: the US experience

In contrast, victim/witness programmes in the US became a major feature of victimological developments as early as the 1970s (Bolin, 1980; Dussich, 1981; Lynch, 1976; Mawby and Gill, 1987; Schneider and Schneider, 1981; Young, 1990). Following the 1967 President's Commission on Law Enforcement and the Administration of Justice, the Law Enforcement Assistance Administration (LEAA) Citizen's Initiative was formed in the early 1970s to encourage public involvement in the 'war against crime' and to foster greater consideration for victims, witnesses and jurors by the criminal justice system. In 1974 the National District Attorney's Commission on Victim Witness Assistance was formed and, with LEAA funding, it developed a series of initiatives that provided the baseline from which court-based services emerged. Eight programmes were initially funded to provide:

1 information for victims and witnesses concerning the courts and procedures involved;
2 direct contact with victim-witnesses to provide details on the current status of their cases;
3 on-call systems to alert witnesses that they were required to give evidence on a specific day;
4 convenience services, such as to improve court facilities, private escorts, and so on.

A range of programmes were subsequently modelled on this early initiative. Essentially they aimed to improve the quality of service offered to victims by building up a better-planned and more effective structure. The chief objectives of this were, however, focused on the interests of the system itself. That is, the new service was intended to reduce costs to the criminal justice system by eliminating waste and, more importantly, to improve conviction rates by encouraging victims and witnesses to co-operate and give evidence. Ironically there is no evidence that the new programmes have encouraged witnesses to co-operate more fully with the system. However, the initiative did lay the basis for the provision of markedly improved services for victims and witnesses.

From 1974 to 1976, victim assistance featured as a central part of the LEAA programme, but by the late 1970s the emphasis within the LEAA shifted to other aspects of law enforcement. Partly as a result of the uncertainty of funding, less than half of the original schemes survived (Duroche, 1980a). In 1979 Congress failed to refund the LEAA and federal funding was phased out, leaving many more of these services in a state of crisis. Of those that survived, many did so through a shift to local government funding. For example, the Pima County Victim/Witness Program was initially funded through the LEAA with a $152,941 grant for its first year of operation in 1976, and was so successful in demonstrating its worth that in 1978 Pima County and Tucson City absorbed the total operating cost into their local government budget (Lowenberg, 1981). In Orange County, California, similarly, federal money was provided for two years but in 1980 this was replaced by state funding under the 1979 Act in California whereby an Indemnity Fund was established with revenue from fines (Binder and Bemus, 1990). In Illinois, similar provisions were made available following the 1983 Violent Crimes Victims Assistance Act (McGuire, 1987). According to Roberts (1990: 46), between 1981 and 1985 as many as 28 states made financial provisions for victim services, the majority of these funding the system through court fines and the rest from the general revenue.

By then, however, additional federal support was available. The Reagan administration had made victims of crime a priority, and in 1981 the President proclaimed National Victim Rights Week, the first of what was to become an annual event. An Attorney-General's Task Force on Crime reported in 1981, followed by the President's Task Force on Victims of Crime (1982) and a further Attorney-General's Task Force on Family Violence in 1984. Of these the most influential was the President's Task Force which, with its emphasis on the prevalence of crime and the problems of secondary victimization, heralded a series of federal legislation aimed at restoring the rights of crime victims: the 1982 Omnibus Victim and Witness Protection Act, the 1984 Victims of Crime Act (VOCA) and the re-authorization of VOCA in 1988. VOCA in particular produced an infusion of funding to victim/witness services, both by providing federal monies and by encouraging local government support (Roberts, 1990: Young, 1990).

Roberts's (1990: 86–7) survey in 1985, which included some victim support services as well as victim/witness programmes, revealed that 95 per cent of initiatives were funded at state, county or city level and 10 per cent from federal sources, and overall suggests a degree of financial support well above that for victim services in other countries. The majority are based in prosecution departments or with the state attorney, who are best placed to liaise between court and victim. What then of the nature of victim/witness programmes?

> [T]he major goal of victim/witness assistance programs is to alleviate the stress and trauma for victims and witness to testify in court. For example, prior to the court date, program staff may accompany a child or elderly victim to an empty courtroom to orient the individual to the physical layout and courtroom procedures. Other services may include transport to court, child care while the victim or witness is appearing in court, appraising the victim of the progress of the court case and changes in the trial date and referral to social services agencies. (Roberts, 1990: 40)

In Roberts's (1990: 47–75) study, almost all the agencies involved had some form of victim/witness notification, 71 per cent said they helped explain the court process, 65 per cent provided escort services, 59 per cent transport to court, and 60 per cent liaised with employers to arrange for witnesses to be given time off; many provided specialist services for specific groups such as the elderly or sexually assaulted victims. 'On call' arrangements, whereby witnesses may be spared the delay of hanging around the courtroom waiting to give evidence, are also common (see also Bolin, 1980; Simon, 1987; Wall, 1991).

In this respect, victim/witness services are to be found among the third, fourth and fifth service elements identified by Young (1990), where the remainder cover crisis intervention, supportive counselling and general advocacy, and services – like crime prevention and public education – that are community focused. The third element concerns 'support during case investigation', the fourth support during prosecution, the fifth support after case disposition; that is:

> It involves providing on-going case status information, participation in diversion, plea bargain, and motions decisions; preparation of a victim-impact statement when needed for consideration in sentencing; providing information on criminal justice procedures and how they apply in the particular case before the system; transportation to and from court; child-care while a victim attends trial or participates in the system; the provision of separate waiting rooms for the victim and the defendant; assistance with developing a restriction plan; and providing a witness call-off system. (Young, 1990: 194)

One issue here, which distinguishes the North American approach from most of those considered elsewhere, is the provision of victim impact statements (VIS). Reflecting the rights emphasis of many US initiatives (Mawby and Gill, 1987), these were the result of local initiatives and subsequently endorsed by the President's Task Force on Victims of Crime (1982). Victim/witness programmes, probation departments or other agencies may be involved in helping victims to make their statements. The 1982 VOCA made VIS mandatory in federal cases where a pre-sentence report was filed with the court, and by the mid-1980s as many as 43 states had their own legislation. VIS allow victims of crime to make personal statements on their offences, but the precise form prescribed for victims' statements varies markedly (McLeod, 1986). Some are restricted to reports on the more objective effects of crime, whilst others allow victims to cite their feelings about the crime, the offender or appropriate sentences. Some may allow, or even oblige, victims to make a formal speech to the court; in some states the nature of victims' involvement varies according to offence-type or whether or not the victim has been defined as 'co-operative'. While the effect of VIS on sentencing is the subject of dispute, there are some indications that they may lead to harsher sentencing (McLeod, 1986: 505). At least 39 states also allow victims some active form of participation at the parole stage (McLeod, 1987). Again there are marked variations between areas: sometimes victims are allowed to attend personally; in other cases to submit a written VIS; the right to be involved may vary according to the offence or the length of sentence, or be restricted to 'co-operative' victims; and the extent to which victims are obliged to keep the system informed of any change of address varies. Here there is little evidence of whether or not VIS influence parole decisions, although McLeod's (1987: 14) study suggests that in one state at least parole may be more likely to be refused where a VIS is presented.

The involvement of victim services at this terminal end of the criminal justice process well illustrates the wide range of services offered by programmes. Roberts (1990: 130–40) provides a useful description of the Milwaukee and Xenia services and Duroche (1980b) gives a similar overview of integrated services in Minneapolis City and Hennepin County. The sheer scale of operations has also made an impression upon British visitors like Simon (1987), a victim support volunteer and magistrate, and Wall (1991), the national secretary of the Police Superintendents' Association. Indeed, as Young (1990) notes, there has been a shift towards agencies that provide a comprehensive service for crime victims, with initial support services integrated with court-based programmes.

The converse of this is however worth stressing, for in the US victim/witness services were the forerunner of these more comprehensive programmes: 'The dissemination of court-related information to witnesses involved in the judicial system was the first service offered by the program' (Lowenberg, 1981: 408). As we shall see, this is the opposite of the situation in the UK where 'victims in court' has been a relatively late addition to the victims' agenda.

Services for victims in court: the British experience

While the problems faced by *defendants* as outsiders to the courtroom processes had been appreciated by Carlen (1976) and Bottoms and McClean (1976), it took a brief and provocative article by the Scandinavian criminologist Nels Christie (1977) to widen the debate to include the victim in court. Indeed, despite the emergence of victim support in England during the 1970s, the main area addressed by policies at the time concerned protection for the rape victim in court. Thus since 1976 evidence on the sexual histories of rape victims, other than where the defendant was involved, has been precluded – in theory not always in practice (Temkin, 1993) – and in the 1988 Criminal Justice Act restrictions on the reporting of the names and addresses of rape victims were more forcibly regulated.

Considering victims in general, the Home Affairs Committee (1984) *Compensation and Support for Victims of Crime* devoted six paragraphs to difficulties faced by victims in court. But, although reference was made to the US victim/witness schemes, the committee's recommendations were rather low key. Accepting that Victim Support did not have the resources to provide a court-based service in other than exceptional cases, the committee recommended that consideration should be given to the way court staff handled witnesses, and suggested that the physical design of courts might be improved. Notably though, while the Parliamentary All-Party Penal Affairs Group's (1984) report on victims had concentrated on reparation, the Home Affairs Committee (1984) focused most of its attention on victim support and compensation (Rock, 1990: 375): the experiences of victims in court received no interest from the former and little from the latter.

The Home Affairs Committee (1984) had received a copy of the report to the Home Office of research by Joanna Shapland, subsequently published as *Victims in the Criminal Justice System* (Shapland *et al.*, 1985). Based on a series of interviews with victims of interpersonal crimes, this showed that many victims were poorly informed about the criminal justice process, including the possibility of compensation. Significantly too, the researchers also discovered that victims began with very positive views of the system's response to their problems, but became more and more critical as their cases progressed further. Subsequently, in a study of police and court perceptions of victims' experiences, Shapland and Cohen (1987) found that senior court officials were considerably less victim-minded than were police management. In magistrates' courts, for example, facilities for all court users were poor (see also Raine and Walker, 1990):

> Facilities for all members of the public attending court are sadly lacking: 52 per cent of courts have no refreshment facilities at all; 51 per cent no interviewing rooms; and 79 per cent no child care facilities. (Shapland and Cohen, 1987: 31)

In the case of victims, such inadequacies were compounded: little attempt was made to ensure that victims/witnesses knew where to go; in a third of courts, no attempt was made to inform them when cases were due to start, and most courts had no separate areas for victims to sit in.

By this time, many victim support schemes had begun to focus on the needs of victims required to give evidence in court. Many responded by providing court escort services in special cases, for example for rape victims, and a few, as in Guildford, initiated court-based services. Of these, perhaps the most notable development took place in North Tyneside, where, using the Rochester USA scheme as a model, Northumbria police set up a working party in 1986 to consider the possibility of providing a courts service.[1] Acting in conjunction with Victim Support the police subsequently successfully applied to the Urban Aid programme for funding, and in 1988 a case-status officer was appointed. As a civilian employee of the police authority, this officer is responsible for providing a service for victims in both magistrates' and crown courts. Victims of specified crimes in the area covered are notified of the arrest of a suspect and asked whether or not they would like to be kept informed of the status of the case or provided with any further information or advice. They are, in any case, subsequently sent details of the outcome of any court case that took place. In the period between March 1989 and July 1990, 562 victims were contacted. Of these 83 per cent replied; 66 per cent asked for advice on court procedures; 59 per cent requested information on bail; and 18 per cent wanted to attend court, with many more seeking information on compensation. There is little evidence of any similar initiatives elsewhere, although Plymouth is currently applying to set up a similar scheme in 1993.[2]

The most significant development with regard to victims in court came with the publication of a report from a working party convened by the National Association of Victim Support Schemes. Set up in 1986 and chaired by Lady Ralphs (1988), the committee spelt out the difficulties facing victims before coming to court, the inadequacies of court buildings, and problems faced both in court and while waiting to give evidence. At the initial stages, the working party noted that victims received inadequate information and recommended that the police should take more responsibility for keeping victims informed. When victims were called to court, the inconvenience of long waiting periods, late adjournments and lack of information on the location of the court and its procedures were highlighted. Buildings were criticized for the lack of separate waiting rooms for prosecution and defence witnesses and lack of refreshment facilities. Victims were inadequately informed of whom to contact on arrival at the court and indeed there was a general lack of any staff with a direct responsibility for helping them. While recognizing the constraints that an adversarial system imposed on any attempts to change the conditions in which victims testified, the working party felt that more could be done to make the process less daunting for witnesses and in particular less degrading for victims. It was recommended that where defence council spoke in mitigation in such a way that the evidence or character of the victims was undermined, there should be a right of reply. Finally it is notable that the committee rejected any suggestion that victim impact statements should be introduced.

One recommendation from the committee – that a leaflet (drafted by the working party) explaining the surroundings and procedures of the court should be routinely sent to prosecution witnesses – was accepted and implemented almost immediately. Others have been adopted as examples of good practice, to be recommended to courts or to be taken on board when new courts are designed. Thus, in sections on 'Going to Court' and 'At Court' the *Victim's Charter* spells out some of the difficulties with instigating change and at the same time urges courts to make improvements. For example:

> Organising court business is difficult . . . The victim (or any other prosecution witness) should let the police know if there are days he or she could not manage to attend . . . These can then be avoided, *if possible,* but there may be occasions when the convenience of individual witnesses has to be subordinate to the interests of justice.
>
> The Home Office produces a leaflet called 'Witness in Court' which tells witnesses who may not have been to court before something about the procedure and what to expect. Witnesses should always receive this with the notice which tells them that they may be needed to give evidence and should attend . . .
>
> *Many* magistrates' courts also distribute their own leaflets showing exactly where they are, how to get there, where there is parking and so on. This is an excellent practice, *to be encouraged* . . .
>
> *Many* magistrates' courts are now trying to list cases in separate blocks, rather than requesting everyone to attend from the start of the day's business. (Home Office, 1990b: 13–15; emphasis added)

One area where significant improvements have been made in the last few years is with regard to child victims, especially in cases involving sex offences (Morgan and Zedner, 1991). Unlike in the US, where the Supreme Court has rejected the possibility, common law allows a screen to be placed between defendant and witness to prevent intimidation, and the practice was endorsed in the Court of Appeal in 1989. Under the 1988 Criminal Justice Act, children aged 14 may be allowed to give evidence by live television video link from outside the courtroom and, following the recommendations of the 1989 Pigot Committee (Home Office, 1989a) the 1991 Criminal Justice Act makes recorded interviews admissible as evidence for children involved in sex or violence offences (House of Commons, 1991).

The innovation that has perhaps had the most significant impact for victims in general, however, is the introduction of Victim Support run services to seven crown courts, begun as a pilot project in 1989, and publicly launched in January 1990. This development is of particular interest in a comparative context since, as Rock (1991b) observes, the main impetus for it came from pressure outside the criminal justice system. Indeed, the national office of Victim Support itself in presenting the case for the funding of such pilot schemes was responding to the *ad hoc* development of court-based initiatives emerging within the grass roots of the organization.

These seven pilot (or 'demonstration') projects were established in crown courts in Teeside, Manchester, Liverpool, Preston, Newcastle, Wood Green and Maidstone. In each of these areas a committee was established to manage the schemes. One of the first tasks of the committee was to appoint a co-ordinator whose job it was to recruit, train and manage teams of volunteers who could provide support to (prosecution) witnesses. These projects followed closely the Victim Support model with a central co-ordinator responsible for establishing general guidelines for the training of volunteers, and so on and disseminating information between the schemes. Interestingly enough, whilst some common features emerged with respect to referral systems for these projects, the individual context in which each was located produced variations in volunteer recruitment, types of cases in which support was offered, and how contacts were made with those in need of support. Wood Green, for example, whilst a new court complex (opened in April 1990) comprised only eight crown courts dealing primarily with burglaries, robberies, thefts and assaults (Rock, 1991b). Liverpool, on the other hand, claims to be the largest court complex in Europe with 28 courts on six floors. Structural or spatial variations such as these clearly make different demands on a service designed to access those in need of support, one consequence of which has been a higher reliance by the Liverpool scheme on an advanced referral system through the police and crown prosecution service than that which appears to have developed elsewhere (Raine and Smith, 1991). Other issues, however, have clearly emerged from the development of victim support services in this context.

Rock (1991a) has commented on the state of 'near privacy' in which the courts conduct their public business. The open involvement of an essentially lay/volunteer organization in this realm of criminal justice systems work brings to the surface some of the structural tensions such involvement highlights. From his research based on the Wood Green project Rock (1991a, 1991b) has commented on the symbolic importance of the spatial and social relationships within the court (relationships which are much more clearly delineated and discernible in a large complex such as Liverpool). These relationships represent more than the conveyance of symbols; they stand for, and indeed are the structural articulation of the idea of a neutral state making a judgment on behaviour which has posed a threat to the prevailing social order. Hence, part-way through the life of the Liverpool project a request was made via the judiciary for the project to change its name from the Victim/Witness Support Project to Witness Support, signalling the necessity for Victim Support to also take on the mantle of perceived neutrality when operating within the confines of the crown court setting. The need to take on this mantle is further articulated by the emphasis within volunteer training on not behaving in any way that might be seen as 'coaching' the witness (this is also commented on by Rock, 1991b).

Whilst the court users may have responded to the presence of Victim Support by efforts to ensure the preservation of the perceived neutrality of the system, the other 'consumers' of that system, the witnesses, appear to have been satisfied with the service offered to them. The research conducted by Raine and Smith (1991) to evaluate the seven court schemes recommended the expansion of crown court services in England and Wales. On the basis of this research, the existing projects have been granted permanent status, with the question of the expansion of the service still under discussion at the time of writing.[3]

The development of these projects and their emergent permanent status mark a significant moment in the recognition of how people as witnesses experience the criminal justice system in England and Wales, but may also mark a further significant development for the parent organization – Victim Support. Prior to this initiative the work of Victim Support *volunteers* was not so open to scrutiny from other professionals working within the criminal justice system. Such scrutiny demands the careful attention of all volunteers involved in these schemes (the management committee as well as the volunteers offering support) and the paid worker. Whilst the work of such schemes clearly smooths a path for the respective roles of the other professionals in the crown courts, it is a path of hazards for the witness support volunteers should they lose sight of their own role in that process.

Reparation initiatives and compensation from the offender

The importance of including provisions whereby offenders may compensate their victims for the harm done is recognized in the United Nations Declaration:

> Offenders or third parties responsible for their behaviour should, where appropriate, make fair restitution to victims, their families or dependants. Such restitution should include the return of property or payment for harm or loss suffered, reimbursement of expenses incurred as a result of the victimization, the provision of services and the restoration of rights. (Quoted in Joutsen, 1987: 311)

Although many European countries operate a sentence similar to community service orders in Britain, whereby the offenders are required to 'pay back' the community or finance victim services (Joutsen, 1987: 229), historically Britain and North America have been distinctly different from continental Europe in making compensation by the offender to the victim an element of the *criminal* sanctions imposed by the court. They have also been more active in developing reparation initiatives, using the principle of mediation, to address the harm done by offenders to victims out of court.

The Victim/Offender Reconciliation Program (VORP) in Kitchener, Ontario, started in 1974, is commonly acknowledged as the forerunner of such initiatives (Peachey, 1989). Taking on board Christie's (1977) critique of modern criminal justice systems, and referring back to the dispute settlement process in primitive societies that we discussed in Chapter 3, proponents of reparation sought to provide alternatives or supplements to adjudication in court by providing mediators to help offenders and victims to reconcile their differences in a less formal setting. By the mid-1980s the VORP model had been applied across a wide variety of areas in both Canada and the US (Chupp, 1989; Dittenhoffer and Ericson, 1983; Umbreit, 1989; Wright, 1991).

In the UK, early discussions were provoked by Chinkin and

Griffiths (1980), following visits to a number of North American schemes, and these gathered momentum in the early 1980s, notably through the writings of Wright (1981) and Harding (1982). In 1984 FIRM, the Forum for Initiatives in Reparation and Mediation (later renamed Mediation UK), was founded, and, given government support (Rock, 1990), major changes might have been anticipated. The government funded projects in Cumbria, Leeds, Wolverhampton and Coventry, which were extensively evaluated (Marshall and Merry, 1990).

However, by the late 1980s it had become apparent that the government's priorities were shifting towards support for Victim Support rather than reparation, and the Home Office (1990d) White Paper on the criminal justice system and subsequent Act of Parliament (House of Commons, 1991) offer little future for mediation and reparation. Despite this, Mediation UK continues as a national umbrella organization and a range of schemes continues to exist, albeit funded on a shoestring. Schemes are, in fact, considerably diverse (Marshall and Walpole, 1985). Many take referrals as an alternative to court action, allied to an official caution. The majority of these, such as one of the earliest, in Exeter (Veevers, 1989), deal with juveniles, although the Kettering scheme (Dignan, 1991, 1992) is for adults and a recent scheme in Plymouth covers all age groups. Others, such as the Coventry initiative, gain referrals from the courts, where cases are adjourned to allow time for assessment by the reparation scheme (Ruddick, 1989). Finally, others like the original Kitchener initiative, link reparation to a sentence such as probation, although in Canada at least this option appears to have become restricted (Peachey, 1989).

Reparation initiatives also vary according to a number of other criteria; such as whether or not face-to-face meetings are common, which agencies run or are involved in the scheme, and whether volunteers are used. Given the restraints on reparation where the case is not cleared up, a somewhat different development also allows for victim/offender groups where the victims of some crime meet a quite different group of offenders (Launay and Murray, 1989; Nation and Arnott, 1991).

Victim/burglar groups such as the one in Plymouth illustrate one of the problems with reparation initiatives: that it seems to many that they start with the interests of offenders, and that the interests of victims are only secondary. In practice, projects may guard against this. Nevertheless, it is perhaps not surprising that, in the UK at least, the government has seen Victim Support and compensation orders as more worthy of its support; it is to the latter that we now turn.

Before focusing on the compensation orders in the UK, we can usefully note the North American experience. In Canada, compensation from the offender can be made a requirement of probation but it can also be required by the court in addition to sentence (Schafer, 1960: 60–61). In the US, by contrast, compensation has traditionally been restricted in being a requirement of probation, nationally through the Federal Probation Act, and locally through various – and varying – state laws (Rosen and Harland, 1990; Schafer, 1960). Currently it is linked in most states to probation, and in many more to parole, work release, suspended sentences and other sentencing options (Goldstein, 1982; Hillenbrand, 1990). A further indication of the heterogeneity of conditions in different parts of the country is the fact that while in some states compensation is allowed for all losses and suffering experienced by the victim, in others there are restrictions. The State of Washington, for example, excludes intangible losses such as mental anguish, pain and suffering (Rosen and Harland, 1990: 239).

The Federal Omnibus Victim Witness Protection Act of 1982 brought with it a significant change in the operation of court-controlled compensation. For the first time it allowed courts to make a compensation order as a sentence in its own right, and also required courts to give reasons why compensation was not given. While again there remain differences between different states, this makes US legislation more akin to that of England and Wales. Given that the problems experienced in the operation of compensation from the offender also appear similar (Hillenbrand, 1990; Rosen and Harland, 1990), in this section we shall take the British example as a case study, and assess its development and current status in more detail.

Historically, it has been possible for the courts of England and Wales to order compensation, both as a condition of probation and in its own right (Mawby and Gill, 1987: 37). However, neither option was regularly used, and in 1970 a working party of the Advisory Council of the Penal System, chaired by Lord Justice Widgery, recommended a change of emphasis (Home Office, 1970). Consequently the 1972 Criminal Justice Act introduced compensation orders as orders of the court *in addition* to sentence, leaving courts with discretion as to when to apply the new order.

One major problem, endemic to the whole notion of compensation from the offender, is of course that it is restricted to cases where the offender is known. Another, and related, problem concerns the ability of offenders to pay compensation to their victims. This is in turn a product of both the offender's personal circumstances and the impact that the sentence has on these.

An offender who is imprisoned or fined may, for example, thereby be restricted in his/her ability to pay compensation. A priori, then, any such system results in an inequality where the ability of the victim to receive compensation depends on circumstances outside the victim's control, more related to the *offender's* circumstances.

Additional problems were identified in early evaluations of the new order (Shapland *et al.*, 1985; Softley, 1978; Tarling and Softley, 1976; Vennard, 1976, 1979). Except in certain cases – most notably offences of malicious damage – sentencers seemed reluctant to make orders; and there was no formal way of reminding magistrates and judges of the appropriateness of compensation in a particular case. Compensation orders were rarely given for violent crimes, or where the offender was fined or imprisoned, and were most likely to be given where compensation was raised as an issue during the trial.

Many of these difficulties stemmed from the fact that no clear guidance was given to the courts on 'the place which compensation of the victim should assume among the aims of the penal system' (Wasik, 1978: 602). In response, the 1982 Criminal Justice Act provided for the imposition of a compensation order as a sentence in its own right, and specified that where an order was given alongside a fine, payment of compensation should take precedence. Then the 1988 Criminal Justice Act made it a requirement that any losses suffered by the victim should be brought to the attention of the court, and required courts to justify not giving compensation.

The precise impact of these measures is yet to be seen. However, the most recent evaluation of the 1982 changes by Newburn (1988) gives little cause for optimism. Newburn notes that compensation orders are rarely given as a sole penalty, that magistrates are reluctant to assess the 'cost' of injury and therefore to make orders in assault cases, and that in real terms the amount of compensation awarded has fallen. Moreover, while it is clear that victims, and the public at large (see also Maguire and Shapland, 1990) approve of the concept, a number of practical difficulties militate against the desirable effects that might be reaped by victims. In particular, Newburn (1988) notes the long-drawn-out process when orders are paid by instalments and the additional problems where offenders fail to complete payment. He echoes other critics, and the conclusions of the Hodgson Committee (Home Office, 1984) that compensation should be taken out of central funds and recovered from offenders afterwards, perhaps supplemented by funding from fines or sale of forfeited property.

While many of these criticisms hold good today, there is some evidence from official sources that improvements have been made, perhaps as a result of the 1988 Act. Figures for 1989 (Home Office,

1991a: 20) show an increase in the use of orders, especially for offences of violence. For example, in 1989, 28 per cent of indictable offenders dealt with in the magistrates' courts and 14 per cent dealt with in the crown courts were ordered to pay compensation, the average amount being £139 and £924 respectively. Moreover, the most marked increase since Newburn's (1988) research is in the use of compensation for violence: in 55 per cent of magistrates' court cases and 28 per cent of crown court cases.

Debates over the appropriateness or otherwise of using criminal sanctions to provide compensation for victims are particularly timely, given that the late 1980s saw a number of other European countries moving to adopt the compensation principle as a criminal sentence. In Sweden, compensation linked to probation or a suspended sentence was introduced in 1988 (Falkner, 1989), while in the Netherlands the recommendation of the 1987 Terwee Committee that compensation, as a combined or sole solution, might be deployed instead of the *partie civile* process, has recently been adopted amidst considerable opposition from the legal profession (Van Dijk, 1989b; Groenhuijsen, 1988). Indeed, as the debate in the Netherlands illustrates, compensation orders provide an apt demonstration of the difficulties involved in 'doing right by the victim' and maintaining a just system for defendants.

State compensation

Whereas compensation from the offender is dependent upon the identification of an offender with the ability to pay compensation, state compensation, whereby compensation is paid to the victim by the state, *appears* preferable from the viewpoint of the victim of crime. It also provides one way in which governments can get across their message that they are concerned to help victims, and, since 1960, it has been espoused in a variety of countries.

State compensation was indeed the subject of a select committee of the Council of Europe, resulting in a convention and its subsequent adoption by the Committee of Ministers in 1983 (Joutsen, 1987: 69–70, 270–72) and is also covered in the UN declaration, paragraphs 12–13:

> When compensation is not fully available from the offender or other sources, States should endeavour to provide financial compensation to:
>
> (a) Victims who have sustained significant bodily injury or impairment of physical or mental health as a result of serious crimes;
>
> (b) The family, particularly dependants of persons who have died or become physically or mentally incapacitated as a result of such victimisation.

The establishment, strengthening and expansion of national funds for compensation to victims should be encouraged. (cited in Joutsen, 1987: 296)

That said, however, there are marked variations in the structuring and operation of state compensation in different countries, and indeed different parts of the same country. We shall therefore focus on England and Wales and Scotland, where state compensation in its contemporary form was first conceived, and then briefly note similarities and differences elsewhere.

In England and Wales and in Scotland state compensation was introduced in 1964 through the creation of the Criminal Injuries Compensation Board (CICB) (Mawby and Gill, 1987: 39–43; Miers, 1978; Rock, 1990: 46–90). The impetus for this came from Margery Fry, a Quaker and one-time secretary of the Howard League, who occupied a key position of influence from outside the Home Office. In some respects, she was led by an appreciation that compensation from the offender might be a more positive, meaningful and effective sentence than was punishment. Additionally, her own personal experience of a purse snatch led her to feel that compensation for victims was long overdue.

But it soon became clear to her that depending on offenders for compensation was fraught with difficulties. In one notable court case in 1951, for example, a victim who was blinded in an assault was granted £11,500 in damages to be paid off by the offender at five shillings per week, which meant that the compensation would have taken 400 years to honour! Margery Fry therefore campaigned for a scheme of state compensation, and, realizing the difficulties of funding such a scheme, restricted her proposals to the victims of crimes of violence. As Chapter 4 stated, although she was unsuccessful in her lifetime, her ideas proved the basis for the system that subsequently emerged. The government White Paper *Penal Practice in a Changing Society* mentioned the possible benefits of reparation (Home Office, 1959: 7) and the subsequent Conservative Party manifesto for 1959 promised that 'a scheme for compensating the victims of violent crime for personal injuries will be considered'. After the Conservative victory in the election, a working party was formed in the same year. Its report was published in 1961 (Home Office, 1961) and, following pressures from within the mainstream Conservative Party, a second White Paper was prepared (Home Office, 1964). As a result, the CICB was formed, not by specific legislation but by administrative fiat.

Since its inception it has been run by a board of administrators under the supervision of the Home Office and, in Scotland, the Scottish Office. It has been subject to a number of reviews – for example by the Home Office (1978) Interdepartmental Working Party in 1978; the Home Affairs Committee (1984) general review of victim services; and, most recently, by a specific review by the Home Affairs Committee (1990). The 1988 Criminal Justice Act moved to place the board on a proper legislative basis, although when this will actually happen, and precisely what differences it might make, are presently unclear. The operation of CICB may be briefly described under a number of headings: the core principles and philosophy of the initiative; the target for the service; the help provided; and the administrative arrangements for the operation of the scheme.

In terms of the core philosophy of the CICB, two issues are fundamental to the ways in which the system is perceived. First, awards are made in recognition that harm has been done, but victims have no *right* to compensation. This was clearly stated in the 1961 and 1964 White Papers. For example:

> Compensation will be paid *ex gratia*. The Government do not accept that the State is liable for injuries caused to people by the acts of others. The public does, however, feel a sense of responsibility for and sympathy with the innocent victim, and it is right that this feeling should find practical expression in the provision of compensation on behalf of the community. (Home Office, 1964: 4)

This quote encapsulates the notion of the 'innocent victim'; more widely than this the CICB was founded on the principle that only certain victims deserved to be compensated. In terms of who benefits, then, claimants were excluded where the offence had not been reported to the police, where the offender was currently a member of the victim's household and where the victim's way of life (for example, a criminal record or a drink problem) in other ways marked him/her off as disreputable. Compensation was also to be reduced where the victim was adjudged partly responsible for the crime. Following the Home Office (1978) working party, the exclusion clause relating to violence within the family was modified, and such victims are now eligible for compensation but only where the offence is especially serious and where the relationship is currently one of estrangement.

In 1990–91 almost two-thirds of applicants received a full award, with 28 per cent of claims rejected, 6 per cent abandoned and 1 per cent of claimants receiving a reduced award (Home Office, 1991b: 4, 25). Indeed, in 1990–91 some 27 per cent of disallowed claims were because the incident was not reported without delay, or there was 'non co-operation' in other respects, 23 per cent due to the applicant's conduct and 12 per cent because of the applicant's character or way of life (Home Office, 1991b: 26).

Examples of claims denied or reduced are fully documented in annual reports of the CICB. For example:

> The applicant, aged 26, alleged that when he was out with his girlfriend and sister, two youths approached them and started to annoy the applicant's sister, who was in a wheelchair. The applicant then tried to stop them at which point they assaulted him by punching him about the face and body. He did not report the incident to the police until one month later. The Single Member disallowed the claim.

> The applicant, aged 52, was in her bed when she was awakened by someone entering her room. She challenged the intruder and was subsequently raped. An award of £6,000 was made but it was reduced by 50% because of the applicant's conviction as it was considered inappropriate that a full award of compensation be made from public funds.

> The applicant, a 32 year old word processor operator, was assaulted by her common law husband after a drunken argument. The applicant stated in her application form that she and the offender may live together in the future 'if things work out'. The Single Member disallowed the claim . . . (Home Office, 1991b: 14–16)

A second feature of the 'target population' is the type of crime for which compensation is available. Following Margery Fry's original concern to minimize costs, compensation is restricted to physical or psychological harm as a result of offences of violence. On the one hand, then, an injured victim of a driving offence is ineligible for compensation; on the other, compensation does not cover financial losses such as damage to clothing or spectacles, or theft, say during a violent robbery. In 1990–91 some 11 per cent of rejected applications were offence related (Home Office, 1991b: 26). It may however cover the concern and worries experienced by a particularly vulnerable victim. It must also be noted that legal costs are *not* included, a relevant issue when we consider the administration of the scheme.

Thirdly, we can focus on the extent of compensation. The British system has never made a maximum award – in 1990 the highest award made was £308,000. However, there has always been a minimum, to exclude the victims of 'minor' crime. In 1964 this was set at £50, and it has been raised at somewhat irregular intervals ever since (Home Affairs Committee, 1990: xv). In 1983, for example, it was raised to £400 or £500 in the case of intra-family violence; in 1990, ironically coinciding with European Victim Day, it was raised to £750, and in late 1991 it was raised again to £1,000. Perhaps of most concern, the decision to raise the minimum is an administrative one, taken by the government in consultation with the board, and is not made subject to parliamentary debate.

In 1990–91 some 19 per cent of claims rejected were considered to involve compensation below the scheme's minimum. These included the following examples:

> The applicant, a 21 year old bakery assistant, was standing at a bus stop when a youth approached him and for no apparent reason head-butted him in the face. His injury was a swollen and bleeding nose. The Single Member disallowed the claim.

> The applicant, aged 21, claimed that as she left a club where she was celebrating her birthday she was confronted by two youths. One of the youths approached her and struck her in the face causing her a black eye and a small cut under the eye. The Single Member disallowed the claim. (Home Office, 1991b: 13–14)

The extent of compensation in specific cases was originally based on the assessment of common law damages, and has since been hardened such that the board works with a 'starting point' of appropriate compensation for specific injuries. In 1990, for example, a fractured jaw was rated at £2,500 and the loss of vision in one eye at £13,000. Whilst in general the CICB is seen as comparatively generous, in some respects there is a degree of controversy over appropriate levels of compensation. For example, civil court levels of compensation for injury in Britain have tended to be low in comparison with claims for libel. Moreover, as illustrated in the Meah case of 1985 (Mawby and Gill, 1987: 45–6), CICB notions of appropriate compensation for rape amounted to less than a quarter of the awards subsequently given in the civil courts, which were themselves criticized as appallingly low.

One final point that is of particular practical relevance *vis-à-vis* the amount of compensation received concerns the relationship between compensation and need. In Britain victims of violent crime are eligible for compensation according to the impact of the offence, *not* their financial circumstances. However, because for social security purposes payment by the board is counted as additional income rather than compensation for a loss suffered, those victims who are dependent upon state benefits may actually have their benefits cut by the amount of the award. Consequently a discriminatory principle operates whereby more affluent claimants receive better compensation from the state than do the poor!

The final issue concerns the administrative arrangements by which state compensation is decided. As noted in the previous chapter, no agency has a direct responsibility for informing victims of the possibility of compensation, and although the *Victim's Charter* (Home Office, 1990b) and Circular 20 (Home Office, 1988) emphasize good practice, it is still the case that by no means all eligible victims apply. At the next stage, moreover, victims may lack expert advice on how to present a claim, or challenge a decision, since they are not entitled to free legal advice and compensation excludes legal costs. Yet it is well accepted that claims are more successful where claimants have legal representation (Home Office, 1978; Samuels, 1973), though some Victim Support workers have developed considerable expertise in this area. A wider issue of access concerns the way in which the board is structured to make it more or less 'consumer friendly'. That is, do applicants find the process of making a claim easy or fraught with difficulties?

The CICB is administered centrally, originally from London although it is currently in the process of transferring most of its operations to Glasgow. It has a board of 40 very senior lawyers, supported by office staff numbering 333 in early 1990 (Home Affairs Committee, 1990), since increased by 60 (Home Office, 1991b). Some applications may be screened out by non-legal staff, but most are dealt with by a board member, so-called 'Single Member' decisions. A minority of more difficult cases will be handled by a panel. Where the defendant objects to a decision, s/he may appeal, in which case there may be an oral hearing before a panel of two board members (reduced from three in 1990):

> At the hearing itself, the chairman will usually invite the applicant to give an account of his or her case and the Board's lawyer will then cross-examine him or her and other witnesses who attend. The proceedings are inquisitorial and informal as the requirement of justice permit and the applicant will invariably be informed of the outcome of the application before leaving the Hearing Centre. (Home Office, 1991b: 6)

Unfortunately, this speed of resolution is scarcely matched by the time taken to arrive at decisions in general and the time taken to arrange hearings. Indeed criticism of the CICB as a bureaucratic monster led the Home Affairs Committee (1990) to carry out its 1989 review, which resulted in a highly critical report. Pointing to poor management practices, the report noted that increasing numbers of applications had resulted in a log-jam; in 1988–9 there were 43,385 applications but just 38,830 resolved cases, with 82,520 applications outstanding; a majority (73 per cent) of cases took over a year from the time the application was made to when they were submitted to a Single Member, much less resolved (Home Affairs Committee, 1990: v, 21). Although additional staff helped the CICB to deal with more claims that it received in 1990–91, 75 per cent of cases took over 12 months to resolve, and where an applicant appealed, two-thirds of appellants waited over a year before an oral hearing was arranged (Home Office, 1991b: 4–7).

While interim payments *may* be made, for most it appears that application to the CICB results at best in an award some considerable time after the event, at worst in rejection. In the light of such criticisms, it is worth considering the situation in other countries: is state compensation handled any better elsewhere?

Using the British notion of compensation, New Zealand actually became the first developed capitalist country to establish a state compensation scheme, which began operation in January 1964 (Brett, 1964). Elsewhere, in Australia the first scheme was started in New South Wales in 1967 (Chappell, 1970) and in Canada, Saskatchewan introduced a scheme in the same year (Edelhertz and Geis, 1974). In the USA, similarly, the federal structure led to the patchy emergence of schemes.

The situation in the US has been extensively documented (see for example Edelhertz and Geis, 1974; Elias, 1983a, 1983b; McGillis and Smith, 1983). The first scheme was introduced in California in 1966 as part of the state welfare system; New York followed in 1967 with an independent board, and by the mid-1970s some 19 states had compensation arrangements of some sort (Meade *et al.*, 1976). There were considerable differences between states, in terms of eligibility criteria, the amount of compensation given and the way in which the scheme was organized (Meade *et al.*, 1976; Schmidt, 1980).

One compounding factor here was the lack of national legislation. Although the possibility of state compensation was mooted in Congress as early as 1965, it was not until VOCA in 1984 that any real central direction was given, when the federal government was mandated to provide 35 per cent of the compensation paid out by states to victims of specified violent crime (Joutsen and Shapland, 1989: 23). Then in the 1988 VOCA states were empowered to claim subsidies in additional cases involving domestic violence and drunken driving (Roberts, 1990: 58).

Nevertheless, by the end of the 1980s there remained considerable regional variations, with six states still having no criminal injuries compensation at all (McCormack, 1989). For those that did, eligibility varied between states in terms of whether or not intra-family crime is included: how soon after the offence it must have been reported; what crimes are covered (for example 37 states include victims of drink-driving offences); and whether legal fees can be claimed. Whilst most states operate a minimum and/or maximum award, the level of these vary considerably, and in some cases there is an annual total for the scheme which, once reached, means that no further claims are considered. Administration of schemes also varies in terms of composition of the board, whether or not claimants are allowed or required to be present, and how the scheme is organized within different regions of the state. McCormack (1989) notes that in some states schemes are centralized, whereas in others such as Colorado committees operate locally, in this case in each of the 22 judicial districts.

The importance of this latter variation is well illustrated in McCormack's (1989) assessment of state schemes. Overall, only 6 per cent of victims of violent crime who reported their crimes to the police actually applied for compensation, and only 56 per cent of these (i.e. 3 per cent overall) received it. At the extreme though, in Colorado, 31 per cent made claims and 29 per cent of victims received compensation and the author suggests that localized arrangements are more successful in encouraging claims. Such findings have implications for policies elsewhere. Ironically they also suggest that whilst the proportion of successful claims in the US is somewhat lower than in mainland Britain, there are even greater variations *within* the US.

What then of the situation in continental Europe? As already noted, the Council of Europe Convention on State Compensation was opened for signature in 1983, and has now been ratified by the UK (in 1990) as well as Denmark, Luxembourg, the Netherlands and Sweden; it has also been signed by Germany, France, Greece, Norway and Turkey (Joutsen and Shapland, 1989). State compensation is also the subject of separate legislation in a majority of Western and Northern European nations. Although developed rather later than in the UK and other common law countries, legislation was introduced in the 1970s in Sweden (1971), Finland (1973), Ireland (1974), Norway (1975), Denmark (1976), the Netherlands (1976), Germany (1976) and France (1977) and in the 1980s in Austria (1982), Luxembourg (1984) and Belgium (1985). Joutsen (1987: 248–76) suggests that the schemes on continental Europe are less restrictive than in the common law countries. There are, however, marked variations between countries, with some schemes extremely restricted and others – the French being a good example – fairly broad.

In Sweden (Falkner, 1989; Joutsen, 1987) the State Compensation Act of 1971 was based on earlier legislation that provided compensation for those victimized by offenders escaping from state institutions, and is restricted to violent crime, although losses and damage as well as injury are compensatable; legal changes in 1988 widened the laws to include certain non-violent offences. In Belgium (Peters and Meyvis, 1989) the 1985 law set up a board comprising legal specialists and civil servants, run centrally from the Ministry of Justice. Compensation, which has a ceiling, is for intentional acts of violence only, and it is stressed that compensation is a discretionary award, not a right. In Germany the 1976 Crime Victim Compensation Act provided compensation for victims of violent crime (Doering-Striening, 1989). Using the administrative apparatus previously set up to provide compensation to war casualties, it is restricted to victims who co-operate fully with the criminal justice system. In an assessment of applications from the State of Northrhine-Westfalia in 1980, Kirchhoff (1984) notes that 89 per cent of claims were rejected and that victims who were considered undeserving were rejected out of hand, taking as one example the case of a homosexual robbed and beaten by a casual sexual partner. Moreover, even where compensation is paid, Kirchhoff (1984) suggests that in many cases it is claimed back by insurance companies, with the result that very few victims actually benefit from the scheme.

Equally strong criticisms have been voiced about the operation of state compensation in the Netherlands. Again this is restricted to victims of violent crime (Penders, 1989). The main complaint here is about the administration of the scheme (Van Dijk, 1989b; Groenhuijsen, 1988; Joutsen and Shapland, 1989). Only some 200–300 awards are made each year, and even then the process is so slow that applicants are on average subjected to a two-year wait, leading to major dissatisfaction.

Perhaps the most widely praised scheme is that operating in France (d'Hautville and Bertrand, 1989; Joutsen and Shapland, 1989; Piffaut, 1989). This was introduced in 1977 but restricted to crime involving physical violence and where the victim was suffering from financial hardship. In 1981 it was extended to cover some property offences, and in 1983 to include all cases of physical violence. Victims of terrorism and traffic accidents are dealt with separately under different legislation. In 1986 the maximum award was raised to 400,000FF. The scheme is financed from a special tax levied on home insurance policies. Victims file applications in their local courts, which are the base for local committees which meet regularly and comprise two judges and one victim specialist. This arrangement, which is very much in line with McCormack's (1989) recommendations for the US, appears to work relatively well, and claims are dealt with reasonably quickly. In 1987 some 700 claims were made. Notably, though, the proportion of claims met is about one half, which is not dissimilar to the US.

Despite the considerable variations between nations, it does seem that a number of principles hold in most of the examples given here. For example, in most cases there is some notion that compensation is not a right, but a reward given to 'deserving' victims. Partly as a result, only a small proportion of victims of reported violent crime, and an even smaller proportion of victims of all violent crime, ever receive compensation, and the administration procedures involved frequently produce irate and dissatisfied claimants, whether or not they are successful. Thus, while in principle it was suggested initially that state compensation might be preferable to compensation from offenders, in general victims appear to prefer the latter (Van Dijk, 1985b; Maguire and Shapland, 1990). Following Miers (1978) many commentators have derided state compensation as 'nothing but a concession to the developing victim movement' (Doering-Striening, 1989: 4), a low-cost example of tokenism (Van Dijk, 1985b), and in its present form state compensation is no vote-winner among victims, even if it appears to be among the general population. Most victims are excluded from its terms of reference; many who are eligible are neither informed of its existence nor encouraged to apply; and those who apply are often disenchanted. Ultimately then, there is a danger of state compensation schemes featuring more as agents of secondary victimization than as sources of justice.

Summary

The problems faced by victims when they are required to give evidence in court, or even when they choose to attend the court, are considerable. Moreover, it appears that even in Europe, where the victim has in theory had more rights *vis-à-vis* the prosecution process, a similar picture emerges. As the inadequacies of the system have become more fully appreciated, there have been moves to improve facilities and provides information, help and support for victims attending court. This is reflected in recent initiatives in Britain, where Victim Support has been notable in its efforts to effect change. Improvements are most advanced in the US, where – in complete contrast – the victims' movement was initially more concerned with addressing problems in court and placed less emphasis on support at the time of the offence. The result, as we shall discuss later, is that many US examples are excellent models of good practice that could be emulated elsewhere.

On a slightly different level, there is the matter of compensation. Of course, one approach to this, which also addresses the problems victims face in court, is to look for out-of-court ways of resolving conflict, notably community- or system-based mediation schemes. Such initiatives, common in North America, were developed during the 1980s in the UK and have taken on board many of the alleged strengths of pre-industrial systems of conflict resolution that we discussed in Chapter 3 (see for example Wright, 1991).

More common alternatives in Western industrial societies have been aimed at sentencing offenders to compensate their victims – through compensation orders either as sentences in their own right or attached to other sentences – and compensation for the victim from the state. In focusing on these, we have made particular reference to the situation in the UK, while noting that similar strengths and weaknesses have been reported elsewhere.

We shall return to these current practices in later chapters where we attempt to build on the experiences of a number of different systems. First, however, we devote the next chapter to the emergence of victim services in Eastern Europe, of particular relevance given the political upheavals of recent years.

Notes

1. North Tyneside Case Status/Victims Support Scheme Liaison Project (1990) Evaluation and Progress Report.

2. This bid was subsequently unsuccessful when the government changed the criteria for funding the urban programme and gave priority to capital rather than revenue bids.

3. It was anticipated that at least 30 crown courts would have witness services by mid 1993 (Victim Support, 1992: 11).

7

Developing an Appreciation of the Victim: Looking to 'Eastern Europe'

In March 1991 the first East–West Conference on Victimology was held in Warsaw. This conference, organized with the support of the Polish Academy of Sciences and the Foundation for Assisting Victims of Crime, was small by European standards. Attended by around 40 people, mostly from Eastern Europe and with a smattering of UK delegates, it represented the opening of a dialogue, which prior to 1989 was, to say the least, difficult. The changes which have occurred in the political map of Eastern Europe during the late 1980s, however, have consequences other than merely facilitating the exchange of ideas at conferences. These changes constitute a fundamental challenge to both structural and individual relationships. Nowhere is this more so than in the challenge these changes pose to the discipline of victimology and those concerned with the development of victim services. This chapter addresses some of the developments which have already occurred in Eastern Europe for victims of crime, the broader impact and context of those developments and the way in which an understanding of them demands a reconsideration of the victimological gaze.

The status of the 'victim' in Eastern Europe

Any discussion of the status of the victim in 'eastern' Europe presumes not only some knowledge about the nature and extent of crime in those countries but also a critical examination of the concepts of victim and victimizer. This discussion, by definition, takes us beyond the conventional criminological and victimological gaze which assumes that both of these questions are given by the criminal law and the criminal justice process (see Chapter 1). It is far more difficult to assume the unproblematic nature of both of these issues when looking to traditional Eastern bloc countries. This is not only a result of recent events which give a greater degree of transparency to the processes underpinning the relationship between the state and the processes of victimization. It is also a result of the higher profile which the West has traditionally given to the violation of human rights issues in the East. This in itself, of course, is a product of unreflective consideration of the behaviour of governments in the West on those same issues. This ideological construction of 'life in eastern Europe' sets a framework which needs to be acknowledged when attempting to evaluate the knowledge and information available concerning the relationship between crime and victimization. Having made that observation, however, it is equally true that more information has been, and is being, made available both within the countries under consideration here (an effect of *glasnost*) and, consequently to observers from the West. It is perhaps worth reflecting on what have been the traditional ways of viewing the 'crime problem' in Eastern Europe before moving on to consider in more specific detail the role accorded to the victim of crime.

Crime in Eastern Europe

As Bienkowska rightly indicates, it is important to set an understanding of the crime problem in Eastern Europe in its ideological context:

> Marxist and Leninist ideology explains crime as a social phenomenon arising from private ownership and the consequent antagonism between social classes. . . . This analysis was the starting point of the socialist view of criminality, namely that the phenomenon of crime was based on the theory of 'capitalist relics'. (Bienkowska, 1991b: 44)

Remove the 'capitalist relics' and the problem of crime was removed.

This position, interestingly, removed some 'crimes' entirely from consideration. Prostitution is a good example of this, it having only recently been recognized as a 'problem' (and subsequently criminalized) in the Soviet Union. It was made into an administrative offence in 1987. Prior to that time it was, officially at least, considered a 'theoretical impossibility'. This seemed to go alongside a neglect of issues relating to women in general:

> Though major economic and political reforms have been introduced over the past few years and though the shortcomings of the Soviet system have been analysed with unprecedented frankness, the status of women has hardly changed and the inequalities they experience at work, in the family and in public life have received little attention from the Party or the press. (Walters, 1989: 15)

Whilst the 'capitalist relics' view of crime declined in significance during the 1950s it was still a commonly held view that crime under socialism was less, and less serious than, crime under capitalism (Bienkowska, 1991b). This constituted quite a different theoretical and ideological basis from which the crime statistics were constructed. The imperative to produce good clear-up rates produced a further effect on those statistics (Shelley, 1990). So there are real problems in comparing the criminal statistics which are increasingly being made available. These problems are compounded by different recording practices and by different processes of legal categorization. However, what appears to be beyond doubt is that crime in Eastern Europe is increasing (Bienkowska, 1991b; Fico, 1991; Mawby, 1990: 123–4) and that this increase is only partly attributable to the greater openness of governments. The social and political turmoil of the Soviet Union during 1990–91 had a particular impact on the number of recorded incidents of violent offences (Shelley, 1990), but the 'true' extent of this impact may remain hidden (Pachulia, 1991). The extent to which ethnic minorities consistently feature as victims of crime, criminal justice processes and state policies is one of the features hidden by these processes, a feature which is not confined to the countries of Eastern Europe (see Albrecht, 1991). Little victimization data, as opposed to crime data, is as yet available, making a fuller documentation of the patterning of criminal victimization difficult. The 1989 International Crime Survey, however, did sample residents of Warsaw, and found that victimization rates there resembled Western Europe rates, with only pickpocketing being more common (Van Dijk *et al.*, 1990: 99). As noted in Chapter 2, the 1992 international crime survey included both Poland and Czechoslovakia. While there were distinctive features concerning crime patterns in each, overall victimization rates were broadly in line with those in West European countries (Van Dijk and Mayhew, 1992), although consumer fraud and corruption by state officials were more common. Comparing these figures with those from parallel surveys in Georgia, Moscow and the Slovenian capital Ljubljana, Siemaszko (1992a) notes the generally higher rates for Moscow and particularly Georgia where the unstable political situation in 1991–2 appears to have contributed to a marked escalation in the crime problem.

The 1989 survey also found that nearly two-thirds of victims in Warsaw would have appreciated assistance from an official agency. Similarly in 1991 some 65 per cent of victims in the Polish survey felt it would have been useful to receive help from a victim assistance agency (Siemaszko, 1992b). In Czechoslovakia victims rarely mentioned receiving any help from welfare or religious agencies, and most commonly said they had been helped by family, friends or neighbours, or by the police. However 40 per cent did feel that a specialist agency would have been useful (Válková, 1992).

Falandysz (1991) has observed that criminologists in Eastern Europe now face two questions: how to advise people on crime prevention and how to advise those people who were victims of state oppression. In other words, the social and political changes have not only exposed areas in which people feel that more assistance might be helpful, they have also identified the state as being crucially and transparently implicated in the processes of criminal victimization.

Whilst it may be difficult to offer a more detailed picture of the patterns of criminal victimization in Eastern Europe, there is no evidence to suggest that such patterns are markedly different to those in the West. The differences which do exist are perhaps more directly associated with the role attributed to the victim in the criminal justice system in socialist societies. It is to an evaluation of those differences which we shall now turn.

The role of the victim of crime in Eastern European criminal justice systems

Joutsen (1987: 283–4) notes that the criminal justice systems in Europe can be categorized in a number of different ways. He makes the distinction between Romano-Germanic, common law and socialist systems. In making this distinction he notes that the German Democratic Republic (as it was), Hungary, Poland and the USSR have all experimented with social courts. These social courts (which are paralleled in Cuba; see Chapter 3) constitute the main avenue through which the goals of mediation and reparation are met.

Bienkowska (1989) describes the role of conciliation boards in Poland. These boards, established in 1960, operate essentially on a neighbourhood basis. They have a very broad brief to deal with 'violations of community life', trespass and health and safety issues in the workplace; in other words, offences deemed to be less serious. These boards, as Bienkowska points out, have the aim of reconciling the parties concerned and are primarily deemed to be 'educational' in their role of meting out 'punishments'. Their effectiveness however, seems to vary from place to place and she concludes that 'they do not play an important role in Poland' (Bienkowska, 1989: 56). Similarly Separovic and Josipovic (1989) comment on conciliatory councils in Yugoslavia, where in 1985 it was made a formal requirement for all private prosecutions to be submitted first to conciliation. And whilst they suggest that research findings point to a 60 per cent or more success rate for conciliation they also recognize that such success is frequently short-lived as further disputes between the same parties often occur. The workings of conciliation councils would, at best, appear to be patchy. Joutsen (1987) however, attributes more significance to the formal role available to the victim in Eastern Europe within the criminal justice system itself rather than that found within the more informal conciliation process.

First Joutsen points out that in socialist states there is a legal requirement for the police to inform victims of their rights and their role. Of course, whether or not this happened in practice given the centralized and militaristic nature of Eastern bloc policing systems (Mawby, 1990) is another matter! The prosecutor is also required, in some socialist societies, to inform the victim if he or she decides not to prosecute so that the victim may pursue a civil claim. The second key observation made by Joutsen (1987) in his overview, is the extent to which the victim is considered a party to the legal proceedings. The precise nature of this role may vary; from Poland and Yugoslavia where a complainant may be appointed as a subsidiary prosecutor to an overall encouragement to take an active role in the proceedings: as a result

> This role means at least he has the right to acquaint himself with the file. From the point of view of the prosecution it is significant that he can generally suggest the collection of further evidence and suggest questions to be asked of witnesses. He also generally has the right to be heard, primarily in the form of giving concluding comments at the end of the trial. (Joutsen, 1987: 191)

A similar situation is described by Bienkowska (1989) with respect to Poland, by Separovic and Josipovoc (1989) for Yugoslavia, and by Fico (1989) with respect to Czechoslovakia. One area of difference between these legal systems, however, appears to lie in the emphasis placed on pursuing claims for restitution simultaneous with the criminal proceedings. This is what has been referred to as the 'adhesion principle' and bears comparison with the model described elsewhere in continental Europe (see Chapter 6).

Fico's (1989) analysis of the restitution process in the Czechoslovakian criminal justice system seems to suggest that the adhesion principle is a key and effective part of that system. Analyses of the Yugoslavian and the Polish systems, however, whilst clearly indicating that there are opportunities for restitution both in the civil courts and through various health and social-security-type regulations, are more circumspect on the question of the priority given to such proceedings in their respective criminal justice systems and their likely success should they be attempted. There is one further aspect to the victim's formal role in the criminal justice systems under discussion here which is worthy of comment. Joutsen (1987) offers a detailed consideration of the nature and extent to which the notion of 'victim precipitation', in the legal sense, acts as a filter on the ultimate outcome of the criminal justice process in a range of European contexts. Many European jurisdictions, including those in Eastern Europe, have legal provision for assigning 'blameworthiness' to the victim. This occurs, for example, by the establishment in law of provocation, self-defence or consent. In some jurisdictions this includes rendering bystanders criminally liable if they fail to take action whilst witnessing a criminal event. This is the case in Poland, Hungary, and what was the Federal Republic of Germany (as well as the German Democratic Republic) for example. In this way the criminal justice systems may be seen to establish some 'balance of responsibilities' for the commission of an act (Joutsen, 1987).

But it is important to note that in seeking just such a balance, it is a balance between the needs of the state in relation to the offender and the victim rather than between offender and victim. That is, the needs of both offenders and victims are sometimes overridden by the considerations of the state. This is a particularly pertinent issue with respect to understanding the nature of the state (see Chapter 8) and those groups in any society most likely to be both criminalized and victimized (see above and Chapter 2). In this context Separovic and Josipovic (1989: 165) comment that 'the protection of women under criminal law in Yugoslavia is not adequate at all'. This refers not only to the range of 'offences' against women that are not criminalized but also to their actual experience of the criminal justice process. There is little evidence to suggest that women, children or people from ethnic minorities fare any better under a socialist criminal justice system. Given the 'balancing act' requirements of the state this comes as a surprise. And although some activity seems to be taking place to address these issues (Gorgenyi, 1991) the question of the availability of compensation for victims of crime seems to be provoking more interest.

In fact, with the exception of Poland, the question of state compensation schemes for victims of crime is relatively undeveloped in Eastern Europe (Joutsen, 1987) allegedly because of the highly developed social insurance coverage in socialist societies which was especially designed to cover personal injury and disability. Interestingly though, Joutsen himself acknowledges that such schemes do not cover everyone, especially not the 'unemployed vagrant'. Moreover:

The receipt of social security benefits in the Soviet Union is not based on an individual's contract with the state, but on a status relationship between the individual and the state. This makes the discretionary powers of the trade unions and the social insurance authorities more important. Despite the comprehensive nature of its social security system, significant numbers of Soviet people remain without provisions. (Dominelli, 1991: 104).

Those without provision include young people, especially offenders who cannot pay contributions while in prison, the congenitally disabled, and those who have accidents outside the workplace, amongst others.

Poland is the exception to this pattern. In 1986 the Foundation for Assisting Victims of Violent Crime became operational. This foundation offers financial assistance to victims of crime in order to lessen the damages caused. Its role is not confined to victims of violence, as with the CICB in the United Kingdom; nor is there a time-limited requirement by which an offence must be reported. But in other respects its working brief looks very similar. Given that Poland also has a system of social insurance, the development of this foundation has been viewed in a very positive light (Bienkowska, 1989) although currently there is some scepticism concerning the extent of aid provided. Similar developments appeared to be on the agenda in Czechoslovakia in 1988–9 (Fico, 1989).

Whilst the question of compensation appears to be arousing some interest, and parallels developments in other parts of Europe and North America, one remarkable difference between those countries and Eastern Europe is the limited response to victims of crime at the time when the crime is reported from within what is traditionally referred to as the voluntary sector. As Bienkowska (1991c: 12) observes, 'The emphasis in the West on the development of services for victims has not really found favour in the East because it was thought that victims' interests were already adequately catered for by the state.' Moreover, despite the emphasis placed in official sources on the role of the community in the law enforcement process (Mawby, 1990) practitioners and academics from Eastern bloc countries to whom we spoke found the notion of voluntary work difficult to comprehend and saw little prospect of an emerging voluntary sector filling the gap in unmet need, as has happened elsewhere. Indeed, the notion of volunteering itself becomes very problematic in societies where individuals may have two or three jobs just to make ends meet. But attitudes may be changing. A Feminist Network was founded in Hungary in the summer of 1990 focusing on rape and domestic violence with the aim of establishing crisis intervention centres; and in November of the same year a

Weisser Ring organization was established along similar lines to that in Germany (Gorgenyi, 1991).

A sketchy picture is emerging not only of the existing legal provision for victims of crime but also of the way in which the political and social changes taking place may be contributing to a re-examination of that provision and the development of alternative models. This is written at a time when the impact of those changes is still in the process of unfolding in more or less dramatic terms. It is clear that the nature of the inter-ethnic conflict in Yugoslavia and the Soviet Union at the present time (1993) could have far-reaching consequences in the political, social, economic and legal domains. This is perhaps an appropriate moment to speculate on the way in which the political changes in Eastern Europe impact on law and order issues in general and issues relating to victims of crime in particular; changes which are also of relevance for developing a meaningful agenda for victimology.

The impact of political change and its relevance for victimology

It has already been observed that the political changes in Eastern Europe have rendered more visible the role of the state and its contribution towards the processes of criminal victimization. This visibility has consequences for both Eastern and Western thinking about these processes. However, those changes also have an impact on law and order in at least five more concrete and policy-oriented ways. First, widespread public unrest has led to an explicit challenge of legal authorities, something that would not have been contemplated three or four years ago. Secondly, changes to the political structure have made the problem of crime more of an issue than in the past, whether because of an actual increase in crime, or a more open review of the extent of crime, or a mixture of both. Thirdly, these political changes have implications for the criminal justice system and its organization; for example with major reviews of the operation and functioning of the police. Fourthly, these reviews have taken place in a context where evaluations of West European and North American models of provision are being made. Finally, shifts away from state monopolies toward a market economy raise a number of questions about the adequacy of welfare policies and the role of the state, private sector, voluntary sector and local community in meeting needs *vis-à-vis* victim services.

In different ways each of these areas of impact may have an effect on the actual policies which are developed with respect to victims of crime. But each of them also highlights the fact that there are now some common problems that could result in the production of what might be termed universal features of responding to victims of crime – the development of state criminal injury compensation schemes might be one such feature. On the other hand it is important not to assume that each of the societies under discussion here necessarily has a common route to follow in developing such responses. That they are all socialist provides only a starting point for appreciating the clear possibility that quite different trajectories could develop stemming from their own historical concerns and influences. It may be that in this process the 'West' would do well to consider what might be learnt from East European traditions with respect to the victim of crime. For example, another look at the feasibility of social courts might prove useful.

Whilst many of these policy possibilities at this time still remain an issue for conjecture and debate, as far as victimology is concerned they represent the unfolding of an empirical reality which has fundamental consequences for the future development of that discipline. These consequences are fourfold.

First, that these events happened at all in the way that they did illustrates more clearly than any theoretical treatise the importance of recognizing the relationship between human actors and social structures. The massive public displays in support of social and political change which occurred across the Eastern bloc from 1989 to 1991 emphasize not only the recursive relationship between agency and structure (Giddens, 1984) but also the ability of human actors, as individuals and in concert with others, to resist those structures. This demands that any discipline which still operates with a functionalist view of the human being should think again (see Chapter 1).

Secondly, these processes rendered more transparent the role of the state as a key determinant of the mechanisms of social control. The state is recognizable in these events as the means by which social change is inhibited or enhanced; not neutrally, but in the interests of economic and ideological processes. In this sense the state is more than the political expression of state power or state control. It is the expression of fundamental interests which are mutually recognizable in both the West and the East. For victimology as a discipline this demands the recognition of the role of the state in the production of the criminal victimization process and consequently requires that a critical appreciation of the relationship between the state and the law be developed.

The state, as has already been suggested, is not neutral. Its partiality is displayed in its patriarchal nature. That this has been as much the case in the Soviet Union as in North America is keenly illustrated in the comparative analysis of social policy offered by Dominelli (1991). In the context of the issues under discussion here, it has been possible to sketch fleeting glimpses of the way in which this has influenced responses to victims of crime. The presumed neutrality of such victims that underpins those responses speaks volumes about their nature. Victims of crime are not foregrounded as women, children, people from ethnic minorities. They are presented as being anyone, a striking similarity with the more conventional (positivist) thinking about victims of crime which has dominated in the West.

It has also been possible to catch glimpses of the central importance of ethnicity to many of the continuing events in the Soviet Union and elsewhere. If any of these events mean anything at all for victimology, they not only indicate the importance of appreciating the extent to which such groups have been marginalized in both the East and the West, but also, unavoidably, place the discipline of victimology on the same plane as the human rights movement.

Whilst it may be possible to debate the precise nature, cause and extent of the changes which have occurred and are still occurring in Eastern Europe, it is also necessary to consider the possible underlying mechanisms to these changes. These may not have the status of causes in the traditional scientific sense; they do however provide an understanding of the strategic options likely to be on the agenda in determining outcomes. The role of the patriarchal state in both Eastern and Western Europe with its capitalist overtones, is one of the mechanisms which helps make sense of these outcomes and the likely responses to victims of crime.

Conclusion

This chapter has highlighted some interesting similarities and differences to the responses to the victim of crime, already constructed and in the process of being constructed, in Eastern Europe when compared with West European and North American equivalents. It has also highlighted the fact that an understanding of those similarities and differences poses questions of the viability of different policy initiatives and also questions of a theoretical nature about victimology as a discipline. The next chapter will consider the lessons to be learnt in both these respects from the overview presented in Chapters 5, 6 and 7.

8

The Principles of a Critical Victimology

The first chapters of this book have been concerned to introduce the reader to some of the features of victimological thinking, empirical findings, and the differential development of victim services in different societies. Chapters 8 and 9 enter the realm of suggesting what kind of policy development emerges from that overview. To this end, this chapter will be concerned to draw together the threads of what might be called a 'critical' victimology. It will focus attention on a number of concepts considered essential to such a framework and which will inform the policy suggestions to be found in Chapter 9. To facilitate this process this chapter will, in the first instance, draw on a consideration of some of the features of the *Victim's Charter*, published for England and Wales by the Home Office in February 1990. This will provide 'case study' material to illustrate the importance of the concepts developed later in the chapter. It will, secondly, draw on the comparative material of previous chapters to elaborate further why such concepts should inform the suggested policy developments.

The production of the *Victim's Charter*, in some respects, marked a continuation of the 'trail-blazing' tradition which Waller (1988a) has particularly associated with victim policy initiatives in the United Kingdom. As such, and as a result of the international interest it has provoked (Joutsen, 1991), it is worth considering in some detail what this charter actually represents. This will serve a number of purposes. It will bring up to date the analysis of the victims' movement discussed in Chapter 4. It will offer the opportunity to place such developments in a broader comparative perspective based on the material presented in the previous chapters. Finally it will constitute a useful case study in which the key concepts of a critical perspective can be highlighted.

Critical victimology: a case study of the *Victim's Charter*

Bottoms (1983) rightly noted the extent to which the 'motif of the victim' had become a powerful symbol within the criminal justice system of England and Wales. Phipps (1988) has also commented on the variable response of the political parties to this motif. In some respects the observations made by these two writers converge in the presentation of the *Victim's Charter*, since it represented both a continuation of the victim motif and a further politicization of the victim (Miers, 1978). There are a number of ways of reading this document: it can be read as a policy document; it can be read as a political document; it can be read as an ideological document; and finally it can be read in its international context, that is comparatively. Before developing each of these readings, it is perhaps worth overviewing the key features of what the *Victim's Charter* actually says.

The charter sets out what is considered to be the appropriate response of the various arms of the criminal justice system to the victim of crime. So, for example, the police will 'respond to complaints of crime with all due courtesy and attention', will pass on the information concerning loss or injury to the crown prosecution service or the court to ensure fair compensation, and will keep the victim informed of significant developments in their case and the outcome of any trial. The crown prosecution service will take into account the interests of the victim in deciding whether a prosecution is in the public interest and will ensure that the police are informed of any defendant involved in a case of personal violence who is subsequently released on bail. The court and court staff will improve listing systems to cut down on the waiting time before witnesses need to give evidence and will give practical information on court layout and procedures. Victim Support volunteers will continue to operate with their code of conduct but will also be prepared to give practical and emotional support to vulnerable witnesses attending court as well as develop special skills to support families of murder victims and rape victims. The media will respect the anonymity of rape victims and the probation service should wherever possible contact victims or their family when a life sentence prisoner is released on licence.

As can be seen from this illustrative list, the charter attempts to establish a thorough and exhaustive statement concerned to focus on improving the response of all agencies within the criminal justice system to the victim of crime. The question which emerges, however, is how this concern is to be understood.

The *Victim's Charter*: a policy document?

The *Victim's Charter*, according to the Home Office press release, 'sets out for the first time the rights and entitlements of victims of crime'. As such, Reeves (1991) suggests that it was 'regarded as a major innovation', a view supported by other commentators (see, for example, Joutsen, 1991). This charter was to be seen as a part of an integrated package on the criminal justice system which placed the victim as the foremost priority. (The other two parts of this package were the government's White and Green Papers on sentencing policy and the supervision of offenders in the community respectively, published at around the same time.) Consequently the charter lays out what is considered to be appropriate practice for the various agencies of the criminal justice system in their relationship with the victim of crime. The spirit in which this practice is presented highlights one of the first difficulties to be faced when considering it as a policy statement.

Much of the *Victim's Charter* is a highly commendable attempt at establishing an integrated framework of good practice across all aspects of the criminal justice system. Little of this framework is, however, backed by legislation. The most striking exceptions to this are the right to anonymity of women who have reported being raped and the requirement of courts to give reasons when a compensation order is not made in cases where this might have occurred. Both of these are covered by the 1988 Criminal Justice Act. Nevertheless, the charter was presented as a statement of rights, so the lack of legislative backing is interesting. The question of 'rights' is an issue which will be returned to. However, even if the *Victim's Charter* is taken as a 'code of good practice' – that is as a statement of 'moral rights' (Spicker, 1988) rather than legal ones – some features of it still remain problematic.

First, as a code of good practice it fails to address the question of discretion which permeates the different levels of decision-making within the criminal justice system. This point was discussed in Chapter 5 where we noted that similar guidelines in the Netherlands, although supported by arguably more legal backing, have failed to produce consistent policies and standards. Such discretion obviously permits variations in interpretation of that practice and allows for the possibility of such variation reflecting stereotypical notions of 'deserving' and 'undeserving' victims.

Secondly it fails to recognize the extent to which the various fiefs (Shapland, 1988) of the criminal justice system jealously guard their own areas of discretion and decision-making. There are no clear guidelines on how these 'fiefs' might act in concert with respect to the charter's guidelines. In addition there is no indication as to which part of the criminal justice system might 'take the lead' in directing such co-ordinated practice.

Thirdly, whilst the responsibilities of the various agencies are outlined in the document there is no sense in which this document provides a framework of accountability should any agency fail to meet its responsibilities in some way and – unlike the Dutch system – there are no strategies for victims to claim redress in cases of such failure. Clearly connected to this third difficulty is a fourth: there is no resourcing base to this document to facilitate the shift in practice focus it assumes the various agencies will embrace.

These questions, alongside the needs/rights debate might provide a more useful basis from which to construct a meaningful policy agenda in the areas which the *Victim's Charter* attempts to cover. Taken together, however, they suggest that reading the *Victim's Charter* as if it were a policy statement reveals its considerable limitations. They also suggest that a political or ideological reading of the document may provide a more fruitful understanding of why it was formulated in the way in which it was.

The *Victim's Charter*: a political document?

The production of the *Victim's Charter* in 1990 marked the end of a very active decade as far as the victims' movement was concerned both in England and Wales and abroad. During that decade Victim Support as a voluntary organization both expanded dramatically and also gained legitimacy and funding from the Home Office (Rock, 1990). The advent of both national and local criminal victimization surveys ensured that not only was the extent of criminal victimization (at least as measured by such surveys) identified, it was also seen to count in establishing policy agendas. Moreover, partly as a result of 'consumer' feedback in those surveys, policing strategies in general became more focused on providing satisfaction with service delivery (Jefferson and Shapland, 1990; Jefferson *et al.*, 1991). This last observation marks the more general political flavour in which the *Victim's Charter* emerged.

The 1980s were marked by the 'politics of Thatcherism'. Thatcherism, as a political and policy agenda, reflected a number of interlinked themes, which, put simply, were concerned to reorient the role and responsibilities of the state in addressing social problems. The developments which took place during the 1980s concerned with victims of crime need to be placed in this broader policy framework. This does not mean, of course, that particular individuals, or groups of individuals, did not have their role to play in prompting the direction and the form of those policy responses. Rock (1990) has more than adequately offered such an account. However, the success or failure of those individually based projects was nurtured in a broader political framework. One of the themes of this framework was a renewed interest in the notion of social citizenship.

This social citizenship, which came to be called 'active citizenship', emphasized the obligations of citizens rather than the obligations of the state. Individuals were encouraged to engage in community action and/or self-help initiatives in their own and their community's interest. One strand of promoting these strategies was the concern to eliminate the 'nanny state' and 'dependency culture'. The encouragement of 'active citizenship' alongside the construction of the citizen as consumer (Edgar, 1991: Jefferson *et al.*, 1991), constitute the broader political context in which the production of the *Victim's Charter* becomes clearer.

The *Victim's Charter*, placing as it does the victim in the foreground of criminal justice practice, represents a particular articulation of the citizen-consumer strategy. It certainly recognizes the importance of quality service delivery which involves taking the victim into account, and thus implicitly recognizes that the victim is a key actor in the overall effectiveness of the criminal justice process. Indeed, in the year following the production of the *Victim's Charter*, the *Citizen's Charter* was published. This was an attempt to 'raise the standard' of responses to the members of the public by public sector employees. Thus the value for money and efficiency of the early 1980s became the quality of service indicators of the early 1990s.

The *Citizen's Charter* rather like the *Victim's Charter* has something to say about every aspect of the criminal justice process which comes into contact with the public, from the police to the court administration service, thus enhancing the idea that the consumers of the criminal justice system are the public/victims of crime, not the offenders. The *Citizen's Charter* and the *Victim's Charter* both offer favourable recognition to Victim Support. Indeed, in the *Victim's Charter* it is recognized as *the* victim service agency in the criminal justice system.

The central inclusion of Victim Support in this way is partly explained by the parallels between its philosophical base and the prevailing anti-dependency, community-based, volunteer philosophy of the Tory Party during the 1980s (see Chapter 4). It is also explained by the perceived political neutrality of Victim Support (Mawby and Gill, 1987; Mawby, 1989). The success of the organization has been attributed to this neutrality (Maguire and Corbett, 1987); a success which was noted earlier and developed on the assumption of an androgynous victim and a successfully nurtured and constructive relationship with the Home Office (Rock, 1990).

The articulation of Victim Support in the *Victim's Charter* as the (neutral) victim support agency, and the assumed neutral image of the victim of crime which underpins this organization, gel with the individualism of the citizen/consumer strategy in a politically safe manner. This also raises a number of interesting questions associated with the future development of service delivery and the basis of that delivery. In other words, the 'service delivery' responses which have emanated from the feminist movement are notable for their absence.

This political reading of the *Victim's Charter* has drawn attention to the need to appreciate the broader political context in which policies are formulated. The key issues to have emerged from this consideration, and which are significant for the development of this chapter, are the questions which underpin that political context. This brief discussion has highlighted two questions of particular concern: the issues which relate to the question of citizenship, and the potential for the political manipulation of the interests of victims' movements. These issues are also related to those highlighted in the earlier reading of the *Victim's Charter* and their mode of articulation may be related to more deeply rooted ideological processes.

The *Victim's Charter*: an ideological document?

The citizen/consumer strategy, highlighted in the previous section, was constructed from a particular interpretation of a range of ideas deeply embedded in the post-Second World War thinking around the welfare state. There are two notions of particular relevance here. First, the distinction which had traditionally been made between the deserving and the undeserving poor; and secondly, the principle of insurance. In the context of victims of crime, these two ideas were particularly influential in the thinking underpinning the formation of the Criminal Injuries Compensation Board (see Chapter 4, and Rock, 1990).

In some respects it is possible to argue that the CICB formed one of the final bricks of the welfare state cemented with post-Second World War ideals. This response to victims of crimes (of violence) may have been 'trail blazing' (Waller, 1988a), and may have constituted the politicization of the crime victim (Miers, 1978), but it also effected a particular view of the crime victim which set the subsequent agenda for policy responses. This view, the structurally neutral innocent victim of crime, has considerable regulatory potential; a potential which becomes more acute as economic stability becomes more suspect.

The *Victim's Charter*, precisely because it places the individual (structurally neutral) victim at the foreground of the practitioners' concerns, permits the perpetuation of such neutral images of the victim. The charter fails to implicate the agencies on which it places the spotlight in the criminal victimization process (see for example, Elias, 1986; Marx, 1983) and yet at the same time it appears progressive. This is especially the case for practitioners struggling on a day-to-day basis with resource shortages and demands for value for money. For them the charter represents a potential justification for both action and inaction.

Understanding the ideological processes that underpin the production of the *Victim's Charter* encourages us to place that statement in a broader historical and economic framework. This does not imply that such processes are always even and successful. It does imply, however, that in order to establish a policy and an academic agenda for victimology, consideration be made of two processes: first, the interconnections to be made between initiatives in the criminal justice system and initiatives in the welfare state; secondly, the connections to be made between these processes and the role of the state, the significance of which was highlighted in Chapter 7.

So far then, it has been established that the *Victim's Charter* can be read in a number of different ways. Development of those readings shows that whilst on the surface such a document appears innovative it is also deeply rooted within well-established political and ideological processes which facilitate an understanding of its surface form. The purpose of developing an analysis of the *Victim's Charter* in this way is not to be deliberately or overly critical of it *per se*, but to use this as a way of illustrating the potential of a more critical edge to victimological work. This analysis has introduced a number of ideas to that end. Before moving to that discussion it is perhaps worth considering briefly what might be learnt comparatively concerning the likely success or failure of such a document.

The *Victim's Charter*: some comparative comments

Chapters 5 and 6 considered a range of policy developments which have occurred with respect to victims of crime in North America and continental Europe. Given the resistance to the introduction of initiatives that have legislative backing (which makes comparison with North American responses less than fruitful), the country that perhaps articulates the response to victims of crime which comes closest to the *Victim's Charter* is the Netherlands. Circulars introduced by the Ministry of Justice in 1986 and 1987 specify certain duties for the police and public prosecutors with respect to their response to victims of crime. Unfortunately available analyses of the impact that such circulars have had is not reassuring. Prosecutors, it appears, rarely use their powers to make compensation a condition of pre-court settlements (Groenhuijsen, 1988), victims' awareness of their rights and available services is low, and despite victim-specific training, the guidelines and various local initiatives, the police do not provide a worthwhile service for victims or indeed refer victims who need help to those who can provide it (Van Dijk, 1985a, 1988; Steinmetz, 1989; Wemmers and Zeilstra, 1991). So whilst the *Victim's Charter* might more easily be seen as the continuation of a European rather than a North American response to victims of crime, in continuing that tradition its likely success as a policy looks rather limited. However, it has been suggested that this document can be read in a number of ways and it is within those other readings that comparisons with the North American tradition become more meaningful.

While the North American response to victims of crime has been much more solidly located in the legal domain it has also been noted that those initiatives have had a less positive side to them. Smith and Freinkel (1988) have pointed out that some women's shelters have been 'defunded', especially if they promote the feminist goals of self-reliance and social change. There is a more general observation to be made concerning this. Both Elias (1990) and Geis (1990) have argued that the victims' movement in the United States has been co-opted by governments and politicians despite the legal changes that have taken place and that this co-option would seem to favour the victims' rights lobby. If this is the case, it must be remembered that it is pursued in a selective and ideologically informed way.

Geis (1990: 259) has argued that the power of this process lies within the power of the victims' movement: 'Inherently, of course, the fundamental basis of the power of the victims' movement lies in public and political acceptance of the view that its clients are good people, done in by those who are bad.' This connects clearly with the observation made above concerning the *Victim's Charter* and elsewhere concerning the nature of responses to victims of crime in general.

The pursuit of individualistically based policies often reflects a structurally blind image of who the victims of crime are and who they are not. For example, victims of corporate crime, in general, remain hidden in the dialogue which has taken place with respect to victims' movements and remain especially hidden from view in the *Victim's Charter*. Such victims are left with out-of-court settlements (for example Bhopal, Piper Alpha) or largely event-based or community-based support funds (for example Hillsborough). In addition, the role of the criminal justice agencies themselves in creating the victimization process is often neglected.

The parallels highlighted here illustrate the similarities to be found in the political and ideological readings of the response to victims of crime between the United Kingdom and the United States. Drawing those parallels in this way does not necessarily mean that such readings cannot be made of the European tradition. It does, however, strengthen the view that while victims are here to stay (Maguire and Shapland, 1990), it is necessary to formulate an understanding of why that is so and what the potential for policy change might be. One way of achieving this is by developing an understanding of the underlying mechanisms which have helped to bring about the more currently centred status of victims of crime and which facilitate an understanding of the nature of that status. In order to achieve this a number of themes will be addressed. These have underpinned some of the policy responses which have been considered here and form the basis of understanding what is meant by a critical victimology.

Key concepts for the further development of a critical victimology

Chapter 1 was concerned, in a general way, to map an alternative approach to the study of victimology and related issues. That chapter encouraged a critical evaluation of the influence of positivism on victimology and the assumptions emanating from such research. It also challenged the traditional distinction made by such research between 'facts' and 'values'. In so doing it suggested a framework for victimological work, informed by realism and feminism, which would incorporate a critical understanding of the role of the law and the state in the victimization process as well as recognizing the potential for human actors both to sustain and to change the conditions under which they act. It was also concerned to ensure that the work which has been produced under the umbrella of the feminist movement should no longer be marginalized by 'victimology'. It is now time to specify more clearly why such framework is seen to be so valuable for the development of victimology, and how such a framework would engage with the key conceptual apparatus of the policy making process.

The initial analysis of the *Victim's Charter* offered above has provided the opportunity for specifying those key concepts and the necessary links to be made between them and the general framework offered in Chapter 1. The key issues to be addressed on the basis of this analysis are the needs/rights debate; the question of citizenship; and the political and ideological dimensions to the role of the state. Whilst each of these will be examined in turn their separation is a heuristic device only.

Do victims of crime have needs or rights? The needs/rights debate is emotive and fraught with political overtones in every area of policy implementation. This also applies to the debate concerning the needs or rights of victims of crime. Earlier chapters have given a taste of this debate. Research has established that victims of crime do have substantive needs, ranging from the need for information from the criminal justice system to the (variable) need for emotional support. Matching needs, however, with service delivery is neither an easy nor a straightforward equation to solve. What is clear is that an approach based solely on the question of meeting needs, without translating any of those needs into rights, is likely to reproduce the individualized discretionary response of earlier charitable eras. This results in a good many victims of crime having unmet needs, and potentially excludes and marginalizes categories of individuals who fail to meet the discretionary and stereotyped criteria of the moment. A rights-based approach may overcome some of these difficulties. There are, however, some difficulties with such a position, which perhaps need to be considered before these principles are developed further.

There are two problems traditionally associated with the question of victims' rights. The first and most obvious one is that the criminal justice system deals with defendants and complainants, not offenders and victims. The structural relationship which is symbolized by this relationship and the consequent role of the state in the criminal justice system has been commented on by McBarnett (1983). An issue not to be forgotten here, of course, is that defendants also have rights. McBarnett's focus on this structural relationship draws attention to a further key dilemma for those pursuing the rights of victims of crime in the legal domain: the use of the term 'victim' itself.

The term victim (or complainant) is generic; that is, it suggests a certain neutrality. This implied neutrality serves to gloss over who are the victims of crime; that is, individuals who share key structural characteristics – women, children, the elderly, and so on. These collectivities and the individuals who make them up do not represent a neutral political or ideological standpoint in policy, or any other, terms. In recognition of this, it makes more sense to construct a claim to rights based upon structural inequities rather than on the basis of criminal victimization alone. But there are difficulties inherent in this line of argument.

Smart (1989) has cogently argued the problems faced by the feminist movement's claim to law as a resolution to the question of rights. The notion of the 'legal man' on which the law is structured renders it very difficult for that discourse to embrace a set of issues which are constructed on a different basis. The law, because of its perceived impartiality, though based on very particular assumptions, can be used to press the case of groups for whom it was not intended. Finally, recourse to the law may result in the stigmatization of those who seek its protection. These difficulties, in part, arise from seeing the question of legal rights as somewhat separate from other questions associated with social citizenship, though in some circumstances a claim to rights structured on the basis of structural inequalities may make better sense than a general claim for victims' rights.

Mawby (1988c: 133) argues for a justice-based approach to the question of victims' rights in which 'the State is obliged to acknowledge the rights of citizens with regard to welfare'. He goes on to suggest that three principles stem from this position for victims of crime: that victims have rights irrespective of need; that such rights should be substantive; and that in constructing these rights attention should be paid to public opinion to ensure that regard is given to what is considered important. In the light of the above discussion, these principles suggest a reasonable starting point for a policy agenda stemming from a critical victimological stance, with a number of provisos.

First, the notion that victims of crime have rights irrespective of need is an idea which has prompted the greater involvement of victims of crime in the criminal justice system in other countries. This idea follows most notably a North American model. In that model those rights have also frequently been substantive, that is, claimable, though there are the usual problems with respect to levels of knowledge of the claimants and the desire to pursue any claim. However, as a principle it sets the question of rights squarely on the policy and academic agenda. Also as a principle, however, it is important to ensure that, in its translation into specific policy initiatives, it is not assumed that all victims possess the same personal or collective power to claim such rights. Put another way, such a principle should not fall into the trap of focusing on a narrowly defined range of criminal victimizations. Children as victims of crime, and individuals as victims of corporate victimization, also require claimable rights if such a principle is to represent a translation of a notion of justice. (At this point it can be seen that the question of victims' rights overlaps with the question of human rights.) Policies would need to clearly differentiate the grounds on which claims were being met and the source of responsibility for meeting those claims.

The notion of incorporating public opinion into the policymaking process also needs clarification. The obvious difficulty here is the problem of unwrapping the different 'publics' which exist, the likely tensions between their potentially opposing concerns, and the level of knowledge on which such opinion might be based. This is a difficult arena, especially if the notion underpinning such a suggestion also implies some notion of democracy. What weight should be given to such information in the policy process is a dilemma faced by the 'left realists' (see Chapter 1); a dilemma which is underscored by the reality of power differentials in any society, democratic or otherwise. There is no easy way out of this except to suggest that its resolution be related fundamentally to the way in which the concept of the 'citizen' is also understood. This is seen as an intrinsic part of Mawby's (1988c) agenda and is one of the key themes to be developed below.

In some instances it might also be argued that public opinion is too fluid a notion on which to base social policy and is too easily subject to media/political manipulation. However, research which has been conducted on other aspects of welfare provision in the United Kingdom, most notably on the health service, points to the remarkable stability of the public's views in an arena of service delivery which is regarded as part of a particular welfare heritage, but perhaps more importantly is also considered to be a priority provision for service delivery. The constancy of those views, despite attempted political manipulation, suggests that in areas where the policy agenda is seen to be a crucial part of the standards of provision within a specific society, then public opinion might well be usefully incorporated into the debate on the provision of rights. The extent to which victims' rights has reached this point, and in which societies, is a question open to discussion.

Although there are a number of difficulties and dangers in translating a rights stance into policy provision, it certainly represents a more meaningful starting point from which to advance a number of more particularistic concerns. This, of course, does not imply that a victim of crime is obliged to pursue such rights but certainly implies that the *Victim's Charter* and its failure to address some of the questions associated with this position (discussed above) will 'continue to cast the victim in a subservient role, as the recipient of services' (Miers, 1991: 3). This stance may constitute a challenge not only to the everyday practice of the participants of the criminal justice system but also to features of the law on which that practice is based, but it is a challenge that needs to be met both within victimology and within the policy arena. The difficulty is that such a route cannot be pursued without acknowledging its connection with a reconsideration of the concept of the 'citizen' alongside the role of the state and its interests in setting a framework for such change. What, then, of the question of citizenship? Different strands of victimological thought reflect differing connections with the concept of citizenship. That this concept was reinvigorated during the 1980s in the United Kingdom in particular was established in Chapter 4, and the vigour of this debate is reflected in the contents of the *Victim's Charter*. But not all societies have moved along the trajectory of citizenship in quite the same way or at quite the same speed. In addition there is some considerable challenge to Marshall's assumptions (discussed in Chapter 4) that such a trajectory was sequential. Despite these difficulties the influence of this renewed interest in citizenship on current sociological concerns is beyond doubt. It is worth reiterating some of the issues associated with this debate before making some general observations on its relevance for understanding (potential) responses to victims of crime.

Walklate (1989) observes that there is a certain symmetry between 'conventional victimology' and the political encouragement given to 'active citizenship' and 'social responsibility'. Chapter 4 observed the additional symmetry between this and the growth of Victim Support. This conservative view of citizenship has been concerned to develop an emphasis on the *obligations* of citizens rather than their *rights* (Plant, 1988), and in particular a 'privatized' view of those obligations (Lister, 1990: 16). That this political strategy is also tied into an economic one – that is, the notion of consumerism – has been commented on elsewhere. What is valuable to observe is that this view of citizenship emphasizes the obligations of the *individual* rather than of the *state*, with problematic consequences:

> the emphasis on the obligations of citizenship serves to obscure and reinforce the inequalities of power, resources and status that an earlier emphasis on the rights of citizenship sought to combat. If the enforcement of the obligations of citizenship is to be just, it must be based on a recognition and strengthening of the rights of citizenship. (Lister, 1990: 21)

This view perpetuates a propertied (and patriarchal) view of citizenship and neglects the complex interrelationship between the question of citizenship and the question of rights. Unfortunately the response of the left within the United Kingdom to the emergence of this view has been somewhat limited.

Walklate (1989) also observes a symmetry between the emergence of a 'realist victimology' and the development of a view of citizenship which emphasizes social rights and social obligations (see Corrigan *et al.*, 1989). There are a number of problems associated with the development of this position. First, it assumes a harnessing of the democratic process in which the community participates in the decision as to what is its interests. This view assumes that 'the community' has the appropriate knowledge to participate in such decision-making, and that the community will participate. But ultimately it is a view of citizenship which is still tainted with liberal principles. Its emphasis on 'social individualism' focuses on the right to work rather than the right to property but it is nevertheless still seen as an individual right and/or obligation. Though this view of citizenship moves away from the 'noblesse oblige' elements of the conservative perspective it neglects to recognize that it perpetuates a work-based, patriarchal view of citizenship.

This debate around the question of citizenship in the United Kingdom has been fuelled by material conditions in which the gap between rich and poor increased notably during the 1980s. The increased marginalization of the poor as consumers during that decade has not been confined to the United Kingdom, as Currie (1990) for example has illustrated in the context of the United States. These processes and the comparative material we have cited elsewhere in this text highlight a number of difficulties which face those seeking to establish a policy agenda focusing on victims of crime based on a notion of citizenship.

The first difficulty lies in an appreciation of the different historical traditions which inform any society's current policy status relating to the question of citizenship. Some of those traditions will be particularistic, especially with respect to the different points at which citizenship rights emerge or change. (See for example the debate on the relationship between warfare and citizenship discussed by Barbelet, 1988: 37–40.) However, other features are more universalistic, especially in the context of Western capitalist societies which have been the main reference for much of this book. This is especially so for understanding the relationship between women as a group and citizenship. It is that issue which presents particular problems for a policy agenda concerned with victims of crime.

Chapter 2 was concerned to establish the nature and extent of criminal victimization. It illustrated that women (for some crimes), children, the elderly, the poor, and those from ethnic minorities were generally subjected to criminal victimization at a higher rate and with severer consequences than the white male. Within these findings it is possible (though not desirable) to construct a hierarchy of 'suffering' from crime. The point here is merely to emphasize that concepts of citizenship have for the most part been constructed on the basis of deeply embedded concerns with social class and unarticulated assumptions of racial and sexual difference. These assumptions have led to a considerable debate on the nature of the relationship between social class and social movements (for example feminism) and their relative contribution to the progress of citizenship. As Mouffe (1988) has argued, this debate represents the tensions between the consideration of citizenship as a possession of individuals and an appreciation of citizenship as a collective and pluralistic construction. Here the difficulties facing those who would argue for a citizenship-based approach to policy initiatives for victims of crime become clearer.

At one level, as Geis (1990) has observed, the victims' movement has succeeded partly because it has encouraged a belief that anyone may be a victim of crime. This strategy has also been a feature of government-sponsored crime prevention campaigns. Such a view has no difficulty in pressing for victims' rights since these rights are seen as essentially individualistic in character and the demand for this stems from pressure groups for whom the term 'social movement' may be inappropriate (Elias, 1990). However, once it is appreciated that the chance of criminal victimization increases markedly in relation to structural characteristics, a claim to rights does not look so neutral and may not be so easily accommodated by the state.

The relationship between citizenship and the state is neither easy nor straightforward. As Barbelet (1988: 110–11) has stated;

> In any event it is crucial to accept that no matter how intense the struggle for citizenship rights, it is the state which ultimately grants them, and it may choose to do so even in the absence of such a struggle. It has to be added that the denial of rights and not simply their extension may at certain times and in certain contexts also enhance a state's rule.

Recognition of this interrelationship of the struggle for citizenship with the role of the state is not intended to imply that a focus on citizenship within the policy arena is misplaced. Indeed it is hoped that the foregoing discussion has highlighted the necessity for such policy strategies to be informed by the limitations inherent in other approaches and to build upon those considerations. It may be necessary to construct policy on the basis of both individual and collective concerns. This discussion has also clearly connected the question of citizenship with the role of the state, which constitutes the third issue in the development of a critical victimology.

What then, of the question of the state? The analysis of the *Victim's Charter* presented in this chapter has explicitly continued the line of argument initiated in Chapter 4 in relation to the importance of the construction of the citizen/consumer strategy during the 1980s in the United Kingdom. This strategy served not only economic and political ends. It also had an ideological purpose. It is the combination of these three features of understanding the role of the state which is crucial to the development of a critical victimology. Arguably, enough has been said here concerning the political and economic dimensions of state activity both in the United Kingdom and elsewhere as a motivator for action or inaction in the context of policy responses to victims of crime. Less attention has been paid to the ideological dimensions. This will be the main focus here.

Offe and Ronge (1975) argued that as the contradictions within welfare state capitalism became increasingly acute stability could be maintained only by 'creating the conditions under which legal and economic subjects' could function as commodities. This process of commodification, occurring at different rates and in different areas, is highlighted in a number of different ways in the context of criminal victimization. Karmen (1990), along with others, has noted the extent to which crime prevention programmes in the United States and elsewhere have shifted emphasis from crime prevention to victimization prevention. One way of understanding the apparent increase in police activity with respect to 'domestic' violence is to place that activity in the context of an increased concern with women as the consumers of public services. Matthews (1991) has commented on the contradictions inherent in the state adoption of rape crisis programmes in the United States. She discusses the actual and possible outcome of co-option of the feminist movement as a result of such adoption. The same issue exists in the United Kingdom, as Victim Support, with its neutral image of the victim of crime, has increasingly moved into supporting women who have been raped and sexually assaulted. The dangers inherent in these processes are twofold.

First, these examples illustrate that the ideological mechanisms underpinning what appears to be a progressive acceptance by the state of the needs and rights of women may not always be progressive in their consequences. This statement implies that the voice of the feminist movement may be marginalized and compromised; and that the real motivation may be other than a concern with women's issues *per se*, which presents the possibility that the state will not actually deliver the appropriate goods.

Secondly, and perhaps, more importantly, these examples may further mask a feature of the state and state activity that often remains hidden from view. In other words the kind of state under discussion is a patriarchal state. Mackinnon (1989: 161–2) comments that

The state is male in the feminist sense: the law sees and treats women the way men see and treat women. The liberal state coercively and authoritively constitutes the social order in the interests of men as a gender – through its legitimating norms, forms, relation to society, and substantive policies.

Mackinnon goes on to argue that one of the basic norms of the state is objectivity; that is, it appears neutral, rational and concerned with the facts. (It is interesting to reflect on the parallels between this observation and the questions raised concerning positivist victimo-logy in Chapter 1.) This appearance assumes gender to be non-existent. Yet, as feminist writers are beginning to illustrate, the patriarchal dimensions to the working of the state make themselves felt in all areas of its activity. This feature of the state, though articulated in different ways and at different moments in the criminal justice systems which have been discussed in a comparative context here, is nevertheless a key feature of similarity. To quote Mackinnon (1989: 170) again: 'However autonomous of class the liberal state may appear, it is not autonomous of sex. Male power is systemic. Coercive, legitimated, and epistemic, it is the regime.' Whilst Mackinnon is here clearly making the point that the state only appears to be autonomous of class, many commentators have more easily considered the class dimensions of state power than the gender dimensions. There are two issues of importance for the development of a policy agenda which recognizes this.

The first is to recognize that the various agencies and agents of the state which implement criminal justice (and other policies) are working from within a system which operates from a deeply embedded patriarchal framework. This does not mean that such a framework cannot be changed or challenged. Rock (1986) has illustrated how the presence of women's voices in the Canadian victims' initiatives programme clearly affected and directed the nature and course of that programme. He has also commented on the significance of the absence of such voices in England and Wales (Rock, 1988). However, to fundamentally change the nature of the framework in which such voices can be heard requires more than the presence of women's voices. This is the second challenge of Mackinnon's analysis of the state which is of relevance here: challenging the law and its perceived objectivity. In the context of victims of crime this rather neatly returns us to the question of the pursuance of legal rights.

As stated earlier, Smart (1989) has argued that the pursuit of legal rights has been double-edged in its consequences for the concerns of the feminist movement. She has also pointed out some important limitations of the position adopted by Mackinnon, in particular her tendency to equate the law with the state. However, the value of Mackinnon's ideas in this context is the attention they give to the legal domain. The pursuit of rights will not ultimately provide an answer for those interested in pursuing the collective rights of women in the absence of challenging the basis of the law.

Conclusion

A critical victimology needs to proceed in the policy arena on the basis of understanding three key concepts: rights, citizenship, and the state. It has been suggested that the actual form which such policy responses take is contingent upon particular historical and social parameters. This was illustrated by the discussion of the *Victim's Charter*. The likely success or failure of the *Victim's Charter*, or of any policy initiative in this area, will be related not only to the actual practices of the agents charged with policy implementation, but also to the extent to which the state plays a role in directing, encouraging or inhibiting policies. Such a role will not be played in a neutral fashion but will be guided by the underlying mechanisms of capitalism and patriarchy. These mechanisms, however, will not necessarily dictate the outcome of policies, but awareness of their importance may lead to a more 'realistic' assessment of what can be achieved by the currently available strategies. The key features which might be the concern of such a policy agenda are the focus of the next chapter.

9

Conclusion: Questions for Policy?

The latter chapters of this book have been largely pessimistic in their critical evaluation of the likely success of recent initiatives within the policy domain with respect to victims of crime, but we retain the view that alternative/or additional policy possibilities have yet to be fully explored. The purpose of this chapter is to map the contours of such possibilities in relation to both policy and practice. First it may be useful to summarize, briefly, what the current experience of the criminal justice system might be like for the victim of crime.

Victim experiences of the criminal justice process

In offering this summary the first difficulty we face is defining what is meant by the victim of crime. As Chapter 2 illustrated, 'common-sense' understandings might lead us to think about the burglary victim or the victim of car theft. That chapter also illustrated the highly problematic nature of such a definition, a definition which takes for granted the gender, age and ethnic dimensions of the victimization experience and frequently fails to recognize the victim of corporate crime. However, there has been a remarkable symmetry between these underlying assumptions and those to be found within policy responses to crime victims. It makes some sense, therefore, to begin our overview of current victim experiences with those assumptions intact.

Let us assume, for the moment, that our victim has been a victim of burglary. Should he or she choose to report the victimization, the key point of entry to the criminal justice process for many such victims is the police. Even if the victim does not report the crime, burglary victims like other victims, can refer themselves to a Victim Support scheme, although in practice this option is rarely adopted. Once the crime is reported to the police the burglary victim may have further contact from the police (for example, a visit from the 'scene of crime' officer) and may also be contacted by Victim Support. Police officers, while gathering information about the incident, are expected, as a matter of good practice, to inform victims that their name and address may be passed on to a local

Victim Support scheme which will offer practical advice and support. How often this procedure is adhered to in practice is open to debate, though Victim Support report few people objecting to their names being passed on in this way. Once referred to Victim Support a burglary victim may be contacted by phone or letter, or may receive a visit from a volunteer. The chance of being in receipt of these various outcomes varies according to the resources of the scheme involved. At this point, if no offender is apprehended, Victim Support may be our burglary victim's last contact with the criminal justice process. If an offender is apprehended our victim may be called to give evidence if this is appropriate. In this eventuality, they will receive a warning notice from the court advising them that they will be required as a witness. This also advises them of the consequences of failure to attend though the notice itself does not specify when attendance is required. Once the date for court has been fixed (the victim is likely to be informed of this by the crown prosecution service and/or sometimes by the police officer involved in the case), the victim/witness may be offered some practical and emotional support by one of the court-based victim support schemes. The availability of such support does vary, dependent upon the area in which the victim lives. If the defendant is found guilty, the court may order compensation to be paid to the complainant/victim. If our victim had sustained an injury as a result of being attacked during the burglary, and if the impact of that injury was costed at £1,000 or higher, and if the victim had been informed of his or her entitlement, our victim may also have lodged a claim with the Criminal Injuries Compensation Board. But since only a tiny minority of burglary victims also suffer criminal assault, the CICB is unlikely to be involved.

Describing the potential experience of the criminal justice process in this way highlights the arbitrary and inconsistent quality of that experience depending upon which part of the country our crime victim lives in. It is clear that the quality of experience is also highly dependent upon the quality of the contact the victim has with key personnel within the criminal justice system and the quality of information received from the system as a whole. As Chapter 8 argued, the *Victim's Charter* and the *Citizen's Charter* both make very explicit recommendations concerning the victim's experience of the criminal justice process, but neither offers any guarantees in respect of improving that experience. The issues this statement raises in policy terms for the criminal justice process are detailed more fully below, but there is a stronger message to be gleaned from this overview of the likely experience of our burglary victim.

The victim of burglary was chosen as illustrative of a 'common-sense' understanding of a crime victim. The above summary clearly illustrates some of the changes which have taken place in the criminal justice system over the 1980s. At the beginning of that decade Victim Support would not have featured so prominently in such a description; nor would the possibility of court-related compensation or the 'victim-oriented' demands of police officers. Yet despite these changes, this example illustrates the gaps in guaranteeing service-oriented provision for what might be considered to be a non-contentious crime victim. What might the experience of the criminal justice process be of a woman who has been raped?

The rape victim is faced with the decision of whether or not to report the incident to the police at all. Whilst Home Office figures suggest that the reporting of rape has increased during the 1980s (such an increase is, rightly or wrongly, often attributed to improvements in police handling of rape 'victims'), many such incidents still go unreported. There are still very few resources available to women outside of rape crisis centres which do not require police involvement before such resources are mobilised. (The St Mary's 'independent' centre is one exception to this rule.) If the rape victim decides to report the incident to the police she may be taken to a police 'rape suite' or 'safe house' where details relating to the incident are recorded and forensic examination is undertaken. Such houses offer more congenial surroundings for information-gathering in such cases and a female police officer is likely to be present. After forensic examination, which may or may not be conducted by a female police surgeon, the woman will be given information about the various support services available and may even be referred directly to Victim Support, with her consent. Of course, which agency she chooses to turn to will depend upon the availability of local resources and the relationship between the police and those local agencies deemed appropriate.

The decision to proceed with the case is dependent upon the nature and the quality of the evidence available. This decision is ultimately taken by the crown prosecution service, influenced by police representation concerning the case. If a prosecution is proceeded with the woman may then be required to give evidence at the committal stage (at the magistrates' court) and subsequently at crown court. This process can take some time. Once at crown court, if there is a witness support scheme in operation at the court in question, the rape victim may receive support during the trial. Whilst her anonymity is legally guaranteed throughout these proceedings (and for the rest of her life) local media interest in such cases is likely to make her feel very uncomfortable, as is the whole process of giving evidence. Again, if she has been given appropriate information, she may also be proceeding with a claim from the Criminal Injuries Compensation Board.

Again, this brief overview illustrates both the changing and unchanging experiences that rape victims might have of the criminal justice process. The 1980s were marked by policy developments in this context with respect to policing practices, increasing commitment to complainant anonymity, and the greater prominence of Victim Support. Little change has occurred in women's actual experiences of the court and the range of services available to them. Rather like the burglary victim – and perhaps more so, given the stability of attitudes towards women who have been raped – such a woman is also likely to leave the criminal justice process with a range of experiences highly dependent upon whom she has met, the availability of support, who has offered her support and from what agency. Both our burglary victim and our rape victim are just as likely to leave the criminal justice process more than hesitant about their willingness to be involved again in the future as to leave it as satisfied customers!

These two examples, while representing considerable diversity in the intensity and impact of their criminal victimization experience (see Chapter 2), highlight a number of common areas where it is clear that service provision for crime victims can be tightened and improved: the police, the courts and support agencies. They also illustrate the usefulness of considering the total impact of the experience of the criminal justice system as a whole and in so doing lend weight to the consideration of the system as a whole. Before considering detailed proposals in each of these areas it is important to say a word about the victim of corporate crime.

Experiences of the criminal justice process have changed for the burglary victim and the rape 'victim' in recent years, but the victim of corporate crime still remains very much outside the criminal justice process. In one sense there is an inevitability about this since, as Chapter 2 illustrated, it is notoriously difficult to document the nature and extent of such victimization given the additional problem of lack of victim awareness in this area. As the 'disasters' which occurred in the United Kingdom towards the end of the 1980s illustrated, victims of corporate crime face two possibilities. If their status as a victim is recognized, they may be offered an 'out of court' settlement. Alternatively they may be faced with a long struggle to gain recognition of their victim status through the formation of a voluntary issue-based pressure group. The likelihood of their case being dealt with by the criminal justice process is very small. When criminal liability on the part of a corporation has been sought within the criminal courts in England and Wales there has been little success. The experiences of such victims and the kind of support available, therefore, remains very much within the domain of self-help.

Improving victims' experiences of the criminal justice process

As Chapter 8 indicated, the basis for victim services may be needs-based, rights-based or a mixture of both. In England and Wales Victim Support and state compensation emerged as a response to the recognition that victims' needs had previously been unmet (Mawby, 1988c; Mawby and Gill, 1987). In contrast rape crisis centres and the feminist based refuge movement, and arguably, compensation orders and mediation/reparation initiatives, are more rights-focused. In continental Europe, conventional victim services such as those provided by the Weisser Ring are needs-based, while the *partie civile* and adhesion court systems appear to be more firmly based on the legal rights of the victim. In the USA, as stressed in Chapters 5 and 6 (see also Mawby and Gill, 1987), victim issues have generally been more rights-oriented.

As Mawby (1988c) has noted (see also Chapter 8) there are a number of problems associated with a needs-based system. Needs are not objective realities; they are subjective experiences underpinned by ideological baggage. If, however, we accept victims' perceived needs as a basis for setting societal standards, then such needs may indeed provide the basis for service provision. On this basis, following Wilson (1977), we might argue that victims' rights should be practicable (i.e. we should be able to guarantee them); they should be of paramount importance (i.e. deprivation of them should be accepted as a grave affront to justice); and they should be universal (i.e. possessed by everyone). In this latter context, then, victims' rights become recognized as an essential ingredient of citizenship, bringing us back in the British context to the *Citizen's Charter* and the *Victim's Charter*.

Earlier Mawby and Gill (1987) argued that there were at least four areas in which victims' rights required strengthening: the right to play an active part in the process of the criminal justice system; the right to knowledge; the right to financial help; and the right to advice and support. As our examples illustrated, these areas still constitute useful focuses for considering the improvement and development of policy. Here we shall reconsider these four areas in the light of policy changes over recent years paying particular attention to the role of the police, the courts and support services in these areas and assessing the British situation in the context of international experiences.

The right to play an active part in the criminal justice system is epitomized, at the extreme, by US initiatives towards mandatory victim impact statements (VIS). Whilst the current British government appears to have toyed with the idea of similar developments here, it is unlikely that any new initiatives of this kind will emerge, nor would we welcome any. If VIS influence sentences then a further inequity is introduced to the system; that is, where the likely impact on the victim was unknown to the offender prior to the offence and the different experiences and attitudes of crime victims lead to different sentences. If VIS do not influence sentences then asking victims' opinions and not acting on them increases victims' feelings of frustration and impotence.

There are, however, other ways in which victim involvement can be facilitated, some of which have been initiated in recent years. We welcome moves by different police forces to seek consumer feedback. Though we also note that the police should seek the views of victims in general (including contentious cases like 'domestic' violence and not merely the relatively 'safe' cases of burglary) and that the results of such feedback and any practice changes made should be relayed to the public. On a rather different level, recent ways in which the courts assess the appropriateness of making compensation orders seem to have improved the position of victims. Such initiatives provide a constructive alternative to VIS, where victims' information is utilized to assess compensation rather than other aspects of sentencing. This, of course, depends on victims receiving adequate information. Moreover, given the increase in cautioning in recent years we are concerned that many victims are effectively becoming 'disenfranchised' where a decision to caution is taken, thus eliminating the possibility of claiming compensation in the court. We recommend that where appropriate compensation be made a condition of caution.

This brings us to the possibility of out-of-court settlements using mediation and reparation. As we noted in Chapter 6, government enthusiasm for such initiatives has waned. In contrast we would recommend the extension of such initiatives and would wish to see Mediation UK develop, with government backing. The possibility of mediation not only provides victims with a means of becoming involved in the process (should they wish to) but also allows for more constructive solutions than are available to the courts. It may also be of value to explore projects where known offenders (rather than sentenced offenders) meet victims of their offence. Such projects would be oriented more to the needs of the victim than the needs of the offender and there is evidence that some victims benefit from such meetings.

Active participation in the criminal justice system is to a large degree dependent upon victims having adequate knowledge of services and procedures. It is here perhaps that most changes have been made in recent years. The police are now more likely than in the past to provide victims with information on available services and to feedback progress (or otherwise) on their case. On the other hand the introduction of the crown prosecution service in England and Wales has created a void whereby neither agency has accepted any responsibility for providing victims with information on cases going to court. Moreover, whilst providing information may be seen as good practice, no sanctions are attached to failure to do so. We therefore recommend that police forces be required to:

1 provide all victims with written details of services available in their area, including state compensation;
2 send all complainants a letter after six weeks outlining progress on the case, and a further letter should there be any subsequent developments;
3 inform all victims when they intend to issue a caution to an offender rather than prosecute;
4 not caution any offender unconditionally where to do so would inhibit the victim's right to compensation.

We would further recommend that where cases are proceeding to court the CPS be required to

1 inform all victims, irrespective of their being required as court witnesses, of court dates;
2 provide all victims with details of their right to claim compensation from the offender.

Such proposals are scarcely original, and echo the spirit of the *Victim's Charter*. However, given the difficulty of monitoring discretion and ensuring consistency, and mindful of the Dutch experience, we would make them the subject of a revised 'victim's charter' given to all victims when they report their crime, specifying their right to claim compensation should the terms of the charter not be met. Such a charter would be quite consistent with the government's current stance on citizens' rights to redress where public services prove inefficient or ineffective.

Turning to victims' rights to financial help, we can see that while the prospect of victims receiving compensation from their offender via compensation orders has increased, and indeed seems to operate better than *partie civile* or adhesion procedures on continental Europe, victims' rights to claim state compensation has been drastically reduced, as the government has raised the minimum award. Yet, as we noted in Chapter 2, much crime is minor, an irritant rather than a disaster, and impacts differentially on the poor, under-insured or non-insured individual. To deny victims compensation in such cases is unjust. We would therefore reduce the minimum award to £200.

Also mindful of the backlog of cases and the inefficiency of a centralized system, and in the light of French and US experiences (see Chapter 6), we would decentralize the system and operate state compensation within police boundaries. Finally, it is clearly unfair that state compensation is counted, for social security purposes, as income. We would change the rules to ensure that victims received compensation proportional to the harm done, not relative to income support.

Of course, state compensation only covers crimes of violence. There are no good grounds, other than cost, why other offences should not be incorporated. The cost burden would, however, be considerable, even if the scheme extended only to traffic crimes, as in many states of North America. We would therefore reiterate the earlier recommendation of Mawby and Gill (1987: 231) that a comprehensive state insurance scheme be formed to provide adequate coverage for all crime victims.

Finally there is the matter of victims' right to advice and support. Broadly this falls within the three time periods of the victimizing event covered in Chapters 5 and 6: immediate response, early support, and support at court. As we noted in Chapter 5, there is a temptation for the police to use Victim Support as an escape clause and avoid providing for some victims by arguing that their role has been taken over by Victim Support. It is important that the *Victim's Charter* acts as a reminder that the police do have a responsibility to serve victims, not merely detect crime. We also welcome the increased emphasis placed on victims' needs in police training. But perhaps the most significant shift has been the emphasis placed on police effectiveness and the monitoring of police performance (Audit Commission, 1990; Horton, 1989; Bunt and Mawby, 1993). As a result evaluation by the police of the services they provide to 'consumers' of their services (notably victims) has increased, and we would recommend that this become the norm.

Early support is also dependent upon efficient policing in that it requires that cases are referred on by the police (or otherwise collated by other agencies) promptly and effectively. As we noted in Chapter 5, while self-referral by victims to agencies like Victim

Support should be encouraged, most referrals are now collected from police files by Victim Support co-ordinators and their aides. Whilst the system now operating in England and Wales appears to be working well, and clearly results in more referrals than in Scotland, it also seems that the gatekeeping process (the decision on how victims are going to be dealt with) has merely been transferred from the police to Victim Support. There appears to be no comprehensive monitoring of how the latter decide on their responses. Of more significance, the opportunity for Victim Support to provide services to more victims is limited by finite resources.

Victim Support, as a voluntary organization, receives limited financial support from the government, and other resources, especially volunteer help, are severely restricted. These constraints obviously act as significant delimiters of the service that Victim Support can offer. Whilst Victim Support in the UK is inevitably going to remain a voluntary organization, we would like to see it shifting its form of organizational provision (Gill and Mawby, 1990) from a reliance on volunteers to an increased reliance on paid workers (co-ordinators, deputies and aides). It seems incontestable that if Victim Support nationally is going to meet the needs of an increasing number of crime victims it cannot do so by relying on volunteers. Volunteers may be sufficient in many rural areas, but in other areas greater flexibility is required to equate provision with need. Only then can victims' rights to help and support be fully addressed.

But Victim Support is not the only answer to service provision, and there is a need for additional funds for other agencies to provide different types of service or services for specific categories of victim. For example, while it is self-evident that many rape or domestic violence victims receive more appropriate support from Victim Support than from some other agencies, for many others rape crisis centres and women's refuges provide more appropriate solutions. Yet to play one agency off against another and fund Victim Support but not its more radical cousins is patently unjust.

In terms of advice and support there is the matter of court-related services. Here, as we noted in Chapter 6, it is clear that many US provisions are a model for the level of services required in Britain. While the continuation of funding for a limited number of crown court programmes is illogical – either victims need help in all crown courts and possibly all magistrates' courts or they do not – we would argue that the pilot studies identify a number of difficulties that require addressing. In particular, a system aimed at victims or prosecution witnesses, rather than witnesses in general, causes some difficulties where in the court building the needs of each overlap. In addition the Victim-Support-based model creates difficulties *vis-à-vis* both relations with Victim Support outside and with professional actors inside the court system. We would recommend that the prosecution service and the court bodies themselves take responsibility for provision in this area in two ways:

1   by providing details of case progress and giving relevant information to attend court with the minimum of inconvenience to all witnesses;
2   by providing facilities and services to be made available separately to prosecution and defence witnesses to allow justice to be felt to be done.

In each case services might be provided through liaison with Victim Support, but we feel that these should become statutory responsibilities and a feature of public sector provision.

The suggestions for policy developments outlined above in some instances address the gaps in existing provision and in others tighten that existing provision. What remains is to consider the policy possibilities which might be put in place to address some of the shortfalls in victims' experiences of the criminal justice system as a whole.

There is a certain inevitability that any policy agenda in this area will start with questions relating to policing and policing practice. The foregoing discussion aptly illustrates this. However, the presumptions which underpin an emphasis on a quality of service orientation demand an effective change in policing priorities. Here recent moves to discover the views of victims, often through consumer surveys associated with the development of quality of service units (Bunt and Mawby, 1993) are to be welcomed. Changing policing priorities, and the consequent change that this implies in relation to the kind of police-work which is rewarded, go hand in hand. Nowhere is this more clearly illustrated than with respect to responding positively to women as 'consumers of a police service'. The difficulties facing such a reorientation should not be minimized, but strategies could be devised to ease this.

We would recommend, for example, following the practice instituted in West Yorkshire in responding to the issue of 'domestic' violence. Here efforts have been made through the constitution of domestic violence forums to bring together all the agencies (both statutory and voluntary) which might have a responsibility for, or make a contribution to, responding to 'domestic' violence. These agencies meet on a regular basis to discuss policy formation, implementation and impact on women with respect to violence in the home. These meetings are not just 'talking shops' (though much could be learnt in terms of appreciation and understanding from just such meetings between the agencies within the criminal justice process); they are policy forums in which priorities are established, agreed and action plans co-ordinated. In the context of the criminal justice system much might be gained in policy and practical terms from the establishment of criminal justice forums. These would include in their membership all those who have a responsibility for and an ability to respond to the victim of crime: the police, the magistracy, the CPS, the judiciary, and voluntary organizations of all kinds. With a specific remit to ensure the prioritization of high-quality service delivery and a framework of accountability, such forums might offer some prospect of real change in relation to how victims experience the criminal justice process. This is not intended to imply that victims are the only 'consumers' of the criminal justice system. Such forums might also effectively debate whose interests are being met by specific policies and how best to balance competing interests.

The suggestion to establish criminal justice forums presumes that victims' interests would be represented by a range of organizations within the voluntary sector. As Chapters 4 and 5 illustrated, Victim Support during the 1980s emerged as *the* victim support organization in England and Wales, having rapidly expanded its brief in the process. As has been noted, this extended involvement to include the families of murder victims, rape victim/witnesses and so on, may not only threaten the perceived neutrality of such an organization but also stretch its effective ability to respond on all fronts. It is also clear that in some areas the extension of the Victim Support web has caused initiatives emanating from the feminist movement to suffer. Given the specific expertise offered by the different emphases within both types of organization, we would recommend the establishment of an umbrella group, rather like NOVA in the United States, whose role would be to represent and sustain the diversity of groups whose focus falls within the remit of criminal victimization. Developments such as these might provide a framework in which different and competing voices could debate the questions of policy and practice with the needs of different victim groups in mind and with a view to ensuring that those needs are met as of right.

Final comment

The proposals for reform that we have listed cover three main areas. First, some are based on a change in the organizational structure through which victim services are provided. Secondly, others are related to the specification of services to which victims are entitled and, most importantly, identification of redress where services prove inadequate. The third area of reform quite clearly posits an expansion of state provision – by the police, the crown prosecution service and the voluntary sector – which carries financial implications. It will obviously be argued that increases in expenditure are unwarranted, or at least impossible in the current economic climate. On the contrary, we would argue that the recognition of the victim as citizen requires that the costs of crime be borne by the community, not by the crime victims who are among the most disadvantaged in the community. To put it bluntly, *crime costs*, in both a personal and a financial sense. At the moment too much of that cost is borne by the victim of crime. In a just system it is appropriate for the state, through all its citizens, to take over that burden.

References

Adleman, C.S. (1976) 'Psychological intervention into the crisis of rape', in E. Viano (ed.), *Victims and Society*. Washington, DC: Visage Press. pp.493–501.

Albrecht, H.J. (1991) 'Ethnic minorities: crime and criminal justice in Europe', in F. Heidensohn and M. Farrell (eds), *Crime in Europe*. London: Routledge. pp.84–102.

Amir, D. and Amir, M. (1979) 'Rape crisis centres: an area for ideological conflict', *Victimology*, 4: 247–57.

Anderson, S., Grove-Smith, C., Kinsey, R. and Wood, J. (1990) *The Edinburgh Crime Survey*. Edinburgh: Scottish Office.

Arbarbanel, G. (1976) 'Helping victims of rape', *Social Work*, November: 478–82.

Archer, D. and Gartner, R. (1981) 'Homicide in 110 nations: the development of the comparative crime data file', in L.I. Shelley (ed.), *Readings in Comparative Criminology*. Carbondale and Edwardsville: Southern Illinois University Press. pp.78–99.

Ash, M. (1972) 'On witnesses: a radical critique of criminal court procedures', *Notre Dame Lawyer*, 48: 386–425.

Audit Commission (1990) 'Effective policing – performance review in police forces', *Police Papers*, 8.

Balkin, S. (1979) 'Victimisation rates, safety and fear of crime', *Social Problems*, 26: 343–58.

Banks, O. (1981) *Faces of Feminism*. Oxford: Basil Blackwell.

Barbelet, J.M. (1988) *Citizenship*. Milton Keynes: Open University Press.

Bard, M. (1971) 'The role of law – enforcement in the helping system', *Community Mental Health Journal*, 7.

Bard, M. (1975) *The Function of the Police in Crisis Intervention and Conflict Management*. Washington: US Department of Justice.

Bard, M. and Sangrey, D. (1979) *The Crime Victim's Book*. New York: Basic Books.

Bastian, L.D. (1990) 'Hispanic victims', *Bureau of Justice Statistics Special Report, NCJ – 120507*. Washington: US Department of Justice.

Bastian, L.D. (1992) 'Criminal victimisation in the United States: 1991', *Bureau of Justice Statistics Special Report, NCJ*. Washington: US Department of Justice.

Bayley, D.H. (1976) *Forces of Order: Police Behaviour in Japan and the United States*. Berkeley: University of California Press.

Berk, R.A. and Newton, P.J. (1985) 'Does arrest really deter wife battery? An effort to replicate the findings of the Minneapolis spouse abuse experiment', *American Sociological Review*, 50: 253–62.

Berman, J. (1969) 'The Cuban popular tribunals', *Columbia Law Review*, 69: 1317–54.

Bienkowska, E. (1989) 'Declaration of basic principles of justice for victims of crime and abuse of power – the Polish experiences', in HEUNI, *Changing Victim Policy: the United Nations Declaration and Recent Developments in Europe*. Helsinki: HEUNI. pp.46–65.

Bienkowska, E. (1991a) 'Victimology in Eastern European countries: the outline of development', paper presented to Eastern–Western European Conference on Victimology, Warsaw.

Bienkowska, E. (1991b) 'Crime in Eastern Europe', in F. Heidensohn and M. Farrell (eds), *Crime in Europe*. London: Routledge. pp.43–54.

Bienkowska, E. (1991c) 'Victims, East and West', *Criminal Justice Matters*, 6 (Summer): 11–12.

Binder, A. and Bemus, H. (1990) 'The university and the development of victim services in Orange County, California', in R. A. Roberts (ed.), *Helping Crime Victims*. London: Sage. pp.147–57.

Binney, V., Harkell, G. and Nixon, J. (1985) 'Refuges and housing for battered women', in J. Pahl (ed.), *Private Violence and Public Policy*. London: Routledge. pp. 166–78.

Blair, I. (1985) *Investigating Rape*. London: Croom Helm.

Block, R. (1983) 'A comparison of national crime surveys', paper presented to World Congress of Criminology conference, Vienna.

Block, R. (1987) 'A comparison of victimization, crime assessment and fear of crime in England/Wales, the Netherlands, Scotland, and the United States', paper presented to American Society of Criminology annual conference, Montreal.

Bolin, D.C. (1980) 'The Pima County victim witness program: analysing its success', *Evaluating Change*, special issue: 120–6.

Bottomley, K., Fowles, T. and Reiner, R. (eds) (1992) *Criminal Justice: Theory and Practice*. London: British Society of Criminology.

Bottoms, A.E. (1983) 'Neglected features of the contemporary penal system', in D. Garland and P. Young (eds), *The Power to Punish*. London: Heinemann. pp.166–202.

Bottoms, A.E. and McClean, J. (1976) *Defendants in the Criminal Process*. London: Routledge & Kegan Paul.

Bottoms, A.E., Mawby, R.I. and Walker, M.A. (1987) 'A localised crime survey in contrasting areas of a city', *British Journal of Criminology*, 27: 125–54.

Box, S. (1983) *Power, Crime and Mystification*. London: Tavistock.

Breci, M.G. (1987) 'Police officers' values on intervention in family fights', *Police Studies*, 10(4): 192–202.

Brenton, M. (1982) 'Changing relationships in Dutch social services', *Journal of Social Policy*, 11(1): 59–80.

Brett, P. (1964) 'Compensation for the victims of crime: New Zealand's pioneer statute', *Australian Lawyers*, 5: 21–7.

Brillon, Y. (1987) *Victimization and Fear of Crime among the Elderly*. Toronto: Butterworths.

Brogden, M., Jefferson, T. and Walklate, S. (1988) *Introducing Policework*. London: Unwin Hyman.

Brown, L., Christie, R. and Morris, D. (1990) *Families of Murder Victims Project: Final Report*. London: Victim Support.

Brown, S.E. (1984) 'Police responses to wife beating: neglect of a crime of violence', *Journal of Criminal Justice*, 12: 277–88.

Bunt, P. and Mawby, R.I. (1993) 'Policing: the quality of service', paper presented to British Criminology Conference, Cardiff.

Burgess, A.W. (1975) 'Family reaction to homicide', *American Journal of Orthopsychiatry*, 45: 391–8.

Burgess, A. and Holmstrom, L. (1978) 'Recovery from rape and prior life stress', *Research in Nursing and Health*, 1: 165–74.

Burnham, D. (1984) 'In the name of reparation', *Probation Journal*, 31: 133–5.

Burris, C.A. and Jaffe, P. (1983) 'Wife abuse as a crime', *Canadian Journal of Criminology*, 25(3): 309–18.

Buzawa, E.S. and Buzawa, C.G. (1990) *Domestic Violence: the Criminal Justice Response*. London: Sage.

Cain, M. (1990) 'Realist philosophy and standpoint epistemologies or feminist criminology as successor science', in L. Gelsthorpe and A. Morris (eds), *Feminist Perspectives in Criminology*. Milton Keynes: Open University Press. pp.124–40.

Carlen, P. (1976) *Magistrates' Justice*. Oxford: Martin Robertson.

Central Statistical Office (1990) *Social Trends*. London: HMSO.

Chambers, G. and Millar, A. (1983) *Investigating Sexual Assaults*. Edinburgh: HMSO, Scottish Office.

Chappell, D. (1970) 'The emergence of Australian schemes to compensate victims of crime', *Southern California Law Review*, 43: 70–7.

Chesney, S. and Schneider, C.S. (1981) 'Crime victim crisis centres: the Minnesota experience', in B. Galaway, and J. Hudson (eds), *Perspectives on Crime Victims*. St Louis: C.V. Molsby. pp.399–404.

Chinkin, C. and Griffiths, R. (1980) 'Resolving conflict by mediation', *New Law Journal*, 130: 6–8.

Christie, N. (1977) 'Conflicts as property', *British Journal of Criminology*, 17: 1–15.

Christie, N. (1986) 'The ideal victim', in E.A. Fattah (ed.), *From Crime Policy to Victim Policy*. London: Macmillan. pp.1–17.

Chupp, M. (1989) 'Reconciliation procedures and rationale', in M. Wright and B. Galaway (eds), *Mediation and Criminal Justice*. London: Sage. pp.56–68.

Clark, L.M.G. and Lewis, D.J. (1977) *Rape: the Price of Coercive Sexuality*. Toronto: Women's Press.

Clarke, R.G., Eckblon, P., Hough, M. and Mayhew, P. (1985) 'Elderly victims of crime and exposure to risk', *Howard Journal*, 24: 1–9.

Clegg, I. and Naitoro, J. (1992) 'Customary and informal dispute settlement in the Solomon Islands', in K. Bottomley, T. Fowles and R. Reiner (eds), *Criminal Justice: Theory and Practice*. London: British Society of Criminology. pp.23–51.

Clifford, W. (1976) *Crime Control in Japan*. Lexington, MA: Lexington Books.

Coates, K. and Silburn, R. (1970) *Poverty: the Forgotten Englishmen*. Harmondsworth: Penguin.

Cobbe, F.P. (1878) 'Wife torture in England', *Contemporary Review*, April: 55–87.

Cole, G.F., Frankowski, S.J. and Gertz, M.G. (eds) (1987) *Major Criminal Justice Systems: a Comparative Study*. Beverly Hills, CA: Sage.

Corrigan, P., Jones, T. and Young, J. (1989) 'Rights and obligations', *New Socialist*, February–March: 16–17.

Counts, D. and Counts, D. (1974) 'The Kalia, Lupunga: disputing in the public forum', in A.L. Epstein (ed.), *Contention and Dispute: Aspects of Law and Social Control in Melaneia*. Canberra: Australian National University Press. pp.113–51.

Crawford, A., Jones, T., Woodhouse, T. and Young, J. (1990) *Second Islington Crime Survey*. London: Middlesex Polytechnic.

Currie, E. (1990) 'Heavy with human tears: free market policy, inequality and social provision in the United States', in I.R. Taylor (ed.), *The Social Effects of Free*

Market Policy: An International Text. Hemel Hempstead: Harvester/Wheatsheaf. pp.299–318.

d'Hautville, A. and Bertrand, B. (1989) 'A better position for victims of crime – legislation and guidelines', in First European Conference of Victim Support Workers, *Guidelines for Victim Support in Europe*. Utrecht: Vereniging Landelijke Organisatie Slachtofferhulp. pp.64–9.

Davis, R.C. and Henley, M. (1990) 'Victim service programs', in A.J. Lurigio, W.G. Skogan and R.C. Davis (eds), *Victims of Crime: Problems, Policies, and Progress*. Newbury Park, CA: Sage. pp.157–71.

Deacon, B. (1983) *Social Policy and Socialism*: London: Pluto Press.

Dignan, J. (1991) *Repairing the Damage: an Evaluation of an Experimental Adult Reparation Scheme in Kettering, Northamptonshire*. Sheffield: University of Sheffield.

Dignan, J. (1992) 'Repairing the damage', *British Journal of Criminology*, 32(4): 453–72.

Dijk, J.J.M. van (1985a) 'Research and the victim movement in Europe', in European Committee on Crime Problems, *Research on Crime Victims*. Strasbourg: Council of Europe. pp.143–64.

Dijk, J.J.M. van (1985b) 'Regaining a sense of community and order', ibid., pp.145–64.

Dijk, J.J.M. van (1988) 'Ideological trends within the victims' movement: an international perspective', in M. Maguire and J. Pointing (eds), *Victims of Crime: A New Deal*. Milton Keynes: Open University Press. pp.115–26.

Dijk, J.J.M. van (1989a) 'Confronting crime: the Dutch experience', paper presented to Crime Prevention Strategy seminar, Adelaide.

Dijk, J.J.M. van (1989b) 'Recent developments in the criminal policy on victims in the Netherlands', in HEUNI (1989), pp.68–82.

Dijk, J.J.M. van (1989c) 'The challenge of quality control: victim support in the Netherlands', unpublished paper.

Dijk, J.J.M. van (1991a) 'More than a matter of security: trends in crime prevention in Europe', in Heidensohn and Farrell (eds). (1991), pp.27–42.

Dijk, J.J.M. van (1991b) 'The international crime survey: some organisational issues and some results', paper presented to Law and Society conference, Amsterdam.

Dijk, J.J.M. van (1991c) 'Affluence, criminal opportunities and property crime: an analysis of correlates of regional victimisation rates', paper presented to Law and Society conference, Amsterdam.

Dijk, J.J.M. van and Mayhew, P. (1992) *Crime Victimization in the Industrialized World*. The Hague, Netherlands: Ministry of Justice.

Dijk, J.J.M. van, Mayhew, P. and Killias, M. (1990) *Experiences of Crime across the World: Key Findings of the 1989 International Crime Survey*. Deventer, the Netherlands: Kluwer.

Dittenhoffer, T. and Ericson, R.V. (1983) 'The victim/offender reconciliation program: a message to correctional reformers', *University of Toronto Law Review*, 33: 315–47.

Dobash, R.E. and Dobash, R.P. (1992) *Women, Violence and Social Change*. London: Routledge.

Doering-Striening, G. (1989) 'The advantages of Weisser Ring's approach to victim support compared with state policy', in First European Conference of Victim Support Workers (1989), pp. 48–51.

Doerner, W.G., Knudten, R., Mead, A. and Knudten, M. (1976) 'Correspondence between crime victim needs and available public services', *Social Service Review*, 50: 482–90.

Dominelli, L. (1991) *Women across Continents: Feminist Comparative Social Policy*. Hemel Hempstead: Harvester Wheatsheaf.

Donzelot, J. (1979) *The Policing of Families: Welfare versus the State*. London: Hutchinson.

Duroche, M. (1980a) 'Helping the victim at national level', *Evaluation and Change*, special issue: 14–15.

Duroche, M. (1980b) 'Helping the victim in a sample city', *Evaluation and Change*, special issue: 16–17.

Dussich, J.P. (1976) 'Victim service models and their efficacy', in E. Viano (ed.), *Victims and Society*. Washington DC: Visage Press. pp.472–83.

Dussich, J.P. (1981) 'Evolving services for crime victims', in B. Galaway and J. Hudson (eds.), *Perspectives on Crime Victims*. St Louis: C.V. Mosby. pp.27–32.

Eckhoff, T. (1966) 'The mediator, the judge and the administrator in conflict resolution', *Acta Sociologica*, 10: 148–72.

Edelhertz, H. and Geis, G. (1974) *Public Compensation to Victims of Crime*. New York: Praeger.

Edgar, D. (1991) 'Are you being served?' *Marxism Today*, May: 28.

Edwards, S.S.M. (1989) *Policing 'Domestic' Violence*. London: Sage.

Elias, R. (1983a) 'The symbolic politics of victim compensation', *Victimology*, 8: 213–24.

Elias, R. (1983b) *Victims of the System*. New Brunswick: Transaction Books.

Elias, R. (1985) 'Transcending our social reality of victimization: towards a new victimology of human rights', *Victimology*, 10: 6–25.

Elias, R. (1986) *The Politics of Victimisation*. Oxford: Oxford University Press.

Elias, R. (1990) 'Which victim movement? The politics of victim policy', in Lurigio *et al.* (1990), pp.251–68.

Epstein, A.L. (ed.) (1974) *Contention and Dispute: Aspects of Law and Social Control in Melanesia*. Canberra: Australian National University Press.

Falandysz, L. (1982) 'Victimology in radical perspective', in H.J. Schneider (ed.), *The Victim in International Perspective*. Berlin: de Gruyter. pp.105–14.

Falandysz, L. (1991) *Personal Communication*.

Falkner, S. (1989) 'Recent legislation in Sweden improving the situation of victims of crime', in HEUNI (1989), pp. 83–92.

Fattah, E.A. (ed.) (1986) *From Crime Policy to Victim Policy*. Basingstoke: Macmillan.

Fattah, E.A. (1989) 'Victims and victimology: the facts and the rhetoric', *International Review of Victimology*, 1(1): 43–66.

Feyerherm, H. and Hindelang, M. (1974) 'On the victimization of juveniles: some preliminary results', *Journal of Research in Crime and Delinquency*, 11: 40–50.

Fico, R. (1989) 'Some comments on the status of the victim in accordance with the Czechoslovak Penal Code and Code of Penal Procedure', in HEUNI (1989), pp.93–110.

Fico, R. (1991) 'Did you know?' *Criminal Justice Matters*, 6 (Summer): 9.

Findlay, A., Rogerson, R., Paddison, R. and Morris, A. (1989) 'Whose quality of life?' *The Planner*, 75(15): 21–2.

First European Conference of Victim Support Workers (1989) *Guidelines for Victim Support in Europe*. Utrecht, the Netherlands: VLO5.

Fitzpatrick, P. (1982) 'The political economy of dispute settlement in Papua New Guinea', in C. Sumner (ed.), *Crime, Justice and Underdevelopment*. London: Heinemann. pp.228–47.

Frederick, C. (1980) 'Effects of natural vs human-induced violence upon victims', *Evaluation and Change*, special issue.

Friedman, L.N. and Shulman, M. (1990) 'Domestic violence: the criminal justice system response', in Lurigio *et al*. (eds) (1990), pp.87–103.

Friedrichs, D.O. (1983) 'Victimology: a consideration of the radical critique', *Crime and Delinquency*, April: 283–94.

Fry, M. (1951) *Arms of the Law*. London: Gollancz.

Galaway, B. and Hudson, J. (eds) (1981) *Perspectives on Crime Victims*. St Louis: C.V. Mosby.

Gaquin, D.A. (1978) 'Measuring fear of crime: the National Crime Survey's attitude data', *Victimology*, 3: 314–47.

Garland, D. (1985) *Punishment and Welfare: A History of Penal Strategies*. Aldershot: Gower.

Garofalo, J. (1979) 'Victimization and fear of crime', *Journal of Research in Crime and Deliquency*, 16: 80–97.

Gay, M.J., Holton, C. and Thomas, M.S. (1975) 'Helping the victims', *International Journal of Offender Therapy and Comparative Criminology*, 19: 263–9.

Geis, G. (1973) 'Victimization patterns in white collar crime', in I. Drapkin and E. Viano (eds), *Victimology: a New Focus, Vol. V: Exploiters and Exploited*. Lexington, MA: D.G. Heath. pp.86–106.

Geis, G. (1990) 'Crime victims: practices and prospects', in Lurigio *et al*. (eds) (1990), pp.251–68.

Genn, H. (1988) 'Multiple victimization', in M. Maguire and J. Pointing (eds), *Victims of Crime: A New Deal?* Milton Keynes: Open University Press. pp.90–100.

Giddens, A. (1984) *The Constitution of Society*. Cambridge: Polity Press.

Gill, M.L. and Mawby, R.I. (1990) *Volunteers in the Criminal Justice System*. Milton Keynes: Open University Press.

Goldstein, A.S. (1982) 'Defining the role of the victim in criminal prosecution', *Mississippi Law Journal*, 82: 515–61.

Gorgenyi, I. (1991) 'Female victims of criminal offences and their assistance', paper presented to First East–West Conference on Victimology, Warsaw.

Gornick, J., Burt, M.R. and Pittman, K.J. (1985) 'Structures and activities of rape crisis centres in the early 1980s', *Crime and Delinquency*, 31: 247–68.

Gottfredson, M. (1984) *Victims of Crime: the Dimensions of Risk*. Home Office Research Study 81. London: HMSO.

Groenhuijsen, M. (1988) 'Recent developments in the Dutch criminal justice system concerning victims of crime', paper presented to Sixth International Symposium on Victimology, Jerusalem.

Groenhuijsen, M. (1990) 'Victim support for road traffic accident victims', paper presented to National Association of Victim Support Schemes, annual conference, Warwick.

Gulliver, P.H. (1963) *Social Control in African Society*. London: Routledge & Kegan Paul.

Gulliver, P.H. (1969) 'Dispute settlement without courts: the Ndendeuli of Southern Tanzania', in L. Nader (ed.), *Law and Culture in Society*. Chicago, Aldine. pp.24–68.

Hafer, B.H. (1976) 'Rape is a four-letter word', in E. Viano (ed.), *Victims and Society*. Washington, DC: Visage. pp.502–10.

Hall, S. (1988) *The Hard Road to Renewal: Thatcherism and the Crisis of the Left*. London: Verso.

Hanmer, J. (1985) 'Violence to women: from private sorrow to public issue', in G. Ashworth and L. Bonnerlea (eds), *The Invisible Decade: UK Women and the UN Decade 1976–1985*. Aldershot: Gower. pp.141–54.

Hanmer, J. and Maynard, M. (eds) (1987) *Women, Violence and Social Control*. London: Macmillan.

Hanmer, J., Radford, J. and Stanko, E.A. (1989) *Women, Policing and Male Violence*. London: Routledge.

Harding, J. (1982) *Victims and Offenders: Needs and Responsibilities*. London: NCVO, Bedford Square Press.

Harding, S. (ed.) (1987) *Feminism and Methodology*. Milton Keynes: Open University Press.

Harding, S. (1991) *Whose Science? Which Knowledge?* Milton Keynes: Open University Press.

Harlow, C.W. (1987) *Robbery Victims*. Bureau of Justice Statistics Special Report, NCJ–104638. Washington: US Department of Justice.

Harlow, C.W. (1989) *Injuries from Crime*. Bureau of Justice Statistics Special Report, NCJ–116881. Washington: US Department of Justice.

Harris Lord, J. (1986) 'Survivor grief following a drunk driving crash', paper presented to World Congress of Victimology, Orlando.

Hauber, A.R. and Wemmers, J. (1988) 'An experiment of victim assistance in police stations in the Hague, the Netherlands', unpublished paper, State University of Leiden.

Hay, D. and Snyder, F. (1989) *Policing and Prosecution in Britain 1750–1850*. Oxford: Oxford University Press.

Heidensohn, F. (1991) 'Women and crime in Europe', in Heidensohn and Farrell (eds) (1991), pp.55–71.

Heidensohn, F. and Farrell, M. (eds) (1991) *Crime in Europe*. London: Routledge.

Hentig, H. von (1948) *The Criminal and his Victim*. New Haven, CT: Yale University Press.

HEUNI (Helsinki United Nations Institute) (1989) *Changing Victim Policy: the United Nations Declaration and Recent Developments in Europe*. Helsinki: HEUNI.

Hillenbrand, S. (1990) 'Restitution and victim rights in the 1980s', in Lurigio *et al.* (eds) (1990), pp. 188–204.

Hindelang, M.J., Gottfredson, M.R. and Garofalo, J. (1978) *Victims of Personal Crime: An Empirical Foundation for a Theory of Personal Victimization*. Cambridge, MA: Ballinger.

Hirschel, D. (1978) 'Providing rape victims with assistance at court: the Erie County Volunteer Supportive Advocate Court Assistance Program', *Victimology*, 3: 149–53.

Hodgson Committee (1984) *The Profits of Crime and their Recovery*. London: HMSO.

Hoebel, E.A. (1961) *The Law of Primitive Man*. Cambridge, MA: Harvard University Press.

Holmstrom, L.L. and Burgess, A.W. (1978) *The Victim of Rape: Institutional Reactions*. New York: Wiley.

Holtom, C. (1989) 'A proposal for a European Association', in First European Conference of Victim Support Workers (1989), pp. 139–44.

Home Affairs Committee (1984) *Compensation and Support for Victims of Crime* (chairman Sir Edward Gardner). HC43. London: HMSO.

Home Affairs Committee (1990) *Compensating Victims Quickly: the Administration of the Criminal Injuries Compensation Board*. HC92. London: HMSO.

Home Office (1959) *Penal Practice in a Changing Society*. Cmnd 645. London: HMSO.

Home Office (1961) *Compensation for Victims of Crimes of Violence*. Cmnd 1406. London: HMSO.

Home Office (1964) *Compensation for Victims of Crimes of Violence*. Cmnd 2323. London: HMSO.

Home Office (1970) *Reparation by the Offender: Report of the Advisory Council of the Penal System*. London: HMSO.

Home Office (1978) *Review of the Criminal Injuries Compensation Scheme: Report on Interdepartmental Working Party*. London: HMSO.

Home Office (1981) *Racial Attacks*. London: HMSO.

Home Office (1983) *Manpower, Effectiveness and Efficiency in the Police Service*. HO Circular 114.

Home Office (1984) *The Profits of Crime and their Recovery* (Hodgson Committee). London: HMSO.

Home Office (1988) *Victims of Crime*. HO Circular 20.

Home Office (1989) Pigot Committee. *Report of the Advisory Group in Video Evidence*. London: HMSO.

Home Office (1990a) *Criminal Statistics for England and Wales*. London: HMSO.

Home Office (1990b) *Victim's Charter*. London: HMSO.

Home Office (1990c) *Domestic Violence*. HO Circular 60.

Home Office (1990d) *Crime, Justice and Protecting the Public*. Cmnd 965. London: HMSO.

Home Office (1991a) *Crime and Justice in England and Wales*. London: HMSO.

Home Office (1991b) *Criminal Injuries Compensation Board: 27th Report*. London: HMSO.

Horley, S. (1990) 'No haven for battered women', *Police Review*, 17 August: 1634–5.

Horton, C. (1989) 'Good practice and evaluating policing', in R. Morgan and D.J. Smith (eds), *Coming to Terms with Policing*. London, Routledge. pp.31–48.

Hough, M. and Mayhew, P. (1983) *The British Crime Survey*. Home Office Research Study, 76. London: HMSO.

Hough, M. and Mayhew, P. (1985) *Taking Account of Crime: Key Findings from the Second British Crime Survey*. Home Office Research Study, 85. London: HMSO.

House of Commons (1990) *Compensating Victims Quickly, the Administration of the Criminal Injuries Compensation Board*. London: HMSO.

House of Commons (1991) *The Criminal Justice Act 1991*. London: HMSO.

Hyland, M. (1989) 'IAVS – welfare and justice', in First European Conference of Victim Support Workers (1989), pp.39–47.

Jaffe, P., Wolfe, D.A., Telford, A. and Austin, G. (1986) 'The impact of police charges in incidents of wife abuse', *Journal of Family Violence*, 1(1): 37–49.

Janoff-Bulman, R. and Frieze, I.H. (1983) 'A theoretical perspective for understanding reactions to victimization', *Journal of Social Issues*, 39(2): 1–17.

Jefferson, T. and Shapland, J. (1990) 'Criminal justice and the production of order and control: trends since 1980 in the UK', paper presented to GERN Seminar on the Production of Order and Control, Paris: CESDIP.

Jefferson, T., Sim., J. and Walklate, S. (1991) 'Europe, the Left and criminology in the 1990s: accountability, control and the social construction of the consumer', paper presented to British Criminology Conference, York, July.

Johnson, J.M. and DeBerry, M.M. (1989) 'Criminal victimization 1988'. *Bureau of Justice Statistics Bulletin, NCJ–119845*. Washington: US Department of Justice.

Jones, S. and Silverman, E. (1984) 'Manpower and efficiency', *Policing*, 1(1): 31–48.

Jones, T., MacLean, B. and Young, J. (1986) *The Islington Crime Survey*. Aldershot: Gower.

Jonker, J. (1986) *Victims of Violence*. London: Fontana/Collins.

Joutsen, M. (1987) *The Role of the Victim of Crime in European Criminal Justice Systems*. Helsinki: HEUNI.

Joutsen, M. (1991) 'Changing victims policy: minimum standards on the role of the victim?' paper presented to British Criminology Conference, York, July.

Joutsen, M. and Shapland, J. (1989) 'Changing victim policy: the United Nations Victim Declaration and recent developments in Europe', in HEUNI (1989), pp.1–31.

Kalish, C.B. (1988) *International Crime Rates*. Bureau of Justice Statistics Special Report, NCJ–110776. Washington: US Department of Justice.

Karmen, A. (1990) *Crime Victims: An Introduction to Victimology*. Pacific Grove, CA: Brooks Cole.

Keat, R. and Urry, R. (1975) *Social Theory as Science*. London: Routledge & Kegan Paul.

Kemp, C. and Morgan, R. (1990) *Lay Visitors to Police Stations: Report to the Home Office*. Bristol: Bristol and Bath: Centre for Criminal Justice.

Kilpatrick, D.G., Saunders, B.E., Veronen, L.J., Best, C.L. and Von, J.M. (1987) 'Criminal victimization: lifetime prevalence, reporting to police, and psychological impact', *Crime and Delinquency*, 33(4): 379–89.

Kimber, J. and Cooper, L. (1991) *Victim Support Racial Harassment Project: Final Report*. London: Victim Support.

Kinsey, R. (1984) *Merseyside Crime Survey: First Report*. Liverpool: Police Committee Support Unit.

Kinsey, R. (1990) 'Victimisation of the silent minors', *The Guardian*, 2 November: 35.

Kirchhoff, G.F. (1984) 'The Germany Victim Compensation Act', *WSV Newsletter*, 3(1): 17–36.

Klein, D. (1982) 'Violence against women: some considerations regarding its causes and elimination', in B.R. Price and N.J. Sokoloff (eds), *The Criminal Justice System and Women*. New York: Clark Boardman. pp.203–21.

Koppel, H. (1987) *Lifetime Likelihood of Victimization*. Bureau of Justice Statistics Technical Report, NCJ–104274. Washington: US Department of Justice.

Krupnick, J.L. and Horowitz, M.J. (1980) 'Victims of violence: psychological responses, treatment implications', *Evaluation and Change*, special issue.

Lägerback, B. (1989) 'Criminally violated – a forgotten group in society?' in First European Conference of Victim Support Workers (1989), pp.35–8.

208   *Critical Victimology*

Lamborn, L.L. (1985) 'The proposed United Nations Declaration on justice and assistance for victims', *WSV Newsletter*, 4(1): 57–70.

Landau, S.F. and Freeman-Longo, K.E. (1990) 'Classifying victims: a proposed multidimensional victimological typology', *International Review of Victimology*, 1(3): 267–86.

Laub, J.H. (1990) 'Patterns of criminal victimization in the United States', in Lurigio *et al.* (1990), pp.23–49.

Launay, G. and Murray, P. (1989) 'Victim/offender groups', in Wright and Galaway (1989), pp.113–31.

Lawton, M., Mahemow, L., Yaffe, S. and Feldman, S. (1976) 'Psychological aspects of crime and fear of crime', in J. Goldsmith and S. Goldsmith (eds), *Crime and the Elderly*. Lexington, MA: Lexington Books.

Lee, J.A. (1981) 'Some structural aspects of police deviance in relation with minority groups', in C. Shearing (ed.), *Organisational Police Deviance*. Toronto: Butterworth. pp.49–82.

Levi, M. (1987) *Regulating Fraud*. London: Tavistock.

Levi, M. (1988) *The Prevention of Fraud*. Crime Prevention Unit Paper 17, London: HMSO.

Lister, R. (1990) *The Exclusive Society: Citizenship and the Poor*. London: CPAG.

Loseke, D.R. and Berk, S.F. (1982) 'The work of shelters: battered women and initial calls for help', *Victimology*, 7: 35–48.

Lowenberg, D.A. (1981) 'An integrated victim service model', in Galaway and Hudson (eds) (1981), pp.404–11.

Lubman, S. (1976) 'Mao and mediation: politics and dispute resolution in Communist China', *California Law Review*, 55: 1284–359.

Lurigio, A.J. (1987) 'Are all victims alike? The adverse, generalized, and differential impact of crime', *Crime and Deliquency*, 33(4): 452–67.

Lurigio, A.J. and Resick, P.A. (1990) 'Healing the psychological wounds of criminal victimization: predicting postcrime distress and recovery', in Lurigio *et al.* 23–49.

Lurigio, A.J., Skogan, W.G. and Davis, R.C. (eds) (1990) *Victims of Crime: Problems, Policies, and Programs*. Newbury Park, CA: Sage.

Lynch, R.P. (1976) 'Improving the treatment of victims: some guides for action', in W.T. McDonald (ed.), *Criminal Justice and the Victim*. Beverly Hills, CA: Sage.

McBarnett, D. (1983) 'Victim in the witness box – confronting victimology's stereotype', *Contemporary Crises*, 7: 279–303.

McClenahan, C.A. (1987) 'Victim/witness services: Vancouver, British Columbia, Canada', paper presented to American Criminological Association annual conference, Montreal.

McCormack, R.J. (1988) 'United States crime victim assistance programs', paper presented to sixth International Symposium on Victimology, Jerusalem.

McCormack, R. (1989) 'United States crime victim compensation: a national system in need of repair', unpublished paper.

McDonald, W.F. (ed.) (1976a) *Criminal Justice and the Victim*. Beverly Hills, CA: Sage.

McDonald, W.F. (1976b) 'Criminal justice and the victim: an introduction', in W.F. McDonald (ed.), *Criminal Justice and the Victim*. Beverly Hills, CA: Sage.

McGillis, D. and Smith, P. (1983) *Compensating Victims of Crime: an Analysis of American Programs*. Washington, DC: National Institute of Justice.

McGuire, S. (1987) 'Victims' rights laws in Illinois: two decade of progress', *Crime and Deliquency*, 33(4): 532–40.

Mackinnon, C.A. (1989) *Towards a Feminist Theory of the State*. Cambridge, MA: Harvard University Press.

McLeod, M. (1986) 'Victim participation at sentencing', *Criminal Law Bulletin*, 22(6): 501–17.

McLeod, M. (1987) 'Beyond the law: an examination of policies and procedures governing the nature of victim involvement at parole', paper presented to annual conference of American Society of Criminology, Montreal.

McPherson, M. (1978) 'Realities and perceptions of crime at the neighbourhood level', *Victimology*, 3: 319–28.

Maguire, M. (1980) 'The impact of burglary upon victims', *British Journal of Criminology*, 20: 261–75.

Maguire, M. (1982) *Burglary in a Dwelling*. London: Heinemann.

Maguire, M. and Corbett, C. (1987) *The Effects of Crime and the Work of Victim Support Schemes*. Aldershot: Gower.

Maguire, M. and Pointing, J. (1988) *Victims of Crime: A New Deal?* Milton Keynes: Open University Press.

Maguire, M. and Shapland, J. (1990) 'The "Victim's Movement" in Europe', in Lurigio *et al.* (eds) (1990), pp.205–25.

Maguire, M. and Wilkinson, C. (1992) *Contacting Victims: Victim Support and the Relative Merits of Letters, Telephone Calls, and 'Cold' Visits*, report to Home Office.

Maine, H.S. (1887) *Ancient Law*, London: Murray.

Marshall, T.H. (1981) *The Rights to Welfare and Other Essays*. London: Heinemann.

Marshall, T. and Merry, S. (1990) *Crime and Accountability: Victim/Offender Mediation in Practice*. London: HMSO.

Marshall, T.F. and Walpole, M.E. (1985) *Bringing People Together: Mediation and Reparation Projects in Great Britain*. Home Office Research and Planning Unit Paper 33, London: HMSO.

Martin, D. (1978) 'Battered women: society's problem', in J.R. Chapman and M. Gates (eds), *The Victimization of Women*. Beverly Hills, CA: Sage. pp.111–41.

Marx, G. (1983) 'Social control and victimization', *Victimology*, 8: 54–79.

Matthews, N.A. (1991) 'State adoption of rape crisis programs: the contradictions of success', paper presented to joint meetings of the Law and Society Association and the Research Committee on the Sociology of Law of the International Sociological Association, Amsterdam.

Mawby, R.I. (1979a) 'The victimisation of juveniles', *Journal of Research in Crime and Delinquency*, 16: 98–113.

Mawby, R.I. (1979b) *Policing the City*. Aldershot: Gower.

Mawby, R.I. (1988a) 'Women and crime: from victimization rates to the crime experience', paper presented to tenth international congress on criminology, Hamburg.

Mawby, R.I. (1988b) 'Age, vulnerability and the impact of crime', in M. Maguire and J. Pointing (eds), *Victims of Crime: A New Deal?* Milton Keynes: Open University Press. pp.101–11.

Mawby, R.I. (1988c) 'Victims' needs or victims' rights: alternative approaches to policy making', in M. Maguire and J. Pointing (1988), *Victims of Crime: A New Deal*. Milton Keynes: Open University Press. pp.127–37.

Mawby, R.I. (1989) 'The contributions of the voluntary sector to a mixed economy of justice', in R. Matthews (ed.), *Privatizing Criminal Justice*. London: Sage.

Mawby, R.I. (1990) *Comparative Policing Issues: Britain and America in International Perspective*. London: Unwin Hyman.

Mawby, R.I. (1992a) 'Trends in research on crime victims in the United Kingdom', in S. Ben David and G.F. Kirchhoff (eds) *International Faces of Victimology*. Mönchengladbach: WSV Publishing. pp.227–43.

Mawby, R.I. (1992b) 'Comparative police systems: searching for a continental model', in Bottomley et al. (eds) (1992), pp.108–34.

Mawby, R.I. and Firkins, V. (1987) 'The victim/offender relationship and its implications for policies: evidence from the British Crime Survey', *Victimology*, 12.

Mawby, R.I. and Gill, M.L. (1987) *Crime Victims: Needs, Services and the Voluntary Sector*. London: Tavistock.

Maxfield, M. (1984) *Fear of Crime in England and Wales*. Research Study, 78. London: Home Office.

Maxfield, M.G. (1987) 'Household composition, routine activity, and victimization: a comparative analysis', *Journal of Quantitative Criminology*, 3(4): 301–20.

Maxfield, M.G. (1988) 'The comparative development of routine activity theories of victimization', paper presented to tenth International Congress on Criminology, Hamburg.

Mayhew, P. (1992) 'England and Wales: summary of results, 1992 International Victimisation Survey', paper presented to International Conference on Understanding Crime: Experiences of Crime and Crime Control, Rome.

Mayhew, P. and Maung, N.A. (1992) 'Surveying crime: findings from the 1992 British Crime Survey', *HORSD, Research Findings no 2*.

Mayhew, P., Elliott, D. and Dowds, L. (1989) *The 1988 British Crime Survey*. Home Office Research Study, 111. London: HMSO.

Meade, A.C., Knudten, M.S., Doerner, W.G. and Knudten, R.D. (1976) 'Discovery of a forgotten party: trends in American victim compensation legislation', *Victimology*, 1(3): pp.421–33.

Meiners, R.E. (1978) *Victim Compensation*. Lexington, MA: Lexington Books.

Melup, I. (1991) 'United Nations: victims of crime', *International Review of Victimology*, 2: 29–59.

Miers, D. (1978) *Responses to Victimization*. Abingdon: Professional Books.

Miers, D. (1989) 'Positivist victimology: a critique', *International Review of Victimology*, 1(1): 3–22.

Miers, D. (1990) 'Positivist victimology: a critique. Part 2: critical victimology', *International Review of Victimology*, 1(3): 219–30.

Miers, D. (1991) 'The responsibilities and rights of victims of crime', paper presented to British Criminology Conference, York.

Minch, C. (1987) 'Attrition in the processing of rape cases', *Canadian Journal of Criminology*, 29(4): 389–404.

Moody, S. (1989) 'Referral methods in victim support: implications for practice and philosophy', in First European Conference of Victim Support Workers (1989), pp.87–96.

Mooney, J. (1993) 'The North London Domestic Violence Survey', paper presented to British Criminology Conference, Cardiff.

Morgan, J. (1988) 'Children as victims', in Maguire and Pointing (eds) (1998) pp.74–82.

Morgan, J. and Zedner, L. (1991) 'Child victims in the criminal justice system', paper presented to British Criminology Conference, York.

Morley, R. and Mullender, A. (1991) 'Preventing violence against women in the home', paper presented to British Criminology Conference, York.

Morris, A., Findlay, A., Paddison, R. and Rogerson, R. (1989) 'Urban quality of life and the North–South divide', *Town and Country Planning*, 58(7/8): 207–10.

Morris, T. (1989) *Crime and Criminal Justice since 1945*. Oxford: Basil Blackwell.

Mouffe, C. (1988) 'The civics lesson', *New Statesman and Society*, 7 October: 28–31.

Nation, D. and Arnott, J. (1991) 'House burglaries and victims', *Probation Journal*, 38(2): 63–7.

National Police Agency, Government of Japan (1984) *White Paper on Police*. Tokyo: Police Association.

NAVSS (1986) *Sixth Annual Report*. London: Victim Support.

Newburn, T. (1988) *The Use and Enforcement of Compensation Orders in Magistrates' Courts*. London: Home Office Research Study 102.

Newburn, T. (1989) 'The police, victims and victim support', *HO Research Bulletin*, 26: 22–5.

Newburn, T. and de Peyrecave, H. (1988) 'Victims' attitudes to court and compensation', *HO Research Bulletin*, 25: 18–21.

Newman, K. (1983) 'The police and victims' support schemes', in NAVSS, *Third Annual Report, 1982/83*. pp.23–5.

Nicholls, M. (1991) 'Sympathy in the right place', *Police Review*, 8 March: 480–1.

Offe, C. and Ronge, V. (1975) 'Theses on the theory of the state', *New German Critique*, 6 (Fall): 139–47.

O'Sullivan, E. (1978) 'What has happened to rape crisis centres? A look at their structures, members and funding', *Victimology*, 3: 45–62.

Pachulia, M. (1991) *Personal Communication*.

Pahl, J. (1978) *A Refuge for Battered Women*. London: HMSO, DHSS.

Paliwala, A. (1982) 'Law and order in the village: Papua New Guinea's village courts', in Sumner (1982), pp. 192–227.

Parliamentary All-Party Penal Affairs Group (1984) *A New Deal for Victims*. London: Parliamentary All-Party PAG.

Pawson, R. (1989) *A Measure for Measures: A Manifesto for Empirical Sociology*. London: Routledge.

Peachey, D.E. (1989) 'The Kitchener experiment', in Wright and Galaway (1989), pp.14–26.

Pearce, F. (1990) *Second Islington Crime Survey: Commercial and Conventional Crime in Islington*. Middlesex Polytechnic: Centre for Criminology.

Pearce, F. and Tombs, S. (1989) 'Bhopal: Union Carbide and hubris of capitalist technocracy', *Social Justice*, 16(2): 116–45.

Penders, L. (1989) 'Guidelines for police and prosecutors: an interest of victims; a matter of justice', in First European Conference of Victim Support Workers (1989), pp.75–86.

Peters, T. and Meyvis, W. (1989) 'Recent projects of victim support and assistance in Belgium', in First European Conference of Victim Support Workers (1989), pp.52–9.

Phillips, D. (1977) *Crime and Authority in Victorian England*. London: Croom Helm.

Phillips, D. (1984) 'Good men to associate and bad men to conspire: associations for the prosecution of felons, England 1770–1860', paper presented to Crime, Law and Society conference, University of Warwick.

Phipps, A. (1988) 'Ideologies, political parties and victims of crime', in Maguire and Pointing (eds) (1988). 177–86.

Piffaut, G. (1989) 'Concrete achievements toward the implementation of the fundamental principles of justice for victims', in HEUNI (1989), pp.113–39.

Pizzey, E. (1974) *Scream Quietly or the Neighbours Will Hear*. Harmondsworth: Penguin.

Plant, R. (1988) 'Citizenship and society', *New Socialist*, December: 7–9.

Police Authority for Northern Ireland and the Royal Ulster Constabulary (1988) *Working together to Police Northern Ireland: Three Years of Progress 1985–1988*. Belfast: Royal Ulster Constabulary.

Powers, E. (1966) *Crime and Punishment in Early Massachusetts, 1620–1692*. Boston: Beacon Press.

President's Task Force on Victims of Crime (1982) *Final Report*. Washington: DC: US Government Printing Office.

Pritchard, C. (1991) 'Tackling child murder', *The Guardian*, 17 April: 22.

Quinney, R. (1972) 'Who is the victim?' *Criminology*, November: 309–29.

Raine, J.W. and Smith, R.E. (1991) *The Victim/Witness in Court Project: Report of the Research Programme*. London: Victim Support.

Raine, J. and Walker, B. (1990) 'Quality of services in the Magistrates' Courts – the user's perspective', *HO Research Bulletin*, 28: 42–8.

Ralphs, Lady (1988) *The Victim in Court: Report of the Working Party*. London: NAVSS.

Rand, M.R. (1989) 'Households touched by crime, 1988', *Bureau of Justice Statistics Bulletin NCJ–117434*. Washington: US Department of Justice.

Reeves, H. (1985) 'The victim and reparation', *WSV Newsletter*, 4(1): 50–6.

Reeves, H. (1991) 'Victims and criminal justice in England and Wales', paper presented to the first East–West European conference on Victimology, Warsaw.

Reiman, J.H. (1979) *The Rich Get Rich and the Poor Get Prison*. New York: John Wiley.

Reiner, R. (1990) 'Policing and social divisions', paper presented to Criminal Justice Studies annual conference, Hatfield College, Durham.

Reiner, R. (1991) *Chief Constables*. Oxford: Oxford University Press.

Reiner, R. (1992) 'Fin-de-siècle blues. Policing postmodern society', professorial lecture, London School of Economics.

Resick, P.A. (1987) 'Psychological effects of victimization: implications for the criminal justice system', *Crime and Delinquency*, 33(4): 468–78.

Resick, P.A. (1990) 'Victims of sexual assault', in Lurigio *et al.* (1990), pp.69–86.

Riger, S., Gorden, M.T. and Bailly, R. le. (1978) 'Women's fear of crime: from blaming to restricting the victim', *Victimology*, 3: 274–84.

Riggs, D.S. and Kilpatrick, D.G. (1990) 'Families and friends: indirect victimization by crime', in Lurigio, *et al.* (eds) (1990), pp.120–38.

Roberts, A.R. (ed.) (1990) *Helping Crime Victims*. London: Sage.

Roberts, A.R. and Roberts, B.S. (1990) 'A model for crisis intervention with battered women and their children', ibid., pp.186–205.

Roberts, S. (1979) *Order and Dispute: an Introduction to Legal Anthropology.* Harmondsworth: Penguin.

Rock, P. (1986) *A View from the Shadows.* Oxford: Clarendon Press.

Rock, P. (1988) 'Government, victims and policies in two countries', *British Journal of Criminology*, 28(1): 44–66.

Rock, P. (1990) *Helping Victims of Crime.* Oxford: Clarendon Press.

Rock, P. (1991a) 'Witnesses and space in a Crown Court', *British Journal of Criminology*, 31(3): 266–79.

Rock, P. (1991b) 'The victim in court project at the Crown Court in Wood Green', *Howard Journal*, 30(4): 301–10.

Rogerson, R., Findlay, A. and Morris, A. (1988) 'The best cities to live in', *Town and Country Planning*, 57(10): 270–3.

Rosen, C.J. and Harland, A.T. (1990) 'Restitution to crime victims as a presumptive requirement in criminal case dispositions', in Roberts (1990), pp.233–48.

Rosenbaum, D.P. (1987) 'Coping with victimization: the effects of police intervention on victims' psychological readjustment', *Crime and Delinquency*, 33(4): 502–19.

Royal Ulster Constabulary (1989) *Chief Constable's Annual Report.* Belfast: Police Authority for Northern Ireland.

Ruddick, R. (1989) 'A court-referred scheme', in Wright and Galaway (eds) (1989), pp.82–98.

Rudé, G. (1985) *Criminal and Victim.* Oxford: Clarendon Press.

Russell, D. (1984) *Sexual Exploitation.* Beverly Hills, CA: Sage.

Russell, D. (1990) *Rape in Marriage*, 2nd edn, New York: Collier.

Russell, J. (1990) *Home Office Funding of Victim Support Schemes – Money Well Spent?* Home Office, Research and Planning Unit paper 58. London: HMSO.

Salas, L. (1985) 'The judicial system of post revolutionary Cuba', in A. Podgorecki, C.J. Whelan and D. Khosla (eds), *Legal Systems and Social Systems.* London: Croom Helm. pp.229–54.

Sales, E., Baum, M. and Shore, B. (1984) 'Victim readjustment following assault', *Journal of Social Issues*, 40(1): 117–36.

Sampson, A. and Farrell, G. (1990) *Victim Support and Crime Prevention in an Inner City Setting.* Home Office Crime Prevention Unit paper no. 21. London: HMSO.

Samuels, A. (1973) 'Criminal Injuries Compensation Board', *Criminal Law Review*: 418–31.

Schädler, W. (1987) 'Crime victim needs', *WSV Newsletter*, 5(1): 78–83.

Schädler, W. (1988) 'Witnesses: the orphans of justice?' *WSV Newsletter*, 6(2): 60–7.

Schädler, W. (1989a) 'Experiences from the victim and witness assistance centre in Hanau', in First European Conference of Victim Support Workers (1989), pp.60–3.

Schädler, W. (1989b) 'The situation of crime victims in the Federal Republic of Germany', in First European Conference of Victim Support Workers (1989), pp.70–4.

Schafer, S. (1960) *Restitution to Victims of Crime.* London: Stevens & Sons.

Schmidt, R.A. (1980) 'Crime victim compensation legislation: a comparative study', *Victimology*, 5: 401–20.

Schneider, A.L. and Schneider, P.R. (1981) 'Victim assistance programs', in Galaway and Hudson (1981) pp.364–73.

Schneider, H.J. (1984) Foreword to special issue: 'Towards a United Nations declaration in justice and assistance for victims', *WSV Newsletter*, 3(2): v–vii.

Schneider, H.J. (1991) 'Victimology: basic theoretical concepts and practical implications', paper presented to First East–West Conference on Victimology, Warsaw.

Schubert, A. (1981) 'Private initiative in law enforcement: associations for the prosecution of felons', in V. Bailey (ed.), *Policing and Punishment in Nineteenth Century Britain*. London: Croom Helm. pp.25–41.

Schwartz, R.D. and Miller, J.C. (1964) 'Legal evolution and societal complexity', *American Journal of Sociology*, 70: 159–69.

Separovic, Z.P. and Josipovic, I. (1989) 'The position of the victim within the framework of the criminal justice system in Yugoslavia', in HEUNI (1989), pp.157–67.

Sessar, K. (1987) 'Participation and restitution: the Siamese twins regarding the victim's role within the criminal process', paper presented to annual conference of American Society of Criminology, Montreal.

Shapland, J. (1984) 'Victims, the criminal justice system, and compensation', *British Journal of Criminology*, 24(2): 131–49.

Shapland, J. (1986) 'Victim assistance and the criminal justice system', in E.A. Fattah (ed.), *From Crime Policy to Victim Policy*. London: Macmillan. pp. 118–236.

Shapland, J. (1988), 'Fiefs and peasants: accomplishing change for victims in the criminal justice system', in Maguire and Pointing (eds) (1988), pp.187–94.

Shapland, J. and Cohen, D. (1987) 'Facilities for victims: the role of the police and the courts', *Criminal Law Review*, January: 28–38.

Shapland, J., Willmore, J. and Duff, P. (1985) *Victims in the Criminal Justice System*. Aldershot: Gower.

Shelley, L.I. (1990) 'The Soviet militia: agents of politics and social control', *Policing and Society*, 1(1): 23–38.

Siemaszko, A. (1992a) 'Eastern European victimization rates: to compare or not to compare', paper presented to International Conference on Understanding Crime, Experience of Crime and Crime Control, Rome.

Siemaszko, A. (1992b) 'Poland: summary of results 1992 International Victimization Survey', paper presented to International Conference on Understanding Crime, Rome.

Simon, S. (1987) 'Victim services – a review of British and American practices with special reference to the victim in court', *Justice of the Peace*, 21 November: 745–7.

Sinclair, I. and Miller, C. (1984) *Measures of Police Effectiveness and Efficiency*, RPU paper 25. London: HMSO.

Skogan, S.W. (1990) *Disorder and Decline: Crime and the Spiral of Decay in American Neighborhoods*. New York: Free Press.

Skogan, W.G. (1986) 'The fear of crime and its behavioural implications', in Fattah (ed.) (1986), pp.167–90.

Skogan, W.G., Lurigio, A.J. and Davis, R.C. (1990) 'Criminal victimization', in Lurigio *et al.* (eds) (1990), pp.7–22.

Smart, C. (1989) *Feminism and the Power of Law*. London: Routledge.

Smart, C. (1990) 'Feminist approaches to criminology; or postmodern women meets atavistic man', in L. Gelsthorpe and A. Morris (eds), *Feminist Perspectives in Criminology*. Milton Keynes: Open University Press. pp.70–84.

Smith, D. (1990) 'Whistling women: reason, rationality and objectivity'. The Harry Hawthorne Lecture, Canadian Learned Societies 25th conference, University of Victoria.

Smith, S.J. (1982) 'Victimisation in the inner city', *British Journal of Criminology*, 22: 386–402.

Smith, S.R. and Freinkel, S. (1988) *Adjusting the Balance: Federal Policy and Victim Services*. Westport, CT: Greenwood.

Soetenhorst, J. (1985) 'The victim issue in the political agenda', *Victimology*, 10: 687–98.

Softley, P. (1978) *Compensation Orders in Magistrates' Courts*. London: Home Office Research Study, 43.

Sparks, R., Genn, H. and Dodd, D. (1977) *Surveying Victims*. Chichester: Wiley.

Spicker, P. (1988) *Principles of Social Welfare*. London: Routledge.

Stanko, E.A. (1990) *Everyday Violence*. London: Pandora.

Steinmetz, C. (1989) 'The effects of victim support', in First European Conference of Victim Support Workers (1989), pp.120–8.

Sumner, C. (1990) *Censure, Politics and Criminal Justice*. Milton Keynes: Open University Press.

Tak, P.J.P. (1986) *The Legal Scope of Non-Prosecution in Europe*. Helsinki: HEUNI.

Tarling, R. and Softley, P. (1976) 'Compensation orders in the Crown Court', *Criminal Law Review*: 422–8.

Taylor, B.M. (1989) *New Directions for the National Crime Survey*. Bureau of Justice Statistics Technical Report, NCJ–11557. Washington: US Department of Justice.

Taylor, I. (1990) 'Introduction: the concept of "social cost" in free market theory and the social effects of free market policies', in I. Taylor (ed.), *The Social Effects of Free Market Policies: An International Text*. Hemel Hempstead: Harvester Wheatsheaf.

Taylor, I. (1991) *Sociology and the Condition of the English City: Thoughts from a Returnee*. Salford Papers in Sociology. Department of Sociology, University of Salford.

Temkin, J. (1993) 'Sexual history evidence – the ravishment of section 2', *Criminal Law Review*, January: 3:20.

Tsitsoura, A. (1989) 'Victims of crime – Council of Europe and United Nations instruments', in HEUNI (1989), pp.197–208.

Umbreit, M. (1989) 'Violent offenders and their victims', in Wright and Galaway (1989), pp.99–112.

Ursel, E.J. and Farough, D. (1986) 'The legal and public response to the new wife abuse directive in Manitoba', *Canadian Journal of Criminology*, 28(2): 171–83.

US Department of Justice (1990) *Criminal Victimization in the United States, 1987*. Washington DC: US Department of Justice.

Válková, J. (1992) 'Czechoslovakia: summary of results, 1992 International Victimization Survey', paper presented to International Conference on Understanding Crime, Experiences of Crime and Crime Control, Rome.

Veevers, J. (1989) 'Pre-court diversion for juvenile offenders', in Wright and Galaway (eds) (1989), pp.69–81.

Vennard, J. (1976) 'Justice and recompense for victims of crime', *New Society*, 19 February: 379–81.

Vennard, J. (1979) 'Magistrates' assessments of compensation for injury', *Criminal Law Review*: 510–23.

Victim Support (1991) *Annual Report 1990/91*. London: NAVSS.

Victim Support (1992) *Annual Report 1991*. London: NAVSS.

Victim Support Scotland (1991) *Annual Report 1990/91*. Edinburgh: VSS.

Vidosa, F.G. (1989) 'Improving the position of the victim of crime in Spain', in HEUNI (1989), pp.209–18.

Viney, A. (1991) 'Assisting victims of crime', paper presented to Eastern–Western European Conference on Victimology, Warsaw.

Walby, S. (1990) *Theorizing Patriarchy*. Oxford: Basil Blackwell.

Walker, L.E. (1984) *The Battered Women Syndrome*. New York: Springer.

Walklate, S. (1986) *The Merseyside Lay Visiting Scheme: First and Second Reports*. Liverpool: Merseyside Police Authority.

Walklate, S. (1989) *Victimology: the Victim and the Criminal Justice Process*. London: Unwin Hyman.

Walklate, S. (1990) 'Researching victims of crime: critical victimology'. *Social Justice*, 17(3): 25–42.

Wall, P. (1991) 'The victim squad', *Police*, 24(4): 30–2.

Waller, I. (1982) 'Declaration on victims of crime', *WSV Newsletter*, 2(2): 88–100.

Waller, I. (1984) 'Declaration on the protection and assistance of crime victims', *WSV Newsletter*, 3(2): 1–14.

Waller, I. (1988a) 'International standards, national trail blazing, and the next steps', in Maguire and Pointing (eds) (1989), pp.195–203.

Waller, I. (1988b) 'The Justice for Victims of Crime Act and other victim initiatives in Manitoba', *WSV Newsletter*, 6(1): 20–7.

Waller, I. (1990) 'The Police: first in aid?', in Lurigio *et al.* (eds) (1990), pp.139–56.

Waller, I. (1992) 'Policy implications related to National and International Surveys', paper presented to International Conference on Understanding Crime: Experiences of Crime and Crime Control, Rome.

Walters, E. (1989) 'Restructuring the "women question": perestroika and prostitution', *Feminist Review*, 33: 3–19.

Wasik, M. (1978) 'The place of compensation in the penal system', *Criminal Law Review*: 599–611.

Wemmers, J.M. and Zeilstra, M.I. (1991) 'Victims services in the Netherlands', *Dutch Penal Law and Policy*, 3: The Hague, Ministry of Justice.

Whitaker, C.J. (1990) *Black Victims*. Bureau of Justice Statistics special report. NCJ–122562. Washington DC: US Department of Justice.

Willis, B.L. (1984) 'State compensation of victims of violent crimes: the Council of Europe Convention of 1983, Virginia', *Journal of International Law*, 25(1): 211–40.

Wilson, E. (1977) *Women and the Welfare State*. London: Tavistock.

Wilson, E. (1983) *What Is To Be Done about Violence against Women?* Harmondsworth: Penguin.

Winkel, F.W. (1989) 'Responses to criminal victimisation: evaluating the impact of a police assistance programme and some social psychological characteristics', *Police Studies*, 12(2): 59–72.

Winkel, F.W. (1991) 'Police responses aimed at alleviating victims' psychological distress and at raising prevention-awareness: some grounded intervention programmes', paper presented to annual conference of Law and Society Association, Amsterdam.

Wootton, B. (1959) *Social Science and Social Pathology*. London: Allen & Unwin.

Worrall, A. and Pease, K. (1986) 'Personal crime against women', *Howard Journal of Criminal Justice*, 25: 118–24.

Wortman, C.B. (1983) 'Coping with victimisation: conclusions and implications for future research', *Journal of Social Issues*, 39(2): 195–221.

Wright, M. (1981) 'Crime and reparation: breaking the penal logjam', *New Society*, 10 December.

Wright, M. (1991) *Justice for Victims and Offenders*. Milton Keynes: Open University Press.

Wright, M. and Galaway, B. (eds) (1989) *Mediation and Criminal Justice*. London: Sage.

Young, J. (1986) 'The failure of criminology: the need for a radical realism', in R. Matthews and J. Young (eds), *Confronting Crime*. London: Sage.

Young, J. (1988) 'Risk of crime and fear of crime: a realist critique of survey-based assumptions', in Maguire and Pointing (eds) (1988), pp.164–76.

Young, J. (1991) 'Ten principles of realism', paper presented to British Criminology Conference, York.

Young, M.A. (1990) 'Victim assistance in the United States: the end of the beginning', *International Review of Victimology*, 1: 181–99.

Young, M.A. and Stein, J.H. (1983) *The Victim Service System: A Guide to Action*. Washington DC: NOVA.

Young, M.W. (1974) Private sanctions and Public Ideology: some aspects of self-help in Kalauna, Goodenough Island, in Epstein (ed) op cit: 40–66.

Young-Rifai, M. (1982) 'Victimology: a theoretical framework', in H.J. Schneider (ed.), *The Victim in International Perspective*. Berlin: de Gruyter. pp.65–99.

Ziegenhagen, E.A. and Benyi, J. (1981) 'Victim interests, victim services and social control', in Galaway and Hudson (eds) (1981), pp.373–83.

Zvekic, U. and del Frate, A.A. (1992) 'Victimization in the Developing World: an overview', paper presented to International Conference on Understanding Crime, Experiences of Crime and Crime Control, Rome.

Index